Origins of the First World War

Origins of the First World War

Revised third edition

Gordon Martel

PEARSON
Longman

Harlow, England • London • New York • Boston • San Francisco • Toronto
Sydney • Tokyo • Singapore • Hong Kong • Seoul • Taipei • New Delhi
Cape Town • Madrid • Mexico City • Amsterdam • Munich • Paris • Milan

PEARSON EDUCATION LIMITED

Edinburgh Gate
Harlow CM20 2JE
Tel: +44 (0)1279 623623
Fax: +44 (0)1279 431059
Website: www.pearsoned.co.uk

First edition published in 1987
Second edition published in 1996
Third edition published 2003
Revised third edition published in Great Britain in 2008

© Pearson Education 1987, 1996, 2003, 2008

The right of Gordon Martel to be identified as author of this work has been asserted
by him in accordance with the Copyright, Designs and Patents Act 1988.

ISBN: 978-1-4058-7431-1

British Library Cataloguing-in-Publication Data
A catalogue record for this book is available from the British Library

Library of Congress Cataloging-in-Publication Data
Martel, Gordon.
    The origins of the First World War / Gordon Martel. – Rev. 3rd ed.
        p. cm.
    Includes bibliographical references and index.
    ISBN-13: 978-1-4058-7431-1
    1. World War, 1914–1918 – Causes.   2. Europe – Politics and government – 1871–1918.
I. Title.
    D511.M269 2008
    940.3'11–dc22

2008005990

10 9 8 7 6 5 4 3 2 1
12 11 10 09 08

Typeset in 10/13.5pt Berkeley Book by 35
Printed and bound in Malaysia (CTP-VVP)

The publisher's policy is to use paper manufactured from sustainable forests.

Introduction to the Series

History is a narrative constructed by historians from traces left by the past. Historical enquiry is often driven by contemporary issues and, in consequence, historical narratives are constantly reconsidered, reconstructed and reshaped. The fact that different historians have different perspectives on issues means that there is also often controversy and no universally agreed version of past events. *Seminar Studies in History* was designed to bridge the gap between current research and debate, and the broad, popular general surveys that often date rapidly.

The volumes in the series are written by historians who are not only familiar with the latest research and current debates concerning their topic, but who have themselves contributed to our understanding of the subject. The books are intended to provide the reader with a clear introduction to a major topic in history. They provide both a narrative of events and a critical analysis of contemporary interpretations. They include the kinds of tools generally omitted from specialist monographs: a chronology of events, a glossary of terms and brief biographies of 'who's who'. They also include bibliographical essays in order to guide students to the literature on various aspects of the subject. Students and teachers alike will find that the selection of documents will stimulate discussion and offer insight into the raw materials used by historians in their attempt to understand the past.

Clive Emsley and Gordon Martel
Series Editors

Contents

Acknowledgements

We are grateful to the following for permission to reproduce copyright material:

Constable & Robinson Ltd for an extract from *Imperialism: A Study* by J.A. Hobson, published by Archibald Constable & Co, pp. 42–44; Cambridge University Press for an extract from the diary of The Chief of the Kaiser's Naval Cabinet published in *The Kaiser and his Court: Wilhelm II and the Government of Germany* by John C.G. Rohl, Cambridge University Press 1994; Pathfinder Press for an extract from *The Balkan Wars, 1912–13* by George Weissmann and Duncan Williams (eds), 1980; and Professor Jonathan Steinberg for his translation of 'The Tirpitz Memorandum of June 1897' published in *Yesterday's Deterrent: Tirpitz and the birth of the German battlefleet* by Jonathan Steinberg, Macdonald & Co 1965. Map 5 from *The Longman Companion to European Nationalism 1789–1920*, reprinted by permission of Pearson Education Ltd (Pearson, R. 1994). Plates 1, 2, 3, and 4 reproduced by permission of popperfoto.com.

In some instances we have been unable to trace the owners of copyright material, and we would appreciate any information that would enable us to do so.

Chronology

1871

10 May Treaty of Frankfurt: end of the Franco-Prussian war.

1873

May First *Dreikaiserbund* [Three Emperors' League] formed.

1875

8 April 'Is War in Sight?' headline in *Berlin Post* precipitates crisis.

1877

24 April Russia declares war on Turkey; Russo-Turkish war begins.

1879

7 October Dual Alliance signed by Germany and Austria-Hungary.

1881

18 June Second *Dreikaiserbund* formed.

1882

20 May Italy joins Germany and Austria-Hungary in Triple Alliance.

1885

30 March Russia occupies Penjdeh, initiating crisis with Britain in central Asia.

1887

February–March   Exchange of notes among Britain, Italy and Austria-Hungary: 'First Mediterranean agreement'.

18 June   Russo-German Reinsurance Treaty signed.

12 December   Second Mediterranean agreement: Great Britain, Austria-Hungary and Italy.

1888

15 June   Wilhelm II becomes emperor.

1889

27 January   General Boulanger flees to Belgium following failure of attempted *coup d'état*.

1890

15 March   Bismarck dismissed.

18 June   Reinsurance treaty not renewed.

1891

27 August   Franco-Russian political agreement.

1892

17 August   Terms of Franco-Russian military convention agreed.

1894

January   Franco-Russian military convention ratified.

1897

27 April   Russia and Austria-Hungary agree to put Balkans 'on ice' for 10 years.

1898

28 March   First German Naval Law.

1899

11 October   Boer War begins.

1900

14 June	Second German Naval Law.
16 October	Anglo-German Agreement on China (the 'Yangtze agreement').

1902

30 January	Anglo-Japanese alliance signed.

1903

2 October	Russia and Austria-Hungary conclude the Murzsteg agreement.

1904

8 February	Japan attacks Russia.
8 April	Anglo-French entente.
28 July	Russo-German Commercial Agreement.
21 October	Dogger Bank incident.

1905

22 January	'Bloody Sunday' in St Petersburg.
31 March	Kaiser Wilhelm II lands at Tangier, Morocco.
30 April	Anglo-French military 'conversations' begin.
6 May	'Fundamental Laws' in Russia establish a constitution and create the Duma.
27 May	Japanese defeat Russian fleet at Battle of Tsushima.
6 June	Delcassé forced to resign position as French foreign minister.
24 July	Treaty of Björkö.
12 August	Anglo-Japanese alliance is revized.
5 September	Treaty of Portsmouth ends Russo-Japanese war.

1906

16 January	Algeciras Conference begins.
7 April	Algeciras Act signed.
5 June	Third Naval Law in Germany ratified by Reichstag.

1907

31 August	Anglo-Russian convention signed.

1908

16 September	Büchlau agreement between Izvolsky and Aehrenthal.
6 October	Bosnia and Herzegovina annexed by Austria-Hungary.

1909

8 February	Franco-German agreement on Morocco.

1911

21 May	French troops occupy Fez, Morocco.
1 July	German gunboat *Panther* arrives in Agadir.
21 July	Lloyd George's speech on Morocco at the Mansion House.
29 September	Italy declares war on Turkey.
4 November	Franco-German agreement on Morocco.

1912

8–11 February	Lord Haldane's mission to Germany.
13 March	Serbia and Bulgaria sign alliance.
22 March	New German naval programme initiated.
29 May	Greece joins Serbia and Bulgaria in 'Balkan League'.
8 October	Montenegro declares war on Turkey.
11–12 October	Serbia, Bulgaria and Greece attack Turkey; First Balkan War begins.
15 October	Italy and Turkey sign Treaty of Ouchy, ending Italo-Turkish war.
8 December	Kaiser Wilhelm's 'War Council' meets at Potsdam.
13 December	Conference of Ambassadors meets in London to settle Balkan War.

1913

30 May	Treaty of London ends First Balkan War.
29 June	Bulgaria attacks Greece and Serbia; Second Balkan War begins.
10 August	Treaty of Bucharest ends Second Balkan War.
4 November	Russia launches the 'Great Military Programme'.

1914

28 June	Archduke Franz Ferdinand assassinated at Sarajevo.
5 July	Kaiser Wilhelm II offers 'blank cheque' to Austria-Hungary.

20 July	Poincaré and Viviani arrive in St Petersburg.
23 July	Austria issues ultimatum to Serbia.
28 July	Austria declares war on Serbia.
28 July	Socialists in France and Germany demonstrate against war.
28 July	Russia orders 'partial' mobilization of four western military districts.
29 July	Austrian artillery shells Belgrade.
29 July	Grey warns Germany that Britain cannot remain neutral in case of war; proposes mediation.
30 July	Russia orders general mobilization for following day.
30 July	Austria orders general mobilization for following day.
31 July	German ultimatum to Russia; kaiser proclaims 'state of imminent war'.
1 August	Germany declares war on Russia.
1 August	France orders mobilization.
2 August	Germany issues ultimatum to Belgium.
3 August	Germany declares war on France.
3 August	Italy declares neutrality.
4 August	German troops cross Belgian frontier.
4 August	Britain declares war on Germany.

Who's Who

Aehrenthal, Count Alois von (1854–1912): Austrian diplomat and states-man; ambassador in St Petersburg, 1899–1906; Austro-Hungarian minister of foreign affairs, 1906–12.

Alexander I (1777–1825): Son of Paul I; tsar of Russia, 1801–25.

Barrère, Camille (1851–1940): French diplomat; ambassador to Italy, 1897–1924.

Berchtold, Count Leopold von (1863–1942): Austrian diplomat and statesman; ambassador in Paris, 1894–99; in London, 1899–1906; in St Petersburg, 1906–12; Austro-Hungarian minister of foreign affairs, 1912–15.

Bertie, Francis (1st Viscount Bertie of Thame, 1844–1919): British diplo-mat; assistant under-secretary of state for foreign affairs, 1894–1903; ambas-sador in Rome, 1903–05; ambassador in Paris, 1905–18.

Bethmann Hollweg, Theobald von (1856–1921): Prussian minister of the interior, 1905–07; German minister of the interior, 1907–09; German chan-cellor, 1909–17.

Bezobrazov, Alexander Mikhailovich (1866–1933): Russian statesman; state secretary and member of Special Committee for the Affairs of the Far East, 1903–05.

Bismarck: Prince Otto von (1815–98): German statesman; elected to Prussian parliament in 1848; Prussian member of federal Diet at Frankfurt, 1851–59; ambassador to Russia and France, 1859–62; minister-president of Prussia, 1862–71; chancellor of North German Confederation, 1866–71; chancellor of Germany, 1871–90.

Boulanger, General Georges (1837–91): French soldier and statesman; minister of war, 1886–87. His appointment of republicans to military posts in place of royalists led to his dismissal, a political crisis and then his exile.

Bülow, Bernhard von (1849–1929): German statesman; foreign minister, 1897–1900; chancellor, 1900–09.

Burns, John (1858–1943): British statesman; elected to House of Commons in 1892; president of local government board, 1905–14; president of the board of trade, 1914; resigned during July crisis.

Cambon, Paul (1843–1924): French diplomat; ambassador to Britain, 1898–1921.

Conrad von Hötzendorf, Count (1852–1925): Austrian soldier; chief of Austro-Hungarian general staff, 1906–11, 1912–17.

Cromer, 1st Earl of (Evelyn Baring, 1841–1917): British colonial administrator; British agent and consul-general in Egypt, 1883–1907.

Crowe, Sir Eyre (1864–1925): British administrator; assistant under-secretary of state for foreign affairs, 1912–20.

Cruppi, Jean (1855–1933): French statesman; minister of foreign affairs, 1911; minister of justice, 1911–12.

Delcassé, Théophile (1852–1923): French statesman; elected deputy, 1889; minister of colonies, 1893–95; foreign minister, 1898–1905; naval minister, 1911–13; foreign minister, 1914–15.

Edward VII (1841–1910): Son of Queen Victoria; succeeded her as king of Great Britain and Ireland and emperor of India in 1901.

Franz Joseph (1830–1916): Emperor of Austria, 1848–1916; king of Hungary, 1867–1916.

Franz Ferdinand: Archduke (1863–1914): Nephew of the emperor Franz Joseph and, from 1896, heir to the throne of Austria-Hungary.

Garibaldi, Giuseppe (1807–82): Italian nationalist and hero of the *Risorgimento*. In 1860 led an invasion of Sicily and later captured Naples, leading to their inclusion in the newly unified Italian state.

Grey, 1st Viscount (Sir Edward Grey, 1862–1933): Elected to British parliament, 1885; foreign secretary, 1905–16.

Haldane, Viscount Richard Burdon (1856–1928): Elected to British parliament, 1885; secretary of war, 1905–12; lord chancellor, 1912–15 and 1924.

Hardinge, Charles (1st Baron Hardinge of Penshurst, 1858–1944): British diplomat and administrator; ambassador in St Petersburg, 1904–06; under-secretary of state for foreign affairs, 1906–10; viceroy of India, 1910–16.

Hobson, John Atkinson (1858–1940): English journalist and economist; author of *The War in South Africa* (1900), *The Psychology of Jingoism* (1901), *Imperialism: A Study* (1902), and *The Science of Wealth* (1911).

Holstein, Friedrich von (1837–1909): German administrator; served in foreign ministry, 1876–1906; although his highest post was as Director of the Political Section, he was very influential in the period 1890–1906.

Izvolsky, Alexander (1856–1919): Russian diplomat and statesman; entered Russian diplomatic service in 1875; foreign minister, 1905–10; ambassador to France, 1910–16.

Joffre, Joseph Jacques Césaire (1852–1931): French soldier and administrator; vice-president of the higher war council, 1911–14; commander-in-chief, 1914–16.

Kiderlen-Wächter, Alfred von (1852–1912): German administrator; foreign minister, 1910–13.

Lambsdorff, Count V.N. (1844–1907): Russian statesman; foreign minister, 1900–06.

Lansdowne, 5th Marquis of (Henry Charles Keith Petty-Fitzmaurice, 1845–1927): British statesman and administrator; secretary of war, 1895–1900; foreign secretary, 1900–05.

Liman von Sanders, Otto (1855–1929): German soldier; led German military commission to Constantinople in 1913; appointed inspector-general of Turkish army, 1914.

Lloyd George, David (1863–1945): British statesman; elected to the British parliament in 1890; entered the cabinet in 1905, chancellor of the exchequer, 1908–15; prime minister, 1916–22.

Loubet, Émile (1838–1929): French statesman; president, 1899–1906.

Metternich, Count Clemens von (1773–1859): Austrian diplomat and statesman; ambassador during the Napoleonic wars; minister of foreign affairs, 1809–48; chancellor, 1812–48.

Moltke, Helmuth von ('the younger', 1848–1916): German soldier; chief of the Prussian general staff, 1906–14.

Napoleon I (Napoleon Bonaparte, 1769–1821): First Consul of France, 1799–1804; emperor, 1804–14.

Napoleon III (Charles Louis Napoleon Bonaparte, 1808–73): Son of Napoleon Bonaparte's brother Louis; elected president of the second republic, 1848; emperor, 1848–71; exiled, 1871–73.

Nicholas I (1796–1855): Son of Paul I, succeeded his brother, Alexander I as tsar of Russia in 1825.

Nicholas II (1869–1918): Son of Alexander III of Russia, became tsar in 1894; abdicated in 1917; shot by revolutionaries in 1918.

Nicholas Nikolayevich, Grand-Duke (1856–1929): Russian soldier and administrator, nephew of tsar Alexander II. Commander-in-chief, 1914–17.

Nicolson, Sir Arthur (1849–1928): British diplomat and administrator; minister in Tangier, 1901–04; in Madrid, 1904–06; in St Petersburg, 1906–10; undersecretary of state for foreign affairs, 1910–16.

Poincaré, Raymond (1860–1934): French statesman; elected deputy, 1887; minister of education, 1893–94; minister of finance, 1894–95, 1906; senator, 1906–13; prime minister, 1912–13; president, 1913–20.

Prinetti, Giulio (1851–1908): Italian statesman; minister of foreign affairs, 1901–03.

Rouvier, Maurice (1842–1911): French statesman; elected deputy, 1871; minister of foreign affairs, 1902–05; prime minister, 1905–06, 1906–11.

Sazonov, Serge Dmitrievich (1861–1927): Russian statesman; minister of foreign affairs, 1910–16.

Schlieffen, Count Alfred von (1833–1913): German field marshal and chief of the Prussian general staff, 1891–1906. Designer of the Schlieffen Plan, the basis of pre-war German military strategy.

Tirpitz, Alfred von (1849–1930): German admiral; secretary of state for the navy, 1897–1916. Strategist responsible for the creation of the 'risk fleet' which began construction in 1898.

Tisza, Count István (1861–1918): Hungarian statesman; prime minister of Hungary, 1904–05, 1913–17; murdered in 1918.

Wilhelm II (1859–1941): Son of emperor Frederick III; emperor of Germany and king of Prussia, 1888–1918; abdicated in 1918, exiled to Holland.

Witte, Serge (1849-1915): Russian statesman; minister of finance, 1892–1903; prime minister, 1905.

Glossary

Anarchism: A socio-political movement that rejects the coercive authority of the state in favour of individual freedom. Based on the ideas of two Russians, Mikhail Bakunin and Prince Peter Kropotkin, anarchism reached the height of its popularity in the decades before the First World War, when it came to be associated with violence and terrorism.

Ausgleich: Literally, 'compromise', this constitutional re-arrangement within the Habsburg monarchy was instituted in 1867. It allowed for separate parliaments (*Diets*) and prime ministers in Austria and Hungary; the empire remained connected by means of a common emperor/king, a common army and navy and a customs unit.

Autocracy: A loosely defined political term usually referring to the absolute or despotic rule by an individual. Most often used in referring to the tsar, 'the autocrat of all the Russias'.

Boxers: Term used to describe those Chinese who violently opposed foreign influence in China, 1899–1900. The name comes from their ritualized exercises known as 'harmony fists'. They attacked Christian missionaries, destroyed European property and besieged foreign legations in Peking for two months in June–August 1900.

Comité de l'Afrique Française: A political association formed to promote French colonialism in Africa. It was a highly influential group, and one of its presidents, Charles Jonnart, became French foreign minister in 1912.

Committee of Imperial Defence: Established by the British government at the end of the South African war in an effort to improve strategic planning and overcome the traditional rivalry between the army and the navy. It proved largely ineffective in accomplishing its goals, although sub-committees did do some useful work.

Dreadnought: A new class of battleship launched in Britain in 1906. Replacing coal with oil as fuel made these ships faster than previous models, and ten

12-inch guns rather than four made it more powerful (and much more expensive). Earlier battleships were rendered obsolete and the Anglo-German naval race was intensified.

Dreikaiserbund: Literally, the 'three emperors' league'. In the first league, formed by Germany, Russia and Austria-Hungary in 1873, the three agreed to consult with one another on matters of common concern. It was replaced by a more formal agreement in 1881 when each promised to remain neutral if one of the three fought a fourth.

Dual Monarchy: The name used to refer to the Habsburg empire following the *Ausgleich* of 1867. It represented an agreement between the dominant Germans of Austria with the powerful Magyars of Hungary.

Duma: The Russian parliament established after the revolution of 1905. Although this represented a significant concession on the part of the Russian monarchy, it was a weak and unrepresentative instititution. Its powers were strictly limited, especially in the areas of defence, foreign policy and finance.

German Confederation: An association (or *Bund*) of thirty-nine states in central Europe formed at the end of the Napoleonic wars in 1815. Dominated by Austria, their representatives met in a Diet in Frankfurt – but this had very little authority. It collapsed when Prussia defeated Austria in 1866.

Holy Alliance: Following the Napoleonic wars, Tsar Alexander I drew up a document proclaiming that European rulers must henceforth be guided by Christian principles; most European states eventually adhered to it. But the phrase is usually used as a shorthand reference to the reactionary policies of Russia, Austria and Prussia.

Italia irredenta: Literally, 'unredeemed Italy'. A popular movement in Italy following the wars of unification to 'redeem' those lands inhabited by Italians but not included within the Italian state (principally Trieste, Trentino, south Tyrol, Istria and Fiume).

Kriegsschuldfrage: Literally, the 'war guilt question'. Following the signing of the treaty of Versailles, in which it was formally asserted that Germany and her allies were responsible for the war, historians and others began to question the assertion, which led to revisionism and a vigorous debate over the question of war guilt.

Magyars: Native name for the inhabitants of Hungary. Those who spoke Magyar were actually a minority in the Hungary that was created by the *Ausgleich* of 1867.

Neue Kurs: Literally, the 'new course'. When Wilhelm II became emperor of Germany in 1888 he was determined to make his mark on foreign policy, which led to Bismarck's dismissal in 1890. When the new chancellor, Caprivi, advised against renewing the Reinsurance Treaty with Russia, Wilhelm agreed, signifying that Germany was no longer dependent on Russian friendship – an essential element of Bismarck's policy.

Nihilism: A radical revolutionary movement that arose in late nineteenth-century Russia, inspired by the teachings of Mikhail Bakunin. Nihilists proclaimed their rejection of all traditional values, particularly those concerning the family and Christianity, and sought to destroy the authority of the state through terror and assassination.

Open Door: The phrase that US secretary of state John Hay gave to his policy in China in 1899. Fearing the partition of China or that European empires would erect barriers to trade in their spheres of influence, Hay issued notes calling for all states to receive equal treatment. He claimed that there was agreement with his principle.

Plan 17: The French war plan of 1911 inspired by General Joffre's belief that the 'spirit of the offensive' was a key to victory. Rather than standing on the defensive and resisting a German attack, the French army was to seize the initiative and attack Germany.

Plan B: The Russian strategic plan for responding to a war with Germany. Based on the Franco-Russian alliance, the Russians were to go onto the offensive in the east, attacking through Poland in order to relieve pressure on the French.

Quai d'Orsay: The location of the French ministry of foreign affairs. Often used by historians as a shorthand reference to the ministry in the same way that British historians will refer to 'Whitehall' for the British Government or American historians to the 'White House' for the US presidency.

Rapprochement: A term used in diplomacy and in diplomatic history to describe the re-establishment of harmonious relations between two states, usually after a crisis or a prolonged period of antagonism.

Realism: A term that is used in contrast to 'idealism'. When used in diplomacy or in diplomatic history, it usually means that individual decision-makers deliberately reject ideology and sentiment in favour of measurable objectives and interests.

Reichsrat: The Austrian Chamber of Deputies, or parliament, established in Vienna in 1907. Based on universal male suffrage, the chamber was relatively powerless as the ministers were not responsible to it.

Reichstag: The German parliament that was established in Berlin by the constitution of 1871. It was based on universal manhood suffrage and it could block certain measures, but it could not initiate legislation. Ministers did not need to be appointed from it, nor were they responsible to it.

Revanche: Literally, 'revenge'. In diplomatic history, the term refers to the desire of the French, after 1871, to avenge their defeat in the Franco-Prussian war. The movement usually focused on the recovery of the 'lost provinces' of Alsace and Lorraine that were taken from France by the treaty of Frankfurt.

Risorgimento: Literally, 'resurgence'. Used by Camillo Cavour as the title of the Piedmontese newspaper (*Il Risorgimento*) that he founded in 1847 with the aim of promoting the unification of all Italian-speaking peoples. Now used by historians to refer to the Italian unification movement generally.

Schlieffen Plan: Devised by Count Alfred von Schlieffen, chief of the Prussian general staff, 1891–1905. Designed in 1895 as a strategic response to the prospect of a two-front war following the formation of the Franco-Russian alliance, the plan was to knock out France quickly by invading through Holland, Belgium and Luxembourg. Although modified, the basic premise remained when Germany attacked through Belgium in 1914.

Slavophilia: A term used to describe the movement in Russia that rejected the policy of westernization that had first been launched by Peter the Great. Popular with many Russian intellectuals in the mid-nineteenth century, the movement led later in the century to a concentration on unifying all slavic peoples, i.e. 'Panslavism'.

Theocracy: A form of government based on the rule of God, in which the laws of the state are those prescribed by religious doctrine or interpretation of the deity's will.

Weltpolitik: Literally, 'world policy'. The term is used to describe the policies of the government of Wilhelm II in which Germany was to take its place as one of the great powers of the world. The policy led to the building of a high-seas fleet and to attempts to gain colonial territories, particularly in Africa and the far east.

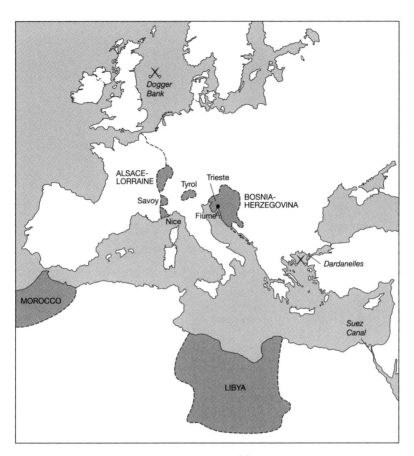

Map 1 Europe and the Mediterranean: trouble spots

Map 2 Central and Eastern Europe

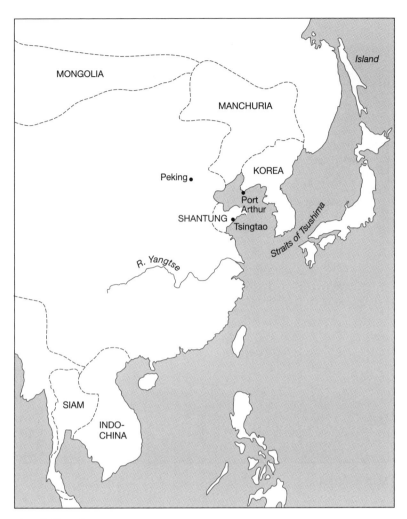

Map 3 East Asia

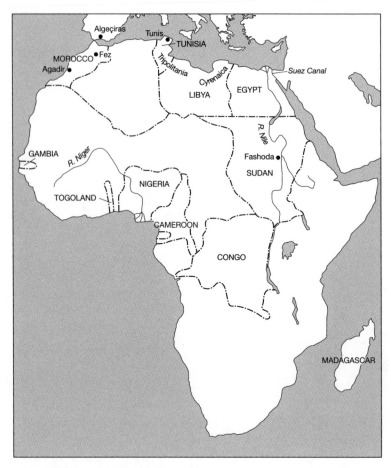

Map 4 Africa

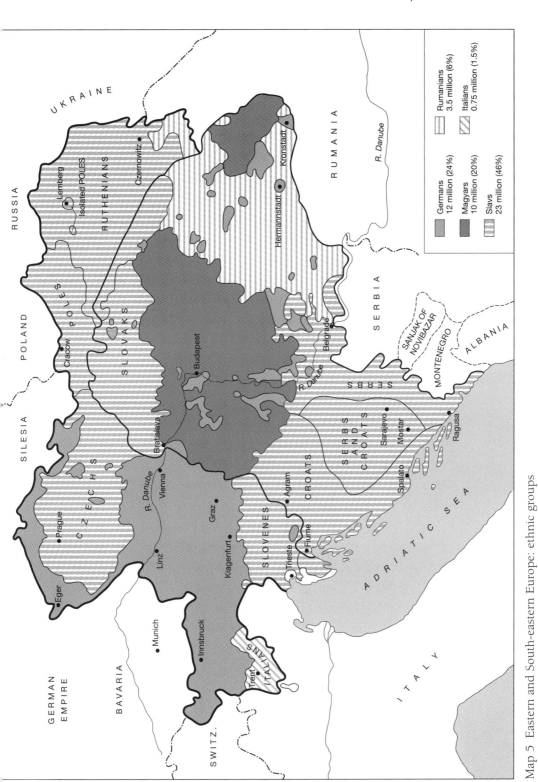

Map 5 Eastern and South-eastern Europe: ethnic groups
Source: Raymond Pearson, *The Longman Companion to European Nationalism 1789–1920* (1994) pp. 50–1

Part 1

ANALYSIS AND ASSESSMENT

1

The Problem

THE OUTBREAK OF WAR

On a summer's morning late in June 1914, the heir to the throne of the Habsburg monarchy arrived at the Bosnian town of Sarajevo for an official visit. While the **Archduke Franz Ferdinand**, his wife and his entourage proceeded through the crowded main street of the city in open motorcars, a young man stepped out of the crowd and hurled something at the Archduke. A bomb exploded, narrowly missing its target, and the would-be assassin was quickly seized. The Archduke, against the advice of his aides, insisted that they continue their journey to the town hall. Here the Austrians endured a fulsome speech by the mayor, saturated with unintentionally ironic references to the loyalty of the Bosnian people and the esteem in which the Archduke was held in the province. When this agony had ended, Franz Ferdinand insisted that he be permitted to visit the hospital to see one of his aides who had been injured by the exploding bomb. As the party retraced its route along the main street, some confusion occurred, which resulted in the Archduke's chauffeur being forced to stop and reverse direction in the middle of the street. Seizing this unexpected opportunity, another assassin emerged, this time with a pistol rather than a bomb; quickly taking aim, he shot Franz Ferdinand in the throat. Within minutes, both the Archduke and his wife lay dead. Before the summer was over, this dramatic event would lead to the greatest war Europe had ever known.

Franz Ferdinand: Archduke (1863–1914): Nephew of the emperor Franz Joseph and, from 1896, heir to the throne of Austria-Hungary.

Few Europeans at the time anticipated that the murder of an Austrian archduke would draw them into a crisis and then into a war: assassinations were not unknown in Europe, but few of them had led to armed conflict. The Balkans seemed far away not only to the English, but to the French and to the Germans as well. Europe had weathered much more threatening crises in the recent past, and the first few days following the death of the archduke were notable mainly for the absence of activity.

Many were surprised by how slowly the Austrians responded to the assassination, which seemed to confirm the impression that the assassination at Sarajevo would soon be forgotten. Franz Ferdinand was not a popular man in court circles in Vienna. There was no sign of a popular outcry for revenge among the peoples of Austria-Hungary. The Archduke himself had dreamt of solving the South Slav question by conciliation when he came to the throne: 'I do not want from Serbia a single plum-tree, a single sheep' (Taylor, 1954: 494). However, as is often the case in the course of diplomatic affairs, this tranquil appearance was misleading. Within the Austrian government there was a strong conviction that Serbia was responsible, that this gunman did not act alone, and that he actually enjoyed the unofficial support of the Serbian government. The Austrians quickly discovered that the assassin and his compatriots were Serbian nationalists, members of a terrorist group called the 'Black Hand', whose ambition it was to incorporate all Serbian peoples within the Serbian state [Doc. 15, p. 102]. Behind the scenes in Vienna, politicians, diplomats and strategists were hotly debating the question of how far and how fast to move in responding to this outburst of Serbian nationalism. Many Austrian officials regarded the nationalism of minority groups to be the greatest threat to the continuing existence of the Habsburg monarchy and they saw in the assassination the perfect opportunity to crush the Serbian-sponsored movement in Bosnia – particularly when the kaiser seemed willing to assure them of German support [Docs 22 and 23, pp. 110–112]. Although they lacked proof of complicity on the part of the Serbian government, the Austrians, after three weeks of negotiation and debate, agreed to despatch an ultimatum that they believed Serbia could not possibly accept [Doc. 27, p. 115]. The terms would end, in effect, Serbia's existence as a sovereign state. The ultimatum was presented at 6 p.m. on 23 July; the Serbs were given only forty-eight hours to comply.

Two days later, three hours before their reply was due, the Serbian government ordered their army to mobilize. But they also presented a note to the Austrian government written in language sufficiently ambiguous to convince some observers that they were, in essence, prepared to accept the terms of the ultimatum. In spite of this uncertainty, the Austrians nevertheless ordered the mobilization of seven army corps against Serbia. The following day the Russian government, which was prepared to support Serbia against an Austrian attack, decided to undertake a series of steps that would enable them to carry out a full mobilization, in the event that Serbia's acceptance of the ultimatum did not go far enough to satisfy the Austrians. At 11 a.m. on 28 July, less than five days after presenting the ultimatum, Austria-Hungary declared war on Serbia.

Later on that same day, during the afternoon of 28 July, Russia announced that she too would mobilize – but only in those districts that would enable her to go to war with Austria-Hungary. This partial mobilization, which was designed to avoid the appearance of threatening Germany, was initiated at midnight, 29 July. But by the following day the Russian government had decided that restricting their mobilization to their Austro-Hungarian frontier would place them in a perilous position, should Germany come into the conflict. On 30 July Russia ordered a full mobilization [Doc. 32, p. 123]. The possibility of localizing the crisis seemed to have evaporated.

Austria-Hungary responded to the Russian decision by ordering a general mobilization on 31 July. War between the Russians and the Austrians now appeared to be inevitable. Consequently, the German government ordered their army to mobilize and despatched an ultimatum of their own to Russia demanding the immediate cessation of all military measures against Germany and Austria-Hungary within twelve hours. When the Russians failed to reply to this ultimatum, the Germans declared war on them at 6 p.m. on 1 August. The French ordered a general mobilization on the same day; the Germans declared war on them two days later. On the morning of 4 August German troops crossed the Belgian frontier; by midnight Germany and Great Britain were at war.

EXPLAINING CAUSES

The preceding summary is a very superficial one; entire books have been written that cover only the details of these events. Nevertheless, students may still begin to have some sense of the complexities involved in answering the deceptively simple question of 'how did the war begin?' No one, not even the Austrians, went to war for the sake of Franz Ferdinand; and yet a direct line can be drawn between his murder, the diplomatic crisis, the mobilizations and the declarations of war. There was clearly more to the July crisis than meets the eye – more than ultimata and mobilizations. Why did the Austrians attempt to eliminate Serbia as a sovereign state? Why did the Russians decide to risk war by mobilizing in support of the Serbs? How did the Germans become involved in a dispute that apparently had little to do with them? Why did the French decide to mobilise their troops when war broke out in the east? Why did the British choose to go to war for the sake of Belgium? Or did they? And where were the Italians? Although a member of the Triple Alliance for thirty-four years, Italy did not enter the war until 1915.

In order to answer these questions we must unravel the diplomatic ties that connected these events to one another; we must understand what the 'alliance system' was and how it bound – or failed to bind – states to one another. In the aftermath of the First World War, many acute observers insisted that it was the system of alliances that led the states of Europe down the slippery slope to war in July 1914. The impression that once the crisis had been provoked by the assassin's bullets the alliance system took over and rendered diplomats helpless became widespread after 1919. The complicated network of political commitments had in turn led the military to produce intricate mobilization plans, which eventually led to *War by Time-Table* – the title of one popular book on the subject (Taylor, 1969).

But statesmen seldom act on the basis of simple legal commitments, and even when we unravel the entangling alliances and alignments that tied the states of Europe to one another, we shall only discover another layer of more fundamental – and more profound – questions that require answers if we are to understand how a great European war began in August 1914. The alliances are, in many respects, the easiest subject to explore when studying the origins of the war: they are well-documented; their terms can be analysed; their effectiveness can be measured. But the Italians managed to avoid living up to their promises, while there was nothing on paper that bound the British to the Russians and the French. So what were the 'underlying' causes of the war? What sentiments and emotions, ambitions and fears prepared governments and peoples alike to gamble their existence in 1914?

Of all the phenomena associated with the outbreak of the war, nationalism is obviously the one that has most fascinated historians. Part of this fascination can be readily explained by the events of July: nationalism was unquestionably the force that propelled the young Serbs of Bosnia into plotting the assassination of Franz Ferdinand; nationalism was unquestionably the phenomenon that the Austrians saw themselves fighting against when they presented their ultimatum; and the feeling of brotherhood based upon a common Slavic identity was unquestionably a factor in leading the Russians to regard themselves as the protectors of the Serbs. But the interest in this phenomenon far exceeds the events of July; almost every historian engaged in writing the history of Europe has identified nationalism as one of the most influential forces that shaped modern history. Or, to put it another way, no historian has argued that the sense of nationality was *not* a factor in the outbreak of war in 1914.

Only slightly less elusive than the idea of nationalism is that of militarism. By the time that the crisis came in July, the continental states of Europe had amassed standing armies of unprecedented size. The conscription of millions of young men by their governments to serve in the armed forces for one, two, or even three years was the rule in pre-war Europe, to which Britain was the exception. This undoubtedly attests to the power of the modern state, both in terms of the power that it can muster, but also in the sense of being able to insist on the compliance of its citizens. Were the young men of Europe forced to the front against their will in 1914? Or does this phenomenon indicate a popular tide of warlike enthusiasm among the peoples of Europe that overwhelmed the statesmen who were unable to stem the tide of the forces that they had unleashed? [**Doc. 33, p. 123**] Even in Britain, with its tiny professional army, amateur militarism was a popular entertainment before the war.

And what was all that marching and drilling supposed to achieve? What were all those symbols of nationality and patriotic zeal supposed to inspire? Did they not all boil down to imperialistic expansionism? The late nineteenth century was the great age of European dominance: Africa had been partitioned, much of Asia was ruled by Europeans; the Ottoman and Chinese empires appeared to be on the verge of collapse. Was the war within Europe really a struggle for spoils beyond it? Did European governments not consciously manipulate their people into supporting their drive to acquire new resources and markets by promoting xenophobia and inspiring war scares [**Doc. 11, p. 98**]? Is it not true that the war within Europe was really a contest to see who would be master outside of it?

Nationalism, militarism and imperialism are the most prominent of the 'underlying' causes of war that historians have investigated in their attempts to go beneath the surface of the events that led to war in 1914. Historians began assessing these factors even before the war ended, and they are assessing them still; students who turn to the 'classic' treatments that appeared between the wars in books by Sidney Fay (1928) and Bernadotte Schmitt (1930) will find these themes clearly being discussed from the beginning. The more detailed, better documented accounts that appeared after the Second World War in books by William L. Langer (1950), A.J.P. Taylor (1954) and Luigi Albertini (1952–57) will find that these themes were not abandoned. It has been apparent from the start that these are the issues that will not go away and that, although it is impossible to assess the relative effect of such factors in some neatly hierarchical manner, it is essential to investigate the factors that altered perceptions, stimulated ambitions and generated fears. Any attempt to explain the origins of the war must take them into account.

One line of investigation not pursued in the English-speaking world until half a century after the outbreak of the war, was the possibility that war arose from the desire on the part of the guardians of the old order to forestall a social conflict at home by engaging in war abroad. This argument was first posed in Germany by Eckhardt Kehr, a radical young historian who, in a number of essays argued for *Der Primat der Innenpolitik* (the primacy of domestic politics). Kehr's argument that the industrialists and landowners of pre-war Germany combined to prevent domestic reform through a policy of *Sammlungspolitik* ('the politics of rallying-together') took hold with a number of influential historians in Germany (Kehr, 1975). This argument was then extended to explain how a crisis – or even a war – would come to be seen by those who were making the decisions to be a more attractive alternative than domestic reform (Mayer, 1967; Gordon, 1974). During the past twenty years historians have applied elements of this thesis to explain the policies of Britain (Offer, 1985), Russia (Lieven, 1983) and Italy (Bosworth, 1979).

It may now be difficult for us to imagine a time and a place in which war was not only acceptable but popular [**Doc. 14, p. 101**]. For students, the greater the gap in time between themselves and their subject, the more difficult it is to recapture the attitudes and the ideas that made up the emotional world in which Europeans lived early in the twentieth century. Two world wars, numerous revolutions, a great depression, the advent of atomic weapons and bloody ethnic conflicts separate us psychologically from the men and women of 1914. The kind of thinking that led people to rejoice at the prospect of war is now difficult to recapture – but rejoice they did: there was dancing in the streets and spontaneous demonstrations of support for governments throughout Europe; men flocked to recruiting offices, fearful that the war might end before they had the opportunity to fight; there was a spirit of festival and a sense of community in all European cities as old class divisions and political rivalries were replaced by patriotic fervour. Students seeking to understand the origins of the First World War must be sensitive to the emotional distance that separates them from their forebears.

But students of history should also understand that distance can be an advantage. The question, 'how did the war begin?' was frequently posed immediately after the war, but in a very different political climate; people were then less concerned with the question of how the war began than they were with determining responsibility for it. In Germany this quest was particularly passionate, where it came to be known as the **Kriegsschuldfrage** (the 'war guilt question'), a question that arose directly from the Paris Peace Conference of 1919. There, the 'Commission on the Responsibility of the Authors of the War and on the Enforcement of Penalties' concluded that the responsibility for the outbreak of war 'lies wholly upon the Powers which declared war in pursuance of a policy of aggression'. Not surprisingly, the victorious powers determined that Germany and Austria (together with their allies, Turkey and Bulgaria) had premeditated the war, and had brought it about by acts 'deliberately committed in order to make it unavoidable'.

No doubt this assessment of blame would in itself have aroused wounded feelings within Germany and Austria. But in inter-war Europe there was more than wounded feelings at stake because the victorious Allies went on to justify their demand for reparations on the basis of the commission's report. So the debate on war origins had a practical as well as an abstract side to it, and the question of war guilt quickly became the most hotly debated

Kriegsschuldfrage: Literally, the 'war guilt question'. Following the signing of the treaty of Versailles, in which it was formally asserted that Germany and her allies were responsible for the war, historians and others began to question the assertion, which led to revisionism and a vigorous debate over the question of war guilt.

historical subject of the 1920s. Those who regarded the Treaty of Versailles as an illegitimate, wicked peace, as a *diktat* imposed upon the vanquished, believed that if they could show that the burden of responsibility rested more with the Allied states than with the Central powers (or at least that responsibility must be shared equally), then the peace settlement might be revised and a morally defensible system of international relations put in its place. Conversely, those who believed that the power of Germany had to be permanently checked, and that the Austro-Hungarian monarchy was an evil and decadent empire that must give way to nation-states, sought to prove that the commission was correct to conclude that the Central powers were responsible for the war.

But with the rise of Hitler, the creation of the Third Reich, the outbreak of the Second World War and the horrors of the Holocaust, the controversy over the origins of the First World War steadily lost its hold on the popular imagination. Professional historians continued their investigations of the subject, exploring what seemed to be an endless supply of new documentary evidence, but the subject had lost its punch. In the 1920s, fresh revelations unearthed in the archives or the appearance of new memoirs had been frontpage news. Led by Germany, each of the combatants began to compile documentary collections of diplomatic correspondence in the hope that these would demonstrate their innocence. It soon became obvious that no one was innocent. The documents revealed an extremely complicated diplomatic system, a network of alliances and alignments and a variety of conflicting ambitions and fears. These complexities made it increasingly difficult to adhere to the view that any one state was responsible for the war.

If the war guilt controversy had any result, it was to give the impression that responsibility was somehow shared by all, that every one of the great powers before 1914 was militaristic and imperialistic, that each had made secret arrangements to come to the aid of friends and allies at a moment of crisis, that each had drawn up elaborate war plans, mobilization schedules and railway timetables which had to be adhered to in 1914. This conclusion seemed to stand in stark contrast with what was generally assumed to be the truth about the origins of the Second World War, where practically everyone agreed that 'Hitler' was the answer to almost every question that almost anyone might ask about responsibility. Thus, by the 1960s, we had a situation in which the two world wars were treated as discrete subjects: the responsibility for the first was very murky but certainly shared by all; the responsibility for the second was very clear and hardly bore investigation. The only connection drawn between the two was that somehow the brutal, unfair and unjustified terms of the Treaty of Versailles had created an environment in Germany that encouraged the development of Nazism, and thereby, in some way, the victorious allies of the First World War were ultimately responsible for the Second.

And then came Fritz Fischer, a German historian at the University of Hamburg whose arguments revived the debate that had lain dormant for more than a generation. When he published *Griff nach der Weltmacht* in 1961 (curiously translated as *Germany's Aims in the First World War* in 1967 – curious, because 'Weltmacht' translates as 'world power') he effectively refocused attention on German responsibility for the war – an approach which had not been fashionable since the 1920s. The book was enormously detailed, piling up mountains of evidence to support the argument that Germany had consciously striven to establish itself as a world power in the era before the First World War, a policy that inevitably led first to competition, then to conflict, with Britain and Russia. This seemed to return the argument to where it had been in the 1920s, when the question of Germany's guilt had been primary. But new zest was given to the debate in the 1960s as a result of Fischer's contention that a clear line of continuity could be drawn between the policies of Wilhelmine and Nazi Germany. Suddenly it became possible to argue that German expansionism could be found at the centre of both world wars. In his next book, *Krieg der Illusionen* (1969; translated and published as *War of Illusions* in 1975), Fischer went farther still, arguing that the German government had decided to go to war as far back as December 1912, and that the declaration of war had only been postponed until circumstances became more favourable – as they did in July 1914. The war upon which Germany then embarked was not the defensive, preventive war that the politicians had claimed; it was not launched out of fear and despair, but rather 'to realize Germany's political ambitions which may be summed up as German hegemony over Europe' (Fischer, 1975: 470).

Not surprisingly, this argument did not go unchallenged, and soon the cause of the First World War was a hot topic again. Things heated up first in Germany, where historians attacked Fischer from almost every angle: Gerhard Ritter, Karl Dietrich Erdmann, Egmont Zechlin and Erwin Hölzle undertook to discredit Fischer by denouncing him in the press, and they succeeded in persuading the government to cancel a lecture tour of the United States on the grounds that he would tarnish the image of Germany in the eyes of Americans. But Fischer did not find himself alone in the face of this criticism: Imanuel Geiss (1966), John Röhl (1973), Volker Berghahn (1973) and others supported his argument and extended the research upon which it was based. It is true, as Holger Herwig has argued (1991), that works on the July crisis published before 1961 are now out of date – telling us more about the times in which they were written than they do about the subject about which they were written – and as such are best treated as a kind of historical archaeology.

The quarter-century that followed the appearance of *Griff nach der Weltmacht* witnessed an explosion of research on the subject of the war's

origins, as well as efforts to arrive at a new synthesis. Detailed and sophisti-
cated works based upon painstaking archival investigation added enormously to both the breadth and the depth of our understanding of prewar
Europe. F.R. Bridge, Richard Bosworth, Keith Wilson, René Girault, Douglas
Porch and Wayne Thompson have revealed new complexities in the political, economic and military processes that set the war in motion; complexities that have, in turn, stimulated fresh controversies far removed from
the Fischer debate. Important new syntheses have been provided by Zara
Steiner, Dominic Lieven, Richard Bosworth and Samuel Williamson in the
Macmillan/St Martin's series on 'The Making of the 20th Century' – although
these have thus far been limited to national perspectives rather than a more
generalized, European one.

   This book is not designed to provide a new synthesis, but rather to introduce the subject to students by summarizing the major themes in a clear and
succinct way. Like most stories, the first, and perhaps the most difficult
choice for historians, is to decide where to begin. In fact, few choices are
more revealing than those first few pages of a book or first few paragraphs
of a scholarly article. Historians writing about the origins of the First World
War have started their stories at almost every imaginable point; a few have
attempted to avoid such a choice by constructing a non-narrative approach.

   In spite of the preceding remarks about the fascination with 'underlying'
causes, some historians have concentrated their attention on the events of the
summer of 1914. Historians who begin here reveal that they do not accept
the argument that the war was the inevitable result of underlying forces. They
resist the suggestion that war was intrinsic to the nature of the European
states system. Instead, they argue that, had it not been for the peculiarities of
the July crisis, war might have been avoided. This view places the burden of
responsibility on one or more of the men who actually made the decisions
that summer: on **Count Berchtold**, the Austro-Hungarian minister of foreign
affairs, because of his determination to crush Serbian independence; on Serge
Sazonov, the Russian minister of foreign affairs, because of his decision to
support Serbia by attempting a partial mobilization of Russian forces;
on **Wilhelm II**, the German emperor, because he pushed Austria into taking
a hard line in the crisis; on **Raymond Poincaré**, the French president,
because he assured Russia of French support for her policy in the Balkans;
and on **Sir Edward Grey**, the British foreign minister, because he failed to
choose between restraining Russia or warning Germany that Britain would
fight alongside Russia and France should war break out in eastern Europe.
Concentrating on the July crisis does not, therefore, imply that any particular state or statesman was responsible for war, but it does reveal an assumption that this crisis could have been managed successfully, as had others in
the past.

**Berchtold, Count Leopold
von** *(1863–1942)*:
Austrian diplomat and
statesman; ambassador
in Paris, 1894–99; in
London, 1899–1906; in
St Petersburg, 1906–12;
Austro-Hungarian minis-
ter of foreign affairs,
1912–15.

Wilhelm II *(1859–1941)*:
Son of emperor Frederick
III; emperor of Germany
and king of Prussia,
1888–1918; abdicated in
1918, exiled to Holland.

Poincaré,   Raymond
(1860–1934):   French
statesman;   elected
deputy, 1887; minister
of education, 1893–94;
minister   of   finance,
1894–95, 1906; senator,
1906–13; prime minister,
1912–13;   president,
1913–20.

Grey, 1st Viscount *(Sir
Edward Grey 1862–
1933)*: Elected to British
parliament, 1885; for-
eign secretary, 1905–16.

Few historians today would choose to focus their attention exclusively on the immediate events that led to war; the most widespread assumption underlying contemporary interpretations of the First World War is that the crisis of July was the logical (if not necessarily the inevitable) culmination of deep-seated antagonisms and fundamental forces. Interest in the July crisis itself has waned: we seem to have reached the point where we know almost everything we are ever going to know about who said what to whom at what moment. But historians have thought this about subjects before and been proved wrong; perhaps the collapse of the Soviet Union and the disintegration of Yugoslavia will produce new revelations.

Students will therefore discover that most narratives begin before the assassination at Sarajevo, and that they take their story at least as far back as 1902–07 and the 'diplomatic revolution' of those years. During this crucial period Great Britain, it is argued, departed from her long-standing policy of 'splendid isolation' during which she remained aloof from the continental alliances. A turning-point was reached when Britain formed an alliance with Japan in 1902. This, it can be argued, led directly to the Russo-Japanese war in February 1904. The conflict between the Russians and the Japanese, by threatening to drag in their respective partners, the British and the French, led directly to the Anglo-French 'entente' in April 1904. The crushing blow that was dealt to the Russian fleet by the Japanese at the Battle of Tsushima led to the Treaty of Portsmouth in September 1905, which signified the rise of Japan and the descent of Russia. This, in turn, led the Russians to give up their imperialist, expansionist designs in both the far east and in central Asia, thus making possible the 'entente' with the British of August 1907. But a focus on the events of these three years usually indicates the belief that they reveal a fundamental change in British attitudes – a change can be interpreted as either an imperialist plot designed to encircle Germany or as a defensive response to the threat of German expansionism in Africa, the Middle East and Asia.

In fact, German expansionism has also been the focus of some who examine these years in particular detail. Germany, they argue, had been undergoing a profound transformation since 1870, but it was not until this period that these changes came to be reflected in her foreign policy: following the turn of the century she adopted a 'world policy', which reflected her determination to break out from the difficult position of being located in central Europe at a time of worldwide expansion on the part of other great powers – a determination that was symbolized by her decision to build an ocean-going battle fleet. The challenge confronting her in these years, declared the chancellor, **Prince Bernhard von Bülow**, was whether Germany was going to be 'the hammer' or 'the anvil' of world politics [**Doc. 97**]. The Moroccan crisis of 1905 was the direct result of this line of thinking within Germany.

Bülow, Bernhard von *(1849–1929)*: German statesman; foreign minister, 1897–1900; chancellor, 1900–09.

When Germany failed to secure the diplomatic victory she sought at the Algeciras Conference in 1906, she concentrated on challenging Britain at sea by escalating her naval building programme. Historians who concentrate on the years 1902–07, by focusing attention on the Anglo-Japanese alliance, the Anglo-French entente, the first Moroccan crisis, the naval race and the Anglo-Russian entente, usually reveal a belief that the First World War was fundamentally an Anglo-German confrontation, a competition for empire outside Europe.

Other historians see the war not as an imperialist confrontation over resources and opportunities outside of Europe, but as the inescapable conflict between the two great alliance systems on the European continent. The roots of this system lay in Europe, and particularly in eastern Europe. Consequently, they begin their story in the period 1879–94. In 1879 the Dual Alliance of Austria and Germany was established, a defensive arrangement in which each of them promised to assist the other if either were attacked by Russia; or to provide assistance in the case of an attack on one of them in which Russia actively co-operated or in which she undertook 'menacing' military measures [**Doc. 1, p. 90**]. When Italy joined Austria and Germany three years later the arrangement was transformed into the Triple Alliance. As long as **Bismarck** was around to guide the alliance, and as long as he was able to remain on good terms with Russia, it seems – at least to most historians – to have posed little danger to peace, and perhaps to have done a great deal to maintain it.

When Wilhelm II ascended to the throne in 1888, however, a **Neue Kurs** ('new course') was initiated in German foreign policy, which soon led to the dismissal of Bismarck and the end of Russo-German harmony. The new kaiser, only twenty-nine years old, looked upon the old chancellor (seventy-three years old) as too conservative for the new Germany. If the only way for Germany to expand her power and her prestige meant offending Russia, then so be it. This terrified Bismarck: 'The young lord wants war with Russia, and would like to draw his sword straight away if he could . . . Woe unto my poor grandchildren' (Röhl, 1998: 758). The resulting estrangement between Germany and Russia was that Russia, determined not to yield her position of dominance in south-eastern Europe, chose to align herself with France by an agreement of 1892. France, determined to take advantage of the Russo-German rift, saw an opportunity to perhaps reverse the decision of her war with Prussia in 1870–71, and by 1894 a formal Franco-Russian alliance had been established [**Docs 7 and 8, pp. 95–96**]. Henceforth Europe was starkly divided into two armed camps, and a spark, falling in the right place, could set off a European conflagration at any moment. The 'alliance system' has, in itself, often been regarded as a cause of the First World War, almost apart from the policies that gave rise to its creation.

Bismarck: Prince Otto von *(1815–98)*: German statesman; elected to Prussian parliament in 1848; Prussian member of federal Diet at Frankfurt, 1851–59; ambassador to Russia and France, 1859–62; minister-president of Prussia, 1862–71; chancellor of North German Confederation, 1866–71; chancellor of Germany, 1871–90.

Neue Kurs: Literally, the 'new course'. When Wilhelm II became emperor of Germany in 1888 he was determined to make his mark on foreign policy, which led to Bismarck's dismissal in 1890. When the new chancellor, Caprivi, advized against renewing the Reinsurance Treaty with Russia, Wilhelm agreed.

More direct responsibility is proposed by those who begin their account in 1870–71, which is regarded as a decisive turning-point because of the dramatic victory of Prussia over France. Those who see the First World War arising logically from the growth of German power – and not from the ambitions of Wilhelm II and his militarist and navalist advisors – are naturally inclined to interpret the creation of the German empire in 1871 as the proper starting-point for their account. The astonishing speed with which France, hitherto regarded as the greatest of European powers, was soundly defeated by Prussia indicated that the new German state might soon be in a position to dominate the continent.

But it is possible to see in 1870–71 a turning-point that focuses attention on France rather than Germany. In this view France, humiliated by her defeat and deprived of Alsace-Lorraine by the Treaty of Frankfurt, followed a policy of **revanche** ('revenge') that would lead to another war with Germany as soon as she felt herself strong enough to win. And a key to this feeling would be an arrangement with Russia that would enable France to avoid the isolation in which she had found herself in 1870. Thus, historians who begin their story in 1870–71 are inclined to regard either Germany or France as the state primarily responsible for war in 1914, although they may also attribute it to the more general breakdown in the balance of power that had kept Europe relatively peaceful since 1815.

Revanche: Literally, 'revenge'. In diplomatic history, the term refers to the desire of the French, after 1871, to avenge their defeat in the Franco-Prussian war. The movement usually focused on the recovery of the 'lost provinces' of Alsace and Lorraine that were taken from France by the treaty of Frankfurt.

The farther back in time historians go in tracing the story of origins, the more likely it is that they see general, underlying causes as the proper explanation of the war: particular personalities and specific events fade against a more illuminating background. Some, for example, choose 1848 as a focal point: the crushing of liberal revolutions in central and eastern Europe bolstered the power of despotic, reactionary regimes in Prussia, Russia and Austria-Hungary. This created a Europe in which militarism and authoritarianism triumphed in the centre and the east, which in turn compelled the liberal, parliamentary regimes of western Europe to defend themselves against their ideological enemies. Others go back as far as 1815 and the Congress of Vienna, where the conservative statesmen responsible for the settlement of the Napoleonic wars attempted to turn the tide of history and repress the legitimate demand of nationalities to form independent states of their own. Most of the international problems in Europe over the following century were caused by nations 'struggling to be free'. This never-ending succession of crises and conflicts could not be localised forever: one of them would inevitably lead to a general conflict. The feeling that Europe was headed for 'Armageddon' grew more persistent throughout the nineteenth century.

There are others who would argue that none of the above approaches are sufficient, that they are all much too limited in their focus. 'Mega historians' insist that it is necessary to go much further back. Studies such as Oswald

Spengler's *Decline of the West* and Arnold Toynbee's *A Study of History*, which were particularly popular in the period between the wars, argue that the First World War was symptomatic of the decline, or the end, of western civilisation itself. They, and others, see Europe slowly heading for disaster since the Reformation – when religious sectarianism shattered the unity of Christendom and led to independent states with conflicting identities; or since the Renaissance – which eroded the spiritual foundations of the West by promoting secular humanism; or since the fall of the Roman Empire – which eliminated the only structure capable of keeping the peace over such a large and variegated variety of peoples; or since the triumph of rationalism in Greece – which replaced a peaceful, matriarchal culture with a warlike, masculine one.

Like all accounts, this one must begin somewhere, and no doubt my choices will reveal something of my own assumptions and prejudices. But I have made an effort to minimise my own views and interpretations; my purpose has been to provide as clear and as succinct a summary of the origins of the First World War as I can. I have chosen to begin with an account of the Great Powers up to 1900. I have divided the chapters along the lines by which the powers were themselves divided by that time: Germany, Austria-Hungary and Italy within Triple Alliance, France and Russia within Dual Alliance, and Great Britain, standing on the periphery. I have then attempted to sketch the broad outlines of the foreign policy pursued by each of the states throughout the nineteenth century, the changes that occurred in the second half of the century, and how these changes led to the creation of the alliance system and to changes in what is usually referred to as the 'Balance of Power'. In attempting to produce this sketch I have made an effort to pay special attention to the question of how 'internal structures' influenced the direction of foreign policy in each of the great powers – a subject that has preoccupied many historians for the past quarter-century. Once I have portrayed the state of affairs that existed in 1900, I have then followed the course of events, the diplomatic rearrangements, crises and wars that led up to the July crisis, and finally to war.

2

The Great Powers to 1900

THE TRIPLE ALLIANCE

The stability of an international system will break down when the growing power of one state destroys the old network of relationships upon which the system was based. In this sense, a state that expands its power through a growth in population, trade, prosperity, industry or territory may be responsible for the breakdown of a system, even if it is not guilty of it. Specialists in the study of international relations refer to this perspective as the 'systemic' level of analysis, in which the whole system is taken into account when attempting to explain why certain events occurred. More important than the policies or the personalities of any given state or its leaders are shifts in the foundations of power, to which governments and statesmen are simply forced to respond.

Nor does the breakdown of a system make a great war inevitable; it does, however, make war more likely as the states that derived benefits from the old system calculate that it is worth the risk of defeat on the battlefield to prevent the establishment of a new system. Therefore, it is important when considering the origins of any great war to determine which states were expanding the base of their power, and which states felt threatened by such a change. It is also worth considering whether or not the state whose power is growing is conscious of the need to create a new pattern of relations, whether there is a sense that without a change in this pattern it will not be permitted to continue to grow, or that it will be prevented from enjoying the benefits of its growth.

There is no doubt that Germany was the most dynamic state within the European system in the half-century leading up to 1914. This is perhaps the one point on which all historians are agreed. Those who lived through the decades leading up to the First World War found it difficult to assess the changing nature of growing states outside Europe: the United States and Japan were puzzling to them, and few believed that these two states were worth analysing in any detail, as their conditions seemed too far removed from those of Europe for useful lessons to be learned. Nor, in the case of the United States and Japan, was it believed that they could ever have much impact upon the European system. But Germany was another matter. No state was more closely watched than Germany after 1870. Anyone interested in military power, in politics, in economic change, felt that they must take the German example into account – if only to criticize and respond to it. Everyone believed that they could learn from the German example, and German thought, literature and music enjoyed an unprecedented popularity outside of Germany. In the years following the wars of unification, the assumption that Germany was capable of upsetting the foundations upon which the international system was built began to spread throughout Europe. The focus of international attention, hitherto located in Paris, shifted to Berlin; Bismarck became the most important statesman in the world.

The three wars that Prussia fought to create the new German empire, against Denmark in 1864, against Austria in 1866, and against France in 1870, demonstrated her military prowess. No one was really surprised when Prussia, in alliance with Austria, defeated Denmark. But the speed and the ease with which Austria was defeated two years later startled observers, who had expected a relatively balanced conflict; and Prussia's victory in the war with France four years later was even more astonishing. Even in the 1860s France had been regarded both as the greatest power in continental Europe and as the state most inclined – by tradition and by ideology – to destroy the European system that had been in place since 1815. Her quick and overwhelming defeat at the hands of Prussia decisively altered everyone's appreciation of the foundations of European relations. Germany would now make things happen; henceforth others would respond to her initiatives.

Prussia's victories were also important because they taught a political lesson that was keenly appreciated by statesmen and students of politics alike: that defeat in war was likely to bring about fundamental changes within the state that lost on the battlefield. Austria's defeat led to the **Ausgleich** ('compromise') of 1867 in which the Germans of the Habsburg empire were forced to share power with the Hungarians. France's defeat led to the destruction of the Second Empire and to the formation of the Third Republic in 1871. Henceforth, those who might be prepared to embark on a policy of adventure would have to weigh more carefully their prospects, because defeat in war could quite possibly lead to the disappearance of the political system for which they were fighting. Ironically, the revolution in the international system caused by the formation of a powerful new German empire simultaneously produced an atmosphere of caution and conservatism.

The new Germany could very easily have come to be regarded as a revolutionary power, as a state prepared to overturn the established international

Ausgleich: Literally, 'compromise', this constitutional re-arrangement within the Habsburg monarchy was instituted in 1867. It allowed for separate parliaments (*Diets*) and prime ministers in Austria and Hungary.

order and to foment radical political change. But this was a role that Germany's chancellor, Prince Otto von Bismarck, was determined not to play. In spite of Germany's tremendous victories, he believed that the new empire faced immediate danger as a result of having defeated two of her three great neighbours. If Germany did not now behave cautiously, she could easily encourage the formation of a coalition of France, Austria-Hungary and Russia, whose combined power would be too much for her to match. Bismarck believed that he had succeeded in unifying Germany only because he had managed to isolate first Denmark, then Austria, and finally France. As strong as the new Germany was, she was in no position to fight a war on three fronts. **General Moltke** confessed that he was 'tormented by nightmares'. The chief of the German general staff envisioned 'the Russians on the Spree and the French on the Main, penetrating from two sides into the heart of the Reich' (Mitchell, 1979: 201), and Bismarck believed that he needed time to consolidate the new empire. This meant upholding the status quo, guaranteeing her neighbours that she had no further ambitions to pursue that would endanger their security or their political systems. Bismarck the revolutionary was transformed into Bismarck the conservative statesman.

Moltke, Helmuth von *('the younger', 1848–1916)*: German soldier; chief of the Prussian general staff, 1906–14.

The method by which Bismarck chose to protect the new empire from the revenge of her neighbours was a system of alliances. He began with the assumption that it would be impossible to make a friend of France. Therefore he had, in the Treaty of Frankfurt, tried to make it as difficult as possible for France to undertake an offensive campaign against Germany: a large indemnity would throw French finances into chaos and consequently deprive her of the funds necessary to fight a great war; the annexation of Alsace and Lorraine would deprive France of rich territory and the most promising ground from which to attack Germany. Neither of these policies would, however, prevent France from undertaking a war of revenge if she thought that she could find the allies necessary to involve Germany in a two-front or three-front war. France, therefore, must be deprived of the allies she required for such a design. Bismarck concentrated his efforts on Austria-Hungary and Russia.

At first, these efforts amounted to no more than vague declarations of friendship expressed by the Hohenzollern, Habsburg and Romanov emperors of Germany, Austria-Hungary and Russia when Bismarck succeeded in bringing them together in 1872–73. Although this **Dreikaiserbund** ('League of the Three Emperors') was far from an alliance, it was nevertheless an important achievement for Bismarck because it publicized the fact that the rulers of Austria-Hungary and Russia did not regard Germany as an international criminal. Moreover, by emphasizing the monarchical ties that bound together the ruling families of central and eastern Europe, Bismarck attained one of his ambitions: to make republican France appear to be the entity that threatened the stability of existing regimes in Europe.

Dreikaiserbund: Literally, the 'three emperors' league'. In the first league, formed by Germany, Russia and Austria-Hungary in 1873, the three agreed to consult with one another on matters of common concern.

Bismarck's satisfaction with his achievement was short-lived. He soon recognized that the French had recovered from the war more quickly than he had anticipated; a great outpouring of patriotic sentiment enabled the French to pay off the indemnity more quickly than anyone had believed possible. The next logical step in his programme was an attempt to deprive France of her most likely ally by offering Austria-Hungary an alliance with Germany. While the French might be able to hold out the possibility of a war that could lead to the dismantling of the new German empire, Bismarck was able to offer something that they could not: a guarantee against attack by Russia. The Austrians, who proved to be more fearful of the prospect of such an attack than they were hopeful of reversing the decision of 1866, signed an agreement with Germany in 1879 [**Doc. 1, p. 90**]. Few would have guessed at the time that the Austro-German alliance would become the most enduring political arrangement between the great powers, remaining in effect for almost forty years. When it disappeared, so did the Habsburg and the Hohenzollern empires.

Bismarck had no intention of going to war with Russia in order to preserve Austria-Hungary. He always believed that the key to Germany's security was good relations with Russia, and he sought to ensure this by drawing Russia into a renewed *Dreikaiserbund* in 1881. The unspoken assumption in this arrangement was that both Russia and Austria-Hungary would forego the adventurous expansionism in south-eastern Europe that was bound to lead them into conflict; and Bismarck, in order to preserve this state of affairs, would act as the 'honest broker' in disputes between the two empires. The final piece of the puzzle was put into place when Italy joined Germany and Austria-Hungary in the Triple Alliance of 1882 [**Doc. 2, p. 90**].

The Bismarckian system of alliances was a complicated series of checks and balances, but it achieved two essential objects: it effectively deprived France of any continental ally and it established the German empire as a responsible and respectable state eager to uphold the new status quo. And this defensive approach to policy was reflected in Bismarck's attitude to empire: 'my map of Africa is here in Europe. Here is Russia and here is France and here we are in the middle. That is my map of Africa' (Craig, 1980; 116–17). Bismarck's limited aims and his desire for respectability were also reflected in the conservative nature of the new empire, which was, in essence, a coalition of the Prussian monarchy and large landowners. These conservative elements had, ultimately, been willing to fight the wars of unification only because Bismarck had persuaded them that they were acting defensively, and that the alternative to his policy was unification from below, led by social revolutionaries. The new state, although it did contain some representative institutions, retained the essential ingredients of the old monarchy, leaving great authority in the hands of the kaiser, especially when it came to the making of foreign and defence policy.

As eager as the conservatives were to contain social revolution and pre-serve the old order, the new empire soon began to develop in such a way as to make this difficult to achieve. Industry, which began to grow quickly, stim-ulated the development of the middle class – which was likely in the future to support liberal ideas of constitutional reform, and of the working class – which was likely in the future to support socialist ideas of revolutionary social change. Both of these forces appeared unsympathetic to the old order. Economic development was making the new Germany less rural and more urban, whereas the political hierarchy was based upon the old agricultural system. The territories of southern Germany, recently incorporated within the empire, were richer, more industrial, more densely populated and more democratic than Prussia. In spite of Bismarck's achievements, therefore, Germany's ruling classes felt that there was a latent internal crisis unfolding within the empire as the new classes created by the industrial revolution came to challenge the basis of the Prusso-German system established in 1871. Social Democrats 'are the country's rats and should be exterminated' Bismarck declared (Gall, 1986 II: 224).

Ironically, this fear of a latent crisis ran parallel to a growing sense of power – a confusing impression of reality that existed most conspicuously in the mind of Wilhelm II, who became kaiser in July 1888. Throughout his reign, which lasted until 1918, Wilhelm was torn between his fears of a social revolution and his ambitions to see Germany become a world power. But some in Germany, such as the founders of the German Navy League, believed 'the revolution' could be avoided through the expansion of power: 'The workers need **Weltpolitik** for a permanent improvement in their conditions of work. Therefore they should be in favour of the fleet' (Eley, 1980: 95). By the time Wilhelm acceded to the throne, Germany was the second most populous nation in Europe (after Russia); she produced more coal, more iron and more steel than any other nation on the continent. The kaiser believed that Germany's new power made it possible for her to break free from Bismarck's cautious preservation of the status quo. Wilhelm II was no longer interested in playing the role of 'honest broker' in disputes between the Austrians and the Russians in the near east. The continuing friendship with Russia was not to be purchased by limiting German ambitions; in the future such a friendship must recognise Germany's right to expand [**Doc. 4, p. 92**].

Bismarck, who regarded the young kaiser as 'a hothead who could not *hold his tongue*, allowed himself to be swayed by flatterers, and could lead Germany into a war without realising or wanting it' (Röhl, 1998: 741) was forced to resign in 1890. The kaiser's new chancellor, Caprivi, launched Germany upon a bold *Neue Kurs* in foreign policy. Germany herself had inter-ests to develop in south-eastern Europe and in the middle east, which Wilhelm symbolized by visiting the sultan in Constantinople in 1889 – a

Weltpolitik: Literally, 'world policy'. The term is used to describe the policies of the govern-ment of Wilhelm II in which Germany was to take its place as one of the great powers of the world. The policy led to the building of a high-seas fleet and to attempts to gain colonial territories.

stark contrast to Bismarck's earlier declaration that the Balkans were not worth 'the bones of a Pomeranian grenadier'. Germany's ambitions could best be developed by strengthening the alliance with Austria and ceasing to worry about the possible repercussions from Russia. Wilhelm gave his personal assurance to **Franz Joseph**, the Habsburg emperor, that in any crisis Germany would mobilize her forces simultaneously with Austria, no matter what the issue; he declined to renew the Reinsurance Treaty of 1887 with Russia in which the two states had promised not to attack one another. The shift from a balanced, tripartite arrangement to one in which Germany was increasingly committed to Austria-Hungary was readily apparent to all observers.

Franz Joseph *(1830–1916)*: Emperor of Austria, 1848–1916; king of Hungary, 1867–1916.

The new course in German policy was undoubtedly instrumental in prompting the Russians to consider seriously the French suggestions for an alliance; within a year the French fleet visited Kronstadt; within two years France and Russia constructed a military agreement. Rather than destroying the principles upon which the *Neue Kurs* was founded, however, this new development in European politics merely served to confirm them. The kaiser, after devouring Mahan's *Influence of Sea Power upon History* vowed 'to learn it by heart' (Sondhaus, 1997: 189) – as it laid down the principles upon which world power was based. He also agreed with the arguments of his general staff that Germany's military might had now reached a level that made it possible to contemplate fighting a war on two fronts, but that such a scenario made it essential for Germany to have an indivisible alliance with Austria-Hungary and an understanding with Great Britain. In the summer of 1892 **General Schlieffen**, the new chief of the general staff, argued that, as a two-front war was now inevitable, Germany had to plan accordingly. As a quick defeat of Russia would be difficult (if not impossible) he proposed to attack France first, defeating her quickly and decisively while remaining on the defensive against Russia in the east. The **Schlieffen Plan** guaranteed that any crisis that led to war with Russia would also lead to a German offensive against France.

Schlieffen, Count Alfred von *(1833–1913)*: German field marshal and chief of the Prussian general staff, 1891–1906. Designer of the Schlieffen Plan, the basis of pre-war German military strategy.

Schlieffen's strategy required a much larger army and he got one in July 1893. But there the expansion of the army stopped. By 1900 the German army was no larger than the French and 300,000 men smaller than the Russian. After the First World War most of the German military blamed the politicians for permitting this relative deterioration of the army to occur. In fact, although Schlieffen himself always advocated an increase in numbers, his colleagues did not and, ultimately, the freeze on the size of the army was according to the general staff's own policies, which were grounded in their fear of a social revolution. Further expansion of the army would have resulted in the admission of 'bourgeois' elements into the officer corps, which would dilute its social exclusiveness while propagating ideas popular with

Schlieffen Plan: Devised by Count Alfred von Schlieffen, chief of the Prussian general staff, 1891–1905. Designed in 1895 as a strategic response to the prospect of a two-front war following the formation of the Franco-Russian alliance, the plan was to knock out France quickly by invading through Holland, Belgium and Luxembourg.

'democratic and other elements . . . not suited to the officer class', – as General Karl von Einem, the German War Minister (1903–09) – put it (Berghahn, 1973: 7). Furthermore, an expansion in the number of conscripts would mean drawing in more men from the urban proletariat – many of whom would be infected with dangerous ideas of socialism. These fears would have counted for less had there not been a widespread expectation of an impending social conflict in which the army alone could safeguard the monarchical-landowner state; if the troops were socialists, or if they were commanded by liberals, the army might prove unwilling to act against revolutionaries in the future.

Germany's diplomacy reflected this awkward combination of strength and weakness. Her policy was predicated upon the assumption that she was strong enough to fight a two-front war, but too weak internally to go on increasing her army to match those of France and Russia. Wilhelm II and his advisors repeatedly resisted opportunities to abandon the principles of the new course, preferring instead to bolster it by means of closer connections with Austria-Hungary, Britain and Italy. They were increasingly dependent on the Austrians who, if they broke away from the alliance, would destroy the keystone of the new course. Britain and Italy were important in this respect: if Austria-Hungary could be certain that, in the event of a war with Russia, Italy would not attack her in the south, and that Britain would neutralise Russia at the Straits and in the Black Sea, then she would be more inclined to remain committed to her alliance with Germany. Because Italy was competing with France for empire in the Mediterranean, it did not seem difficult to keep her within the fold of the Triple Alliance. Britain proved more difficult to persuade.

Wilhelm II favoured a closer understanding with Great Britain from the beginning of his reign. If Germany's future lay in the middle east, through south-eastern Europe, Russia was clearly marked as her main competitor. As Anglo-Russian antagonism had been the most consistent element in international relations since the War of Greek Independence in the late 1820s, it seemed reasonable to assume that the British would be happy to join an anti-Russian coalition. This was to reverse Bismarck's strategy: he had encouraged the Russians to expand into Asia where they would clash with the British: 'It is the aim of German policy to bring about between Russia and England hostile, rather than too intimate, relations' (Fuller, 1922: 14). Even with the French alliance, the Russians would not be in a position to withstand the combined efforts of Germany, Austria-Hungary and Britain along her eastern and southern frontiers. This arrangement would be so advantageous to the British, who must recognize the inevitability of an Anglo-Russian war over the future of Asia, that they should be prepared to make concessions to the

Germans outside Europe. Such co-operation would symbolize the success of the new course.

The British, however, refused throughout the 1890s to be drawn into the alliance, and the Germans gradually became convinced that the British would be persuaded to join only if the consequences of remaining aloof became too dangerous. Herein lies the diplomatic origin of the 'risk fleet': Germany could build a naval force strong enough to ensure that Britain would not dare run the risk of war with her. This would draw the British into the alliance and encourage friendly behaviour in Asia and Africa, where territorial concessions would provide the German government with examples of the success of its foreign policy. Advocates of German sea power, such as **Admiral von Tirpitz [Doc. 9, p. 96]**, also emphasized the defensive advantages of a navy, without which, he said, Germany was 'like a mollusc without a shell' (quoted in Hale, 1971: 229). Finally, a fleet-building programme offered political advantages inside Germany, by holding out to businessmen engaged in heavy industry the promise of reliable, long-term profits through the increasing demand for iron and steel. In this way the monarchical state might be able to rely upon the support of industrialists as well as landowners.

Tirpitz, Alfred von *(1849–1930)*: German admiral; secretary of state for the navy, 1897–1916. Strategist responsible for the creation of the 'risk fleet' which began construction in 1898.

By 1900, therefore, Germany had maintained, and even extended, the principles underlying the new course in foreign policy that had begun with the accession of Wilhelm II. She had reaffirmed her commitment to Austria-Hungary, developed war plans based on the assumption of a two-front war, and increased her interests in the near east and in colonial expansion. Germany was the most dynamic element in the international system, and most of her leaders were convinced that they were at a crossroads, one of which led to world power and empire, the other to the minor status of a relatively small state in the centre of Europe. The question facing Germany, as Bernhard von Bülow, the chancellor in 1899 would soon put it, was whether or not she would become 'the hammer or the anvil' of world politics [**Doc. 10, p. 97**].

The alliance formed between Austria-Hungary and Germany in 1879 ought to be regarded as one of the most surprising events in modern diplomatic history. It is certainly a mistake to assume that the sharing of German language and culture somehow drew the two states together into some close political connection; in fact, throughout the first half of the nineteenth century, nationality did much more to divide the two empires than it did to unite them. The Habsburg rulers of Austria (and then Austria-Hungary) recognized that any promotion of the idea of nationality as the principle upon which states should be erected would doom their empire to extinction, and no one saw this more clearly than **Count Clemens von Metternich**, the leading conservative statesman in Europe from 1815 to 1848. Metternich

Metternich, Count Clemens von *(1773–1859)*: Austrian diplomat and statesman; ambassador during the Napoleonic wars; minister of foreign affairs, 1809–48; chancellor, 1812–48.

defined the spirit of diplomacy between the Congress of Vienna and the revolutions of 1848 in much the same way that Bismarck did between the Schleswig-Holstein crisis and the accession of Wilhelm II.

The Habsburg empire owed its creation to traditional dynastic practice; it was an empire made by marriage and inheritance, wars and diplomacy, and it is best thought of as a loose agglomeration of Habsburg 'lands', an inter-connected series of properties belonging to the ruling family, not as a 'nation-state'. Although the Habsburg family and the ruling élite around them was German, the empire, by 1815, included Hungarians, Magyars, Poles, Czechs, Slovaks, Rumanians, Croatians, Serbs and Italians. The empire may have been a state ruled by Germans, but it did not regard itself as a German state. Moreover, the Germans of the empire were overwhelmingly Roman Catholic – which set them apart from the mainly Lutheran Germans of the German empire.

Metternich was especially anxious in the years following the Congress of Vienna to prevent the idea of a 'German nation' from spreading. When Napoleon had cobbled together a series of petty principalities, fiefdoms and bishoprics in southern Germany into what he had called the 'Confederation of the Rhine', he provided further impetus to the idea being broadcast by philosophers like Herder and Fichte that the German people ought to be brought together within a single state. These territories remained linked to one another after 1815 in the new **German Confederation** to achieve the very practical purpose of providing what strategists hoped would be a more successful barrier against renewed French expansion than the old, disorganized German states had been. But the Confederation, designed for practical purposes, was soon fulfilling an ideological one: it became the seed-bed of liberal nationalism. Groups of university students, *Burschen-schaften*, were particularly active, thus attracting the attention of Metternich who undertook to quash their movement. In other words, the Habsburgs were determined not only to avoid leading the unification of the German people, but to prevent it altogether.

German Confederation: An association (or *Bund*) of thirty-nine states in central Europe formed at the end of the Napoleonic wars in 1815. Dominated by Austria, their representatives met in a Diet in Frankfurt – but this had very little authority. It collapsed when Prussia defeated Austria in 1866.

Habsburg policy following 1815, therefore, was guided by a reasonably coherent and consistent set of conservative ideas. Metternich supported or proposed various interventions on the part of European governments to put down liberal and nationalist revolts in Spain, Italy and Greece, on the assumption that, if the principle of representative, constitutional, nationalist regimes took root along the frontiers of the empire, it would be only a matter of time before the contagion spread within the empire itself. Italian nationalism was particularly worrying in this respect. The settlement of 1815 had awarded Lombardy and Venetia, the two most prosperous and highly developed territories of the Italian peninsula, to the Habsburgs. Once again, the object was strategic: to provide the Austrians with a more defensible frontier against a renewed French bid for hegemony. The remainder of Italy was to remain divided: the Kingdom of Sardinia, Parma, Modena, the Papal States, Tuscany and the Kingdom of the Two Sicilies provided the Habsburgs with a feeling of security on their southern frontier. As long as these political divisions existed, the Italians would be in no position to pose a threat. If, on the other hand, the Italians demanded, and achieved, the unification of Italian-speaking peoples, this would simultaneously deprive the empire of two rich provinces and leave her vulnerable to attack from the south. Although the prospect of successful revolution caused Metternich to flee Vienna in 1848, his system survived the challenge. As late as 1860, the empire was surrounded, on three sides, by a succession of rather weak states: Bavaria, Saxony and Switzerland to the west; Sardinia, Parma, Modena and the Papal States to the south; the essentially autonomous Ottoman provinces of Bosnia, Serbia, Wallachia and Moldavia to the south and east. The only states in a position to place the Habsburg empire in jeopardy were Prussia and Russia, to the north and north-east. It is hardly surprising then that nationalism, especially of the German and Italian varieties, was perceived to be the main threat to this happy state of affairs.

The glaring exception to this strategically beneficial situation was in the east, where there loomed the enormous potential of the Russian empire. The main reason why Metternich had, in the 1820s, gone along with **Tsar Alexander I's** rather muddle-headed proposal of a '**Holy Alliance**' of Christian princes was his desire that Russia should firmly adhere to the principle of monarchical solidarity. The Holy Alliance became, in effect, a loose association of the Habsburg, Romanov and Hohenzollern emperors to uphold the settlement of 1815 in the face of nationalist and liberal pressures.

Alexander I *(1777–1825)*: Son of Paul I; tsar of Russia, 1801–25.

Holy Alliance: Following the Napoleonic wars, Tsar Alexander I drew up a document proclaiming that European rulers must henceforth be guided by Christian principles. But the phrase is usually used as a shorthand reference to the reactionary policies of Russia, Austria and Prussia.

The Greek revolt of 1828 opened a fissure between Austria and Russia that never closed, and which foreshadowed the future of their relationship in south-eastern Europe. When the tsar decided, on the grounds of religious principle, to support the demands of the Orthodox Greeks for independence from the Muslim Turks, Metternich objected. He preferred to treat the sultan as a respectable monarch and as a necessary component of the international system: legal sovereignty and political authority were more important than religious identities and linguistic affiliations. Support for Greek independence might well unleash similar demands on the part of other subject peoples – Serbs, Bulgars, Rumanians – in the near east, some of whom were to be found in the Habsburg empire. Moreover, if the rather weak and remote Turkish regime were to disappear from the Balkans, and if this were to be replaced with Russian-sponsored regimes, the Habsburg empire would become much more difficult to defend. This underlying fear for the future of the Balkans proved to be one of the most dominant features in the pattern of international relations throughout the nineteenth century.

The fissure in the Holy Alliance was closed, temporarily, as a result of the revolutions of 1848. The Habsburg empire was nearly blown to pieces: violence erupted in almost every city, and in Milan, Prague and Budapest, nationalist forces seized control, with Italians, Czechs and Hungarians leading the demand for independence or autonomy. The Italians and the Czechs were suppressed only when the army resorted to the most brutal measures. But the strength of the army was not sufficient to suppress the **Magyars** of Hungary, who were defeated only when the tsar dispatched a force of some 200,000 men to assist his fellow monarch. Russia, in contrast, remained quiet, practically immune from the upheavals of the year of revolution. The conclusion seemed to be that the Habsburg empire was going to find it very difficult to survive in the face of these disintegrative pressures and that she would have to learn to rely more and more on the Russians propping her up.

Magyars: Native name for the inhabitants of Hungary. Those who spoke Magyar were actually a minority in the Hungary that was created by the *Ausgleich* of 1867.

The behaviour of Austria during the Crimean War therefore came as a shock to Russia. The Russians assumed, after 1848, that the Habsburg empire was both weak and friendly. She proved to be neither. Austria, rather than supporting Russia in her war with Britain and France, chose to exploit the advantages of the situation in which she found herself: she insisted that Russia must withdraw her forces from the principalities of Wallachia and Moldavia; otherwise Austria would join Britain and France. The Crimean War thus provided the Austrians with the opportunity of barricading the Balkans from further Russian adventures: the principalities were given their independence and re-named Rumania; Russian troops were not to be permitted to advance through them to Constantinople. With the revolutionaries of 1848 either in prison or in exile, and with the Balkans cut off from Russia, Austria appeared, by 1856, to be in a much safer position than she had ten years previously.

But the failure of the revolutions of 1848 convinced many nationalists in the small states of Italy and Germany that they would never be successfully united from below, that it would take war and the connivance of one or two great powers to create a unified state. In the Italian case, this meant that the kingdom of Piedmont-Sardinia had to fight the Austrians for control of Lombardy and Venetia, and, if she were to succeed in this fight, that she needed the active co-operation of France. This story is a particularly complicated one, but the result was that Austria was defeated in battle, lost the two provinces, and ceased to be an 'Italian' power. There remained, however, a distinctive Italian population in the Tyrol, which could prove a focal point of future Austro-Italian disputes.

Within three years the Habsburgs had also ceased to be a 'German' power. The war with Prussia in 1866, which Bismarck adroitly manoeuvred the Austrians into starting, was really a struggle for the future of Germany; it was to decide whether the German states were to be united under the aegis of

Prussia, or whether they would remain a loose association of independent entities, informally presided over by Austria. Defeat on the battlefield was quick, decisive and final, and after 1866 it was clear that Austria was no longer in a position to compete with Prussia as an equal. Bismarck's moderate peace terms (in contrast with the terms imposed on France five years later) reflected the real purpose of the war: the German Confederation was to be dissolved and Austria was to be excluded from German affairs. If Austria were to seek revenge, therefore, it would not be to recover 'national' territory or to relieve the burden of harsh financial and military terms; a war of revenge would mean that Austria had decided to renew the fight to establish her predominance within Germany.

The perfect opportunity for a war of revenge came in 1870 when Prussia went to war with France. But the Austrians did not take advantage of the opportunity; instead, they stood by and waited to see if the French could succeed in turning back the Prussians on their own. There was always the chance that France could, in essence, win Austria's battle for her: if Prussia were soundly defeated her newly established predominance in the German states of the old confederation would surely evaporate. When this possibility was destroyed on the battlefield, so were any remaining Austrian dreams of a recovery in Germany. Austria's acceptance of the new German empire as an irreversible feature of European politics constituted one of the essential foundations of international relations between 1871 and 1914.

The events of 1866–70 had thus caused a profound re-evaluation of Austria's position in Europe; they also caused Austria to be transformed into 'Austria-Hungary', henceforth referred to as the '**Dual Monarchy**'. Following the loss of Lombardy to Piedmont in 1859, the emperor had attempted to strengthen the empire by creating a representative assembly, the **Reichsrat**. This reform failed to satisfy the leading nationalities of the empire however: the Magyars, Italians and Croatians boycotted it; the Czechs, Poles, Serbs and Slovenians opposed it; the new assembly proved unworkable and was held partly responsible for the military failure of 1866. The following year a new system was introduced, a compromise (*Ausgleich*) that transformed the empire into an association of two autonomous states, Austria and Hungary, who were to share the Habsburg emperor as their head of state. They were to have a common foreign policy, defence and finances, and a unique – and cumbersome – process was created to accomplish this. Every ten years the two states were to agree on the expenses necessary to sustain their common foreign policy and defence; the ministers of foreign affairs, defence and finance were to be jointly appointed to both states, and these ministers were to meet once a year with the 'Delegations' (executive committees) drawn from each of the two parliaments – which communicated with one another only in writing. The system of 1867, which was untidy and invited dispute,

Dual Monarchy: The name used to refer to the Habsburg empire following the *Ausgleich* of 1867. It represented an agreement between the dominant Germans of Austria with the powerful Magyars of Hungary.

Reichsrat: The Austrian Chamber of Deputies, or parliament, established in Vienna in 1907. Based on universal male suffrage, the chamber was relatively powerless as the ministers were not responsible to it.

was manageable only because the cabinet was not responsible to parliament, but to the emperor, and because emergency decrees provided that a cabinet could govern for some time without the support of the legislature.

The hope of accommodating the Magyars of Hungary to the empire was the primary objective of these new constitutional arrangements. Austrian strategists believed that the threat of a renewed revolution in Hungary had forced them to fight with a severe handicap against the Italians in 1859 and against the Prussians in 1866. But permitting the Magyars to take the place of equals within the empire inevitably led to some fundamental changes in policy. The Magyars were not interested in the states of western and northern Germany and they were unwilling to make any sacrifices for the recovery of the monarchy's position there. This made an improvement in relations with the new German empire much easier to achieve after 1867. On the other hand, the Magyars and the Germans alike were sensitive to the fact that almost one-half of the people of the empire were Slavic, which led them to fear that the spread of Panslavism would lead to the dismemberment of the newly constituted Dual Monarchy. Given these attitudes, it is not surprising that the earlier tendency of Austria to see Russia as an enemy was confirmed, while the defeat at the hands of Prussia was soon forgotten or overlooked.

The alliance with Germany that was signed in 1879 was the logical culmination of this new direction in the policy of Austria-Hungary [**Doc. 1, p. 90**]. An alliance with a strong Germany now seemed to offer the best protection against Russia. Once Russia was defined as the principal threat to the Dual Monarchy, Austria-Hungary became anxious to expand her alliance with Germany to include Italy. The Austrians had been compelled, when fighting the Prussians in 1866, to keep a large army in the south; although they had defeated the Piedmontese forces at the second battle of Custoza, their ability to defend themselves against the Prussians had been seriously hindered, and they were forced to cede most of Venetia to a united Italy in 1866. As the same dilemma would almost certainly confront them if they ever went to war with Russia, the Austrians were eager to ensure that their southern frontier would not need to be defended. If, by means of the Triple Alliance, Italian ambitions could be turned in the direction of France and the Mediterranean, the Italian population of the Dual Monarchy was less likely to prove troublesome. Italy was welcomed into the alliance in 1882 [**Doc. 2, p. 90**].

Austrian foreign policy had, since the Congress of Vienna, been a tangle of complicated and often conflicting interests in Germany, Italy and on the eastern frontier; now policy became unusually simple and straightforward. The aim of the Dual Monarchy was to protect itself from disintegrating through the pressures being placed upon it by the forces of Panslavism and

Balkan nationalism. Austria-Hungary thus became the leading supporter of the status quo in the middle east – a policy that culminated in two 'Mediterranean' agreements with Italy and Britain in February/March and December of 1887. The Austrians were as eager as the Germans and the Italians to draw Britain into the Triple Alliance; but by 1896, after repeated refusals on the part of Britain, the Austrians came to believe that they were running too many risks for the sake of Britain and they declined to renew the Mediterranean agreement. In its place they substituted an arrangement with Russia in May 1897 whereby the two powers agreed neither to disturb the status quo in the Balkans, nor to permit anyone else to do so; the Balkans were, for the next ten years, 'put on ice'. By 1900 Austria was firmly committed to the Triple Alliance – but as long as the Balkans remained quiet and Russia behaved cautiously, it was most unlikely that the connection with Germany would lead the Austrians to undertake an adventurous policy.

No less surprising than the decision of Austria-Hungary to join Germany in the Dual Alliance of 1879 was the decision of Italy to join Austria-Hungary in the Triple Alliance of 1882. The Austrians had led the opposition to Italian unification throughout the nineteenth century: the Italian lands of Lombardy and Venetia were recaptured from the Austrians only by force of arms, and the Austrians had frequently intervened against the liberal and constitutional movements in the peninsula since 1815. A considerable change in outlook was necessary in order for the Italians to overlook the recent past.

Moreover, Italian unification had not been completed in the wars of 1859 or 1866; **Italia irredenta** ('unredeemed Italy') remained. The Austrians continued to hold on to the Tyrol, Trieste and Fiume – all areas densely populated by Italians. In the eyes of some, therefore, Austria remained Italy's principal enemy. But others had grievances against France. In exchange for French assistance to Piedmont-Sardinia in the war of 1859 against Austria, the Piedmontese had ceded Nice and Savoy – each with sizeable Italian populations – to France. Some nationalists believed that Italy would not be complete until these territories were recaptured. The French had also damaged themselves in Italian opinion by maintaining and defending the papal possessions in and around Rome; in 1867 they had actually fought off an attack led by **Giuseppe Garibaldi**, the great Italian patriot, and then sent him into exile. Only when the French needed all available manpower in their war with Prussia in 1870 did they withdraw their troops from Rome, thereby permitting the Italians to capture it. In northern Italy, therefore, there remained lingering grievances against both Austria-Hungary and France, although most nationalists felt that the grievances against France were rather minor by comparison.

Dreams of neo-Roman greatness in the Mediterranean divided Italy from France more than the hope of recapturing Nice and Savoy, more than the

Italia irredenta: Literally, 'unredeemed Italy'. A popular movement in Italy following the wars of unification to 'redeem' those lands inhabited by Italians but not included within the Italian state (principally Trieste, Trentino, south Tyrol, Istria and Fiume).

Garibaldi, Giuseppe *(1807–82)*: Italian nationalist and hero of the *Risorgimento*. In 1860 led an invasion of Sicily and later captured Naples, leading to their inclusion in the newly unified Italian state.

Risorgimento: Literally, 'resurgence'. Used by Camillo Cavour as the title of the Piedmontese newspaper (*Il Risorgimento*) that he founded in 1847 with the aim of promoting the unification of all Italian-speaking peoples. Now used by historians to refer to the Italian unification movement generally.

issue of French troops guarding the papacy. One of the symbols of the Italian **Risorgimento** ('resurgence') was the past greatness of Rome, which seemed to show what the Italian people could achieve if they were united with one another and free from foreign interference. Even the most fervent nationalists did not go so far as to suggest that it was possible to re-establish the Roman empire in Europe, but they did believe that Italy had a special mission to spread civilisation – and the Mediterranean territories of north Africa, where the Ottoman empire was steadily disintegrating, offered an attractive site for the demonstration of Italy's renewed greatness. The strongest component of Italian imperialism was backward-looking: visions of a *mare nostrum* were always stronger than coldly rational calculations of financial and economic benefits. 'There is something greater than material interests' declared the Prime Minister, Crispi, responding to critics of his colonial aspirations in 1888: 'this bourgeois habit of always counting the cost is unpatriotic'; the dignity of Italy 'and the interests of civilisation' required that Italy succeed in its imperial mission (Lowe and Marzari, 1975: 57).

Italy, following unification, was more concerned with questions of prestige and status than was any other great power. Indeed, the fundamental question facing Italy after 1866 was whether or not she was in fact a 'great' power. She had been united by war, but not by victories: defeats on the battlefield were compensated for by victories in diplomacy. Judged by any measurable criteria Italy was certainly 'the least of the Great Powers' in 1900: she had the smallest army; she was the least populous; her iron and steel production was not only the smallest, but amounted to only one-fifth of Austria-Hungary's, and one-tenth of Russia's. Italy was still an agricultural nation, yet she did not produce enough food to feed herself; her railway system was undeveloped and inadequate; her ports had not been modernized; she could not supply her own energy needs. It is difficult to believe that Italy could be regarded as a great power when Spain and Belgium were not; and yet Italian politicians were determined to achieve this status by behaving in the way that a great power was supposed to behave.

An empire in the Mediterranean would go far to establishing Italy's claim to great-power status, and this was the essential factor in drawing Italy into the combination with Austria-Hungary and Germany. Membership of the Triple Alliance by itself did much to support Italy's claim to this status, and the terms of the 1882 agreement were highly attractive to Italy. In return for promising to support Germany, were Germany to be attacked by France, Italy received a guarantee of German and Austrian support should France attack her. The only real concession that Italy made to her alliance partners was her promise to remain neutral if one of them came to be engaged in a war with a single power: in other words, she would not take advantage of a war between Austria-Hungary and Russia to attack the Austrians in the hope of redeeming Tyrol, Trieste and Fiume. In this first phase of the alliance, Italy's role was clearly defensive [**Doc. 2, p. 90**].

But Italy, in spite of the practical limitations she faced, had great ambitions. The original version of the Triple Alliance, which did nothing to promise that any of these ambitions would be fulfilled, would have to be revised if Italy were to succeed with her dreams of expanding along the southern shores of the Mediterranean. Some hint of this was given in 1887 when the Triple Alliance was renewed and a new agreement was arranged between Italy and Austria-Hungary that promised 'reciprocal compensations' should the status quo of the Balkans be altered. This did something to satisfy Italian hopes of expanding along the shore of the Adriatic. More encouraging still was a new agreement with Germany that promised both military assistance to Italy, should she become embroiled in a war with France over Tunis or Morocco, and diplomatic assistance in securing for Italy improvements in her frontier security and maritime position: i.e. the irredentist claims against France in Nice, Savoy and Corsica, and the Mediterranean ambitions in Tunis. After 1887 it appears that Italy stood to make substantial gains in the event of hostilities with France or a disturbance of the Balkan status quo. Italy was not one of the states determined to uphold the current territorial and political arrangements in Europe.

Italy's ambitions were limited only by her lack of power and her vulnerable geographical position. In spite of the favourable diplomatic arrangements with Germany and Austria-Hungary, few Italians believed that they could afford to engage in a war in which Great Britain was an enemy. Many of Italy's largest cities (Naples, Palermo, Genoa, Venice), were open to naval bombardment; much of her railway system (as underdeveloped as this was) hugged the coastline; she depended on maritime commerce to make up for her inability to feed herself and for the absence of coal supplies with which to fuel her industry. Italy had to be certain, therefore, that in a war with France she could count on British assistance or at least her neutrality. This hope seemed to have been realised in the Mediterranean agreement of February 1887 which, although referring rather vaguely to consultation and co-operation, did draw Italy and Britain closer together. Italy, even more than Austria-Hungary and Germany, needed Britain to join the Triple Alliance.

The question facing Italy in 1900 was whether or not her continued membership in the Triple Alliance would enable her to fulfil some of her ambitious plans for expansion. As long as Britain remained even an informal friend of the alliance it seemed a useful instrument. But, were Britain to switch sides, it would be a dangerous policy for Italy to run the risk of a war with both Britain and France. The other members of the Triple Alliance were keenly aware that Italy always had the alternative of joining France and Russia and focusing her ambitions in the Tyrol and the Adriatic rather than in the Mediterranean. Italy was apparently locked into the Triple Alliance; in reality she would be tempted to disengage if it appeared too dangerous or if a more attractive offer were made.

THE DUAL ALLIANCE

The joining together of France and Russia in the Dual Alliance of 1894 was a revolutionary event in the history of European diplomacy, and one that fundamentally altered the pattern of relations. Few observers had believed such an alliance to be possible. Philosophically, France and Russia represented opposite ends of the political spectrum: France stood for revolution and republicanism, Russia for stability and despotism. Nor was this clash of ideas purely symbolic. Russian statesmen believed that all threats to the tsarist regime and to the stability of European politics emanated from Paris; French statesmen believed that their republican system and a morally legitimate European order would always be imperilled by the existence of the Russian **autocracy**. Nor were these fears purely imaginary: France had invaded Russia twice during the nineteenth century, in 1812 and in 1854; Russia had led the anti-revolutionary movement, creating the Holy Alliance in 1815 and crushing the Hungarian revolution in 1848. When the two states committed themselves to assist one another if either were to be attacked, therefore, they implicitly announced the triumph of interests over ideas. In order to understand the origins of the First World War it is essential to understand what these interests were and how each of these two great powers believed their alliance would provide for their achievement.

Foreign observers of nineteenth-century Russia were invariably struck by two features of Russia as a great power. Those from western Europe, especially from Britain and France, were struck by the nature of the tsarist autocracy, which seemed to them to give a distinctive colouration to Russian foreign policy, designed as it was to uphold the legitimacy of the regime. They were also sensitive to the enormous power of Russia, although observers from central Europe, especially from Prussia and Austria, were more likely to be fascinated by this feature. Whether this power was real or imagined, and whether or not the autocratic nature of the Russian regime predetermined the direction of her policy were crucial questions for European diplomats in the late nineteenth century.

The part played by Russia in the destruction of the empire of **Napoleon I** contributed enormously to her reputation as a great power up to the time of the Crimean War. Although Napoleon had defeated each of the states of continental Europe and proven himself invulnerable to the continuing hostility of Great Britain, his *grande armée* had been annihilated when he had

Autocracy: A loosely defined political term usually referring to the absolute or despotic rule by an individual. Most often used in referring to the tsar, 'the autocrat of all the Russias'.

Napoleon I *(Napoleon Bonaparte, 1769–1821):* First Consul of France, 1799–1804; emperor 1804–14.

attempted to invade Russia. From the original invasion force of 600,000 only 100,000 had returned. Europeans as a whole drew two conclusions from this, the most destructive military episode in European history before the First World War: that the territorial expanse of Russia was so immense that a successful invasion was almost unimaginable; and that the population of Russia was so huge that she could suffer the most appalling losses and live to fight another day. Thus, although Napoleon penetrated as far as Moscow, and although he managed to capture the city, and although Russia lost 200,000 men in a single battle at Borodino, Russia was not defeated. Within three years of Napoleon launching his invasion of Russia, she had 30,000 of her troops participating in the allied occupation of France.

The advantages in population and territory that had enabled Russia to withstand the French invasion persisted, or grew, throughout the century. Her territory dwarfed that of continental Europe. Her population, in 1900, was twice as large as that of her nearest rival, Germany, and was almost equal to the combined population of Germany, Austria-Hungary and Italy. In 1900 the Russian empire comprised some 16 million square miles and contained approximately 125 million people.

The raw components of power seemed to suggest that Russia was capable of overwhelming any potential opponents on the European continent, and the Germans and Austrians were certainly sensitive to the dangerous proximity of the Russian giant. But power, in order to be effectively applied, depends on more than size alone, and here contemporaries in 1900 were much less certain about the actual strength of Russia. Modern armies and navies were in the process of becoming industrial machines. They required railways and coal to move them, iron and steel to arm and supply them, and, in these components of power, Russia was noticeably behind the other great powers. In 1910 European Russia had less than one-tenth the length of railway per square kilometre of Britain or Germany. In 1900 her coal production was one-half that of Austria-Hungary, one-tenth that of Germany; her pig-iron production amounted to 40 per cent of the German, 33 per cent of the British; steel production to 30 per cent of the British, 20 per cent of the German. Given Russia's limited industrial development, it was questionable whether she would be able to utilize her advantage in manpower, and it was clear that the most difficult operation for her to mount would be one that required her to go quickly onto the offensive.

Critics of the regime blamed Russia's weakness on her autocratic system of government. In the decade prior to the revolution of 1905 a wide range of opposition groups emerged, all of them demanding fundamental changes in the nature of the regime. Marxists established the Russian Social Democratic Labour Party in 1898, which aimed to overthrow the tsar by harnessing the revolutionary potential of the proletariat. Liberals published a newspaper,

Liberation, beginning in 1902, and organised the Union of Liberation in 1904, which aimed to abolish the autocracy and establish constitutional government. Populists united several factions in 1901 when they organized the Party of Socialist Revolutionaries, dedicated to the triumph of the 'will of the people' which was to be achieved through the use of terror and by mobilizing the peasant masses of the countryside.

Political opposition and social movements were not the only threats to Russia's future as a great power. The very things that made Russia so frightening to outsiders – her enormous population and her vast territory – might also tear her apart. The 1897 census showed that non-Russians outnumbered the Russians: 55.7 per cent of 122.6 million people were not Russian, including over 13 million Turkic people of Muslim faith. Catholic Poles cherished their religion and their national identity; during the Russo-Japanese war a leading Polish nationalist (Pilsudski) attempted to secure Japanese arms and aid in order to rise up against Russian rule; in August 1914 he raised a legion in Galicia to fight the tsarist armies.

As varied as these opposition groups were, and in spite of their political and cultural differences with one another, they were nevertheless united in their belief that social justice was impossible under the tsarist autocracy. Moreover, they believed that Russia could never be transformed into a modern state as long as the tsar and his landowning aristocracy remained in control. Thus, the Russian people would continue to find themselves at the mercy of their better-organized and better-equipped neighbours, as they had during the invasions of 1812 and 1854.

The tsar, by contrast, rested much of his right to govern on the claim that he and his ancestors were responsible for the creation of the Russian state, and that the autocracy, in alliance with the gentry, was essential to the maintenance and defence of the state. This claim made the tsar and his advisers peculiarly sensitive to international questions. If the regime suffered a defeat in diplomacy the reverberations might shake the autocracy to its foundations: disenchantment within Russia was most intense in the immediate aftermath of disastrous foreign adventures – following the Crimean War of 1855–56, the war with Turkey of 1877–78, and the war with Japan in 1905. The tsar was fully aware of the dangers that lurked within any policy of adventure, especially after 1905, but he was also aware that his other claim to authority, his leadership of the Christians of the Orthodox church, would suffer if he failed to act on behalf of his brethren when they were endangered by the Muslims of the Ottoman empire. Too cautious a policy might be as dangerous as one that was too adventurous.

These twin claims to authority, the traditional powers of the monarch and the leadership of the orthodox church, neatly fused together in the Holy Alliance created by Tsar Alexander I in 1815. The alliance, which was a highly informal arrangement, initially included Russia, Austria and Prussia, and was supposed to guarantee that Christian principles would provide the foundation for rule in these states, and that the monarchs would work together to maintain peace and justice. Monarchical solidarity was to take the place of revolutionary republicanism and nationalism, while the right to rule was to be based on Christianity rather than the Rights of Man or the General Will. In the years following the Congress of Vienna, Russia came to be regarded as the bastion of reaction, and the upheavals that did occur – in Spain, in Italy and even in Germany – were far removed from her own frontiers. Never was the strength of tsarist rule so vividly demonstrated as in 1848, when, practically free from the revolutionary uprisings that swept across Europe, **Tsar Nicholas I** was able to dispatch 130,000 troops to assist the Habsburg emperor in crushing the Hungarian revolt.

Nicholas I *(1796–1855)*: Son of Paul I, succeeded his brother, Alexander I as tsar of Russia in 1825.

The idea of the Holy Alliance was an attractive one to Russia, both because it upheld the principle of the Christian monarchy and because it offered protection against attack by her neighbours. It also appeared to provide a barrier against revolutionary infection from western Europe or against another Napoleon. It should not be surprising to discover, therefore, that some Russians in the decades before 1914 longed for a return to the peace and security of the Holy Alliance, to a policy of co-operation with Germany and Austria.

In spite of the alliance, an underlying tension between Russia and Austria had emerged early in the century, as the growing aspirations of Balkan Christians to set themselves free from Turkish rule and form their own states began to distinguish the politics of south-eastern Europe [**Doc. 17, p. 105**]. Where Austria, following Metternich's principles, preferred to suppress upheavals and crush revolutions of any kind, Russia usually chose to support the demands of the Christians. This policy led to a particularly acute difference of opinion over the question of Greek independence in 1827. The tsar's inherited role of protector of the Christians in the Ottoman empire also led to war with France and Britain in 1854, when Nicholas I came to believe that **Napoleon III** was attempting to replace him as spokesman for the Christians at Constantinople; if this new Napoleonic strategy were to succeed, it could result in the sultan becoming a puppet of France and Britain. But where this would seem to have reinforced Russia's determination to rely upon the Holy Alliance against the western powers, the Crimean War destroyed that arrangement as an attractive strategy for Russia. Austria refused to act as the friend of Russia – in spite of Russian intervention having saved her from dissolution six years earlier – and took advantage of her position to exploit the situation to her own advantage. During the war, and at the peace conference, Austria demonstrated that the principle of monarchical solidarity no longer mattered to her, and that she was more concerned with restraining Russian ambitions in the Balkans and in the Black Sea.

Napoleon III *(Charles Louis Napoleon Bonaparte, 1808–73)*: Son of Napoleon Bonaparte's brother Louis; elected president of the second republic, 1848; emperor, 1848–71; exiled, 1871–73.

After the Treaty of Paris brought the Crimean War to a close in 1856, Russian foreign policy became more 'realistic', less concerned with principles such as monarchical solidarity and orthodox rights, more concerned with the interests and the security of the Russian state. The Crimean War had shown that Russia was more vulnerable to attack than the precedent of the Napoleonic invasion had indicated; France and Britain had avoided the disasters of 1812 by attacking in the south through the Straits. The naval strength of the western allies had enabled them to control the lines of communication and supply, which were practically invulnerable to counterattack from Russia, and almost impervious to the Russian winter. Thus, the treaty of 1856 had attempted to perpetuate Russia's exposed position by 'neutralizing' the Black Sea, by disallowing both Russian and Turkish warships from operating there. Like most neutrality arrangements, this one gave France and Britain a distinct advantage.

The lessons of the Crimean War laid new foundations for Russian foreign policy. Austria now came to be regarded as unreliable or unfriendly, while Britain emerged as Russia's real competition. The political course of the war led to the conclusion that the British, and not the Russians or the French, had achieved paramount influence at Constantinople. Moreover, Britain's strategy in the eastern Mediterranean made it appear that she was willing to use this influence to threaten Russia in the Black Sea whenever she found it useful to do so. The new **realism** in Russian policy meant establishing a counterpoise to Britain in the Black Sea by undertaking a forward policy in central Asia in order to threaten the British empire in India.

Realism: A term that is used in contrast to 'idealism'. When used in diplomacy or in diplomatic history, it usually means that individual decision-makers deliberately reject ideology and sentiment in favour of measurable objectives and interests.

The new realism also meant working closely with Bismarck. Prussia had not joined the Crimean coalition and, especially after the Austro-Prussian war of 1866, she seemed to offer a useful counterpoise to Austria. A strong tradition of friendship with Prussians existed at the Russian court (where many nobles were married to Germans); Prussia seemed to have no ambitions in the Balkans or in the Black Sea, and the two states had a history of co-operation in subduing their Polish subjects whenever trouble broke out. Russia's new realism was rewarded in 1870 when, in return for remaining neutral during the Franco-Prussian war, Bismarck led the way in securing international agreement to the annulment of the Black Sea clauses. As long as Bismarck was prepared to keep a close rein on Austria in the Balkans and to act as the 'honest broker' in Austro-Russian arguments, the Russians were happy to co-operate with him – a state of affairs that was most clearly symbolized when Alexander II and Franz Joseph met with Wilhelm I in Berlin and declared their friendship in the *Dreikaiserbund* (Three Emperors' League) of 1873.

But the meeting of the three emperors did not renew the Holy Alliance. After the betrayal of 1854–56, Russia would never again trust Austria, and, insofar as Russian policy retained any ideological foundation, this moved away from monarchical solidarity and in the direction of Panslavism, away from 'Europe' towards 'Asia'. Dostoevsky's Russian nationalism led him to condemn Europe as the land of the bourgeoisie and the Jews, which contrasted with 'the protesting Russian soul, to which European culture . . . has always, ever since Peter, been hateful' (Williams, 1997: 14). The second half of the nineteenth century witnessed the rise of the 'Slavic idea' which saw Russia as a state culturally and politically distinct from the states of western and central Europe. Russia, according to this view, had a historic mission to protect and promote – perhaps even to unite – all Slav peoples, which meant defending the interests of Bulgars, Serbs and Montenegrins.

The panslav idea, which was a more extreme, modernised, version of the older notion of an Orthodox brotherhood of believers, became increasingly popular among Russian educated classes, even though it inevitably meant antagonism with both the Ottoman and Habsburg empires. The most influential publicist of the movement, Danilevskii, insisted in his popular *Russia and Europe* that Russia could only serve her interests by joining forces with other Slavs in protracted military struggle against the rest of Europe. Russia was too strong and powerful to be merely one of the great European powers, and could occupy 'a place worthy of herself and Slavdom' only as the 'head of a special independent system of states and by serving as a counterweight to Europe as a whole' (Thaden, 1964: 111). When Wilhelm II acceded to the throne in 1888 and quickly launched Germany on its new course in foreign policy, a large part of which involved the expansion of German interests in the Ottoman empire and more straightforward support of Austria-Hungary, the germanophiles in Russia found it increasingly difficult to maintain the connection with Germany in the face of these **slavophile** sentiments.

The new course in German policy also reflected the changing nature of the balance of power in Europe, which further altered Russia's perception of the position she occupied in that balance. Germany's decisive victory over France in 1870–71 showed that she was now the pre-eminent military state on the continent and, over the next twenty years, the gap between Germany and France continued to grow. Russia's professional diplomatists increasingly became convinced that Germany intended to harness this new strength; and, if Germany crushed France altogether, she would be free to pursue a much more aggressive policy in the east. This was particularly true given the signs that the Habsburg empire was being transformed into a German satellite, rather than an equal partner, and that Britain was co-operating with the Triple Alliance in the middle east and in the Mediterranean. A strong and independent France, even if she did follow the dangerous creed of republicanism, was seen by Russian diplomats as a necessary counterbalance to

Slavophilia: A term used to describe the movement in Russia that rejected the policy of westernization that had first been launched by Peter the Great. Popular with many Russian intellectuals in the mid-nineteenth century, the movement led later in the century to a concentration on unifying all slavic peoples, i.e. 'Panslavism'.

German power. Overcoming a century of tradition, therefore, Russia agreed in 1891 to the principles of an alliance with France [**Doc. 6, p. 94**], and then, in 1893–94, to a military convention that provided for mutual defence against a German attack, or an Austrian attack (on Russia) that was supported by Germany, or an Italian attack (on France) that was supported by Germany [**Doc. 7, p. 95**].

The French found it as difficult to overcome their aversion to the tsarist autocracy as the Russians had found it to overcome their horror of revolutionary republicanism. Throughout the nineteenth century, no state had so clearly symbolized the decadence of the *ançien régime* as Russia. The Russian emperor claimed that his right to rule came from God, whereas both Napoleon I and Napoleon III claimed that their mandate came from the people. Russia was still stuck in the mire of unenlightened, **theocratic** ideas: the Orthodox church was the most backward in Europe; no representative institutions existed whereby the people could make their will known; ordinary people were treated as chattels, not as citizens. 'Barbarism lit by gas' was how one French politician (Gambetta) saw Russia as late as the 1880s (Bury, 1982: 193). The French came to believe that an implicit connection existed between the survival of the autocracy in Russia and the unregenerate nature of the whole European system. The failure of the principles of the French revolution could be traced to the strength of the tsarist regime; its disappearance could open the door to a new Europe.

In the nineteenth century Paris became the home of Russian revolutionaries: **anarchists**, **nihilists** and communists organised secret societies, published newspapers, and plotted the overthrow of the tsar, none of which could have happened without the tacit support of the French government – as the kaiser delighted in pointing out to the tsar [**Doc. 5, p. 93**]. The cause of Polish nationalism in particular was close to many French hearts; the partition of Poland in the era before the French Revolution, carried out by the despots of the east against the wishes of the Polish people, symbolized the wickedness of the old regime. France became the champion of the cause of Polish independence and the home of the movement. When the people of Paris erupted in the final days of the Franco-Prussian war and formed a revolutionary commune, and when this was followed by the establishment of the Third French Republic, it seemed to confirm the impression that France would always be inflammable, chaotic and fanatical.

Bismarck certainly counted on this continuing to be the case. Assuming that the French would do anything to avenge the humiliating defeat they had suffered at the hands of the Prussians, he regarded Russian fears of revolution as one of the tools he could use to keep them away from the French. Moreover, the habitual instability of the French political system ought to provide insurance against a cohesive national campaign to recover their strength.

Theocracy: A form of government based on the rule of God, in which the laws of the state are those prescribed by religious doctrine or interpretation of the deity's will.

Anarchism: A sociopolitical movement that rejects the coercive authority of the state in favour of individual freedom. It reached the height of its popularity in the decades before the First World War, when anarchists came to be associated with violence and terrorism.

Nihilism: A radical revolutionary movement that arose in late nineteenth-century Russia. Nihilists proclaimed their rejection of all traditional values, particularly those concerning the family and Christianity, and sought to destroy the authority of the state through terror and assassination.

Although the Franco-Russian alliance proved that differences in political ideology were not sufficient to overcome calculations based on strategic interest, the idea that France was in decline before the First World War, and that this was one of the fundamental factors that determined the international politics of the period has become indelibly etched upon the history of Europe from 1871 to 1914.

Like most legends, that of French decline has much to support it. At the time of the Franco-Prussian war, the two states had been roughly equal in population, but by 1914 Germany was almost double the size of France – which was now only slightly larger than Italy, and somewhat smaller than Austria-Hungary. In both iron and steel production France and Germany were equals in 1870–71, but by 1914 France produced only 30 per cent as much iron and only 25 per cent as much steel. The balance that had appeared to exist when the Franco-Prussian war broke out had clearly disappeared by 1914. Contemporary observers concluded that France was no longer in a position to dominate Europe, and that her place as the dominant European power had been taken over by Germany.

But the weakness of France is easily exaggerated, and it is important to recognise that few Frenchmen believed their nation to be finished as a great power in the era before 1914. The French people in general and republicans in particular, attributed the defeat of 1870–71 to the corruption and incompetence of Napoleon III and his advisers. According to this view, France and Prussia had been equals in 1870–71, so defeat on the battlefield was not predetermined by factors beyond anyone's control: on the contrary, the politicians of the Second Empire (and those they appointed to positions of military command) had been corrupted by their appetite for wealth and power. The leaders of the new republic denounced their predecessors as depraved seekers of pleasure and luxury; they sought instead to create a regime that would be moral, efficient and unified, a regime in which all Frenchmen could take pride and which, consequently, would benefit from a renewed patriotic fervour.

The first problem confronting the new republic was the payment of the huge indemnity provided for in the Treaty of Frankfurt; until this was paid a German army of occupation would remain in France. Bismarck had hoped that the indemnity would throw French finances into such disorder as to make their recovery long and hard. The French people, however, unlike the Germans after 1919, chose to regard payment as a matter of national honour and, against all expectations, paid the indemnity in a little over two years – six months ahead of schedule. Nor did this impoverish the nation. Over the next forty years the French showed that, in spite of their lagging industrial productivity, they enjoyed sufficient reserves of capital (as a result of the national preoccupation with saving rather than spending) to remain a leading participant in the European economy. Iron and steel do not account for everything, and the ability of the Paris *bourse* to float loans was an important factor in the events that led up to the Franco-Russian alliance.

French money also made it possible to expand and modernize the army with unexpected speed, and to an extent that frightened Bismarck. Within a year of the French defeat, the new republican Chamber of Deputies agreed that they could afford to introduce compulsory five-year military service for all men between the ages of twenty and forty. For the next thirty years France consistently spent more money on her army than Germany did, and at least twice as much on her navy. By 1900 France's regular army was slightly larger than Germany's. The tremendous growth of Germany's economy and population undoubtedly provided her with a potential greater than that of France – but this might count for little if she could be defeated quickly on the battlefield.

The French national recovery – at least as it was measured in troops and armaments – was achieved at a tremendous cost, however, as French tax-payers regularly paid almost twice as much as their German counterparts. The cost of military parity no doubt contributed to the gap in the economic development of the two nations, which continued to grow each year. Nevertheless, French patriotic pride (combined with gold reserves) gave France a military standing almost equal to that of Germany in 1900.

The revival of patriotism after 1871 also stimulated colonial expansion. At the time of France's defeat, her overseas empire consisted of no more than a handful of ports and islands along the coasts of Africa and China; by 1900 the French had expanded their empire to the extent that it comprised four million square miles – an empire second only to that of Great Britain and more than twenty times the size of France itself. Vast territories were marked out in north Africa, west Africa and Indo-China, and a large navy was built to defend the new possessions. Until the late 1880s France was spending almost as much as Britain on her navy, and more than Germany, Austria-Hungary, Italy, Russia and the United States combined.

The new imperialism in France, the reformed and expanded army, the new and modern navy, the readiness to use accumulated capital for political purposes, along with pride in the political achievements of the Third Republic, contributes to a rather different picture of France from 1870 to 1900. Far from resembling a state whose citizens were conscious of its steady decline, France can be seen as spirited and determined, eager to overcome the reputation for weakness and corruption that she had acquired as a result of the debacle of 1870.

The great revival following 1870 was neither simple nor straightforward. Colonial expansion encouraged quarrels with Britain, and one of these, the Fashoda crisis, almost led to war in 1898, whereas those who sought *revanche* persisted in seeing Germany as the real enemy, which led the

Germans to anticipate that any conflict in Europe would encourage the French to attack them. Those who looked overseas for the future of France as a great power usually saw Britain as the enemy, and therefore supported the building of a large fleet; logically, it also ought to have led them to support a **rapprochement** with Germany in Europe. Some important figures like Jules Grévy (President of the French National Assembly) believed that 'France must not think of war. She must accept the fait accompli, she must renounce Alsace' (Keiger, 1983: 9). Others believed that French power and dignity could be restored only by recapturing the lost provinces of Alsace and Lorraine. Renan, the great French historian and republican politician wrote that his dream of an intellectual, moral and political alliance between France and Germany had been smashed in 1871, opening an abyss between the two that centuries would not fill. Even philosophers 'cannot be insensible to the cry of two million men whom we were obliged to throw into the sea in order to save the rest from drowning'. Henceforth, France had 'a point of steel embedded in her flesh which will no longer let her sleep' (Buthman, 1970: 15). They regarded Germany as the enemy, and therefore supported the creation of a large army; logically, it also ought to have led them to support the settlement of colonial differences with Britain overseas.

Rapprochement: A term used in diplomacy and in diplomatic history to describe the re-establishment of harmonious relations between two states, usually after a crisis or a prolonged period of antagonism.

From 1870 to 1900, however, the French attempted to pursue continentalism and colonialism simultaneously. There was no clear or consistent leadership to provide a systematic approach to foreign affairs. Although the republic itself proved to be stable, successfully withstanding challenges from monarchists and Bonapartists alike, the governments of the republic were much less so: they lasted for little more than a year at a time in the first two decades after 1871. France had thirteen foreign ministers in the nineteen years between 1871 and 1890. This political instability resulted in a confused policy that managed to antagonize both Germany and Britain, which, in turn, contributed significantly to the Anglo-German harmony that prevailed throughout most of this period.

Anglo-French relations, which had improved dramatically after 1871, were seriously damaged when the British occupied Egypt in 1882. A financial crisis had caused the bankruptcy of the Egyptian government in 1876, whereupon France and Britain had agreed to participate in joint financial control. But this broke down in 1882 when a nationalist revolt seemed to threaten the security of the Suez Canal, leading the British to intervene by force. However, the French, who had agreed to act jointly with Britain, were prevented from participating when the government lost a vote in the chamber. Although the deputies were not prepared to undertake the expense of a joint occupation, there was widespread resentment at the establishment of British predominance in Egypt. Ever since Napoleon's invasion of 1798 the French had come to regard themselves as having a special mission to perform

Quai d'Orsay: The location of the French ministry of foreign affairs. Often used by historians as a shorthand reference to the ministry in the same way that British historians will refer to 'Whitehall' for the British Government or American historians to the 'White House' for the US presidency.

in Egypt. One of the glories of Napoleon III's Second Empire had been the building of the Suez Canal, and French investment in Egypt had continued to grow since 1871. Even if the deputies were not keen on a new French intervention in Egypt, the permanent officials of the **Quai d'Orsay** (the French foreign ministry), who really managed policy in the absence of strong governments, were mostly keen colonialists. Many officials believed that the way to restore the greatness of France was to establish a great empire in north Africa that would stretch from Morocco to Egypt, thus transforming her into the greatest power in the Mediterranean. For twenty years following the British intervention, therefore, the foreign ministry was preoccupied with prying the British out of Egypt.

The Germans, not surprisingly, welcomed the Anglo-French antagonism over Egypt, and Bismarck encouraged the French to enlarge their interests in Tunisia, Morocco, Nigeria, Madagascar and Indo-China. Consequently, the years immediately after 1882 were ones of Franco-German détente. But French policy was inconsistent: *revanche* was not dead. Although a growing number of responsible French politicians were inclined to forget the lost provinces, few dared to proclaim this publicly; the cause of Alsace and Lorraine still fired the imaginations of too many Frenchmen for this to be a practicable programme, a point which was illustrated in the '**Boulanger** affair' of 1889.

Boulanger, General Georges *(1837–91)*: French soldier and statesman; minister of war, 1886–87. His appointment of republicans to military posts in place of royalists led to his dismissal, a political crisis and then his exile.

General Boulanger was an outspoken nationalist who, as minister of war in 1886–87, initiated further reforms and expansion of the army. He became an immensely popular figure, especially with those extreme patriots who believed that France had already recovered sufficiently to launch a war of revenge on Germany. Bismarck was particularly worried by his popularity, because it seemed to presage the kind of Bonapartist revival that might prove a real threat: a strong man who could unite the country in an anti-German crusade. Although Boulanger lost his nerve and abandoned the idea of a *coup d'état* against the republic, his momentary fame led to an expansion of the German army, and to talk of a preventive war against France.

The Boulanger affair made it clear to the Germans that any détente with France was likely to be short-lived; in spite of their colonial aspirations, the French, it seemed, would never be persuaded to think of Germany as anything but an enemy. By the 1890s few Frenchmen were prepared to undertake an aggressive campaign to restore the lost provinces – but neither were they prepared to abandon them permanently to Germany. The war-scare that arose from the Boulanger affair led the French to fear that the Germans would attempt to confirm their possession of Alsace-Lorraine by launching a new war against them.

In spite of the revival of French spirits, finances and military forces following 1871, France remained as isolated diplomatically as she had been during the war itself. Where Bismarck had succeeded in building the Triple Alliance and bringing Russia and Britain into association with it via the

Dreikaiserbund and the Mediterranean agreements, the French had managed only to antagonize Britain and Italy. In the first instance, the great attraction of an alliance with Russia was that it would not force the French to choose between their colonial ambitions and her hopes of recovering the lost provinces: the Russians had been consistently anti-English since 1856, and, with the abandonment of the Russo-German Reinsurance Treaty in 1890, the Russians were prepared to consider French suggestions for a defensive alliance against Germany. The alliance really did nothing to provide for *revanche*, but it did offer security against another German attack [**Doc. 7, p. 95**]. Security in Europe encouraged the French to become more aggressive overseas, and within a few years they found themselves on the brink of war with Britain.

The French colonialists believed, after almost twenty years of fruitless diplomatic efforts to persuade the British to leave Egypt, that they must find some way to prod them into serious negotiations. The strategy they resolved upon was to send a military expedition through the Congo into the Sudan. Here they could, by occupying a position at the headwaters of the Nile, threaten the British position in Egypt. They believed that only a threat would be necessary – but they were mistaken. When the French force arrived at Fashoda in September 1898 it was challenged by a superior British force, and the British government instantly made clear its determination to go to war rather than permit the French to remain in the Sudan. The French, who were not prepared for war with the British in Africa or on the high seas, had no choice but to back down and retreat from the Sudan.

By 1900, therefore, French policy was still somewhat uncertain, although almost everyone who mattered now regarded it as essential that the alliance with Russia be maintained. The colonial party used the example of Fashoda to encourage a rapprochement with Germany and to argue that the alliance with Russia ought to be expanded to include the contingency of war with Britain. The Franco-Russian alliance was, accordingly, altered in this way in 1899. The object of the alliance was also expanded to provide for the maintenance of 'the balance of power in Europe' in the hope of forestalling direct German control of the Habsburg monarchy. Whether the French ought to concentrate their attention on the German threat to their security in Europe or on the British competition to their ambitions in Africa had not yet been resolved. Temporarily, the French hoped that their alliance with Russia would prove strong enough to permit them to pursue both objects simultaneously.

GREAT BRITAIN

By 1900, continental Europe had been clearly divided into two rival alliances, but one great power had refused to join either side. Instead, Britain was at that moment engaged in fighting a war in South Africa – a fact that led some critics of the government to deplore the 'isolation' that left her not only without allies, but practically without friends. Critics worried that this isolation would render Britain vulnerable, that the animosity felt for the British cause in the Anglo-Boer war might lead to the formation of a 'continental league' aimed at the British empire, and perhaps to a new version of Napoleon's continental system. After all, they pointed out, France and Russia, Germany and Italy, all coveted territories contained within the empire. Nor was isolation necessary: Germany, Austria-Hungary and Italy had been attempting to persuade Britain to join the Triple Alliance for a decade or more. Britain, however, had steadfastly refused to join, and leading members of the government were, by the time of the Anglo-Boer war, proclaiming that her isolation was 'splendid'.

Was it a sign of British strength or weakness that she was isolated in 1900? Continental observers of Britain in the late nineteenth century were particularly struck by three aspects of Great Britain as a great power: her industry, her empire and her navy. These components were understood to work in close conjunction with one another: British industry provided the appetite for empire, the desire for the resources and markets that her possessions in Africa and Asia, in North America, the Caribbean and Australasia provided; industrial prosperity and technological proficiency enabled the British to construct a large, modern navy; mastery of the seas enabled them to defend their empire against all opponents. This simplistic picture may be misleading, but the idea that British power was fundamentally industrial, and that British interests were essentially imperial, was entertained by most observers of Victorian Britain. What was debatable at the turn of the century was whether or not British power was sufficient to enable her to continue to stand aloof from the system of European alliances and alignments.

British industry was still pre-eminent in the Europe of 1900. She produced more coal than the five powers of the continent combined. She produced as much iron as the Triple Alliance, and only Germany produced more steel. In spite of the advantage she still enjoyed, however, the continental states in general, and Germany in particular, were rapidly closing the gap. In 1870 Britain had produced five times as much coal as all of Europe, and twice as much iron; in 1880 she had produced twice as much steel. Although British production in all of these vital sectors of the economy rose steadily in the fifty years prior to 1914, by the time war broke out Germany was producing almost as much coal, more iron and twice as much steel. In the newer, more technically oriented chemical and electrical industries Britain was outdistanced from the start, and was falling farther behind each year.

This changing pattern of industrialization has led some commentators to argue that the First World War was simply an Anglo-German contest for industrial predominance and the trade that followed from it. But Russia too was making rapid strides in catching up with Britain and, outside Europe, the United States had already surpassed Britain in all of the vital industrial components by 1900. In spite of the continuing prosperity of British industry in 1900, therefore, it cannot be argued that it any longer provided her with a clear advantage over potential rivals.

The British empire, on the other hand, appeared in a quite different light. Without the empire Great Britain was a state not much bigger, either in territory or in population, than Italy; with the empire she was bigger than Russia. The enormous extent of the empire – over ten million square miles – gave Britain potential reserves of manpower and resources not available to the continental states, and most particularly not to the central powers. Colonial groups in Germany, France and Italy argued that they too must acquire empire in order to compete with Britain.

But the apparent advantages of empire might also be misleading, and possession of these vast territories could be interpreted as a source of weakness. They were certainly a source of danger: Russia and the United States could threaten various parts of the empire much more easily than Britain could defend them; France apparently aimed to make trouble everywhere she could, especially in Egypt and Indo-China. Britain, who had fought wars against each of these states in the course of the nineteenth century, was forced to take expensive measures to defend her possessions against these threats. And now, near the end of the nineteenth century, new competitors emerged on the scene: Germany, Japan and Italy had also developed an appetite for empire, and they were now in a position to cause trouble and even greater expense to Britain, should they choose to do so. The British, in order to prepare to meet any or all of these threats (whether real or imagined) were compelled to erect fortifications and maintain defences in the far east, in central Asia, in Egypt, in the Mediterranean, in South Africa, on the Pacific coast of North America and elsewhere.

Critics of empire within Britain, of whom **J.A. Hobson** was the most famous, argued that the expense of such undertakings was out of all proportion to the benefits gained, that empire was a source of weakness, not strength. The greatest expense arose from the necessity of building a large navy to defend imperial possessions, and Hobson argued that naval interests – the Admiralty, shipbuilders and port towns – were among the select groups that actually benefited from empire; everyone (especially the working classes) paid the taxes that were necessary to sustain the empire, but only special interests reaped the rewards [**Doc. 11, p. 98**]. Radicals also argued that a large navy was not really essential for the defence of the British Isles, that a small navy and defensive fortifications were sufficient to deter an invasion; so Britain would be safer and more prosperous without the empire.

Hobson, John Atkinson *(1858–1940)*: English journalist and economist; author of *The War in South Africa* (1900), *The Psychology of Jingoism* (1901), *Imperialism: A Study* (1902), and *The Science of Wealth* (1911).

As the existence of the empire meant preparing for an imperial war, it was not enough that the British be superior to only one European competitor: the Royal Navy must be stronger than any possible combination of European navies. In the 1890s this meant building to the 'Two-Power Standard' in order to meet the threat of a combined Franco-Russian attack. But, after the German naval laws of 1898, 1900 and 1906, Germany too had to be taken into account, and the new dreadnought class of battleship meant a further increase in the already enormous expenditure. By 1910 Great Britain was spending almost as much on her navy as Germany, France and Russia combined, and more than all six European great powers had spent in 1890.

Naval building and imperialism had become controversial subjects in Britain by 1900, and the debate over the Anglo-Boer war had divided the Liberal party into distinct factions. Public controversy over the course of foreign policy was not a new feature of British political life, however, and foreign observers had noted throughout the nineteenth century the extent to which the British parliamentary system encouraged division and debate. The government was required to inform, explain and defend its foreign policy to members of parliament, but whether this was a source of strength or weakness in the making of policy, or a factor encouraging isolation rather than commitment, is very difficult to judge. Most members of Parliament believed that they must conduct themselves cautiously and responsibly when it came to questions of foreign policy, that the foreign secretary and his advisors had access to better sources of information than they, and that the public would disapprove if criticism weakened the government's ability to negotiate successfully.

Ironically then, while there was more open discussion and criticism of foreign policy in Britain than anywhere in Europe (with the possible exception of France), there was also more continuity and coherence. Changes in government seldom meant dramatic changes in policy, and the party in power could usually be quite certain that the nation as a whole would support its policies. This coherence was largely the result of the widespread acceptance within the British ruling class of certain basic assumptions that were to guide British relations with Europe. Such debates as there were usually focused on methods, on questions of administration and organisation; the principles of the balance of power, of a strong navy and of avoiding commitments that would draw Britain into a European war were generally supported by both political parties and most politicians. A century of unparalleled power and prosperity had furnished convincing evidence that adherence to these principles had accounted for Britain's success; it would be reckless to abandon them now.

The Napoleonic wars had clarified the dangers with which Britain would be faced should one state succeed in establishing hegemony in Europe.

Britain's economy had been severely disrupted by the interruption of trade with her best markets – which, in spite of the empire, were always to be found in Europe – and through the necessity of spending enormous sums on defence. Furthermore, there was little question that, had Napoleon succeeded in establishing real dominance and bending the whole of the European economy to suit the needs of France, he would eventually have been able to mount an effective challenge to Britain's overseas possessions, especially in India. No responsible Englishman believed that Britain could survive as a great power if Europe came under the control of France. Finally, economic hardship combined with inflammatory political ideas to produce the greatest danger of social revolution in Britain since the seventeenth century.

Security, prosperity and social harmony all seemed to depend upon what the British referred to as 'the balance of power'. This was a concept that was rooted in the eighteenth-century enlightenment, and especially in the Newtonian concept of the physical universe. Ideally, the balance of forces among both heavenly bodies and states would regulate itself; but in the heavens divine intervention was sometimes necessary, as was occasional British intervention in European politics. The experience of the Napoleonic wars furnished another lesson here: for intervention to be successful Britain needed to find one or more European allies – on her own she would not be able to defeat a continental power that possessed a great army. For the balance of power to work, therefore, Britain had to assume that one or more European states would always find it in their interest to counterbalance the power of the strongest; ideally, they would choose to do this on their own; if necessary, Britain would have to encourage them to do so.

In the forty years that followed the Congress of Vienna in 1815, the British demonstrated their belief in the principle of the balance of power. The French, once they accepted their 'historical' frontiers and gave up their ambitions to dominate Europe, became, in British eyes, respectable participants in the European system once again. The danger to the balance was now thought to come from Russia, which seemed to be in a position to dominate both eastern Europe, as her intervention in Hungary in 1848 demonstrated, and the middle east, as her policy in the crisis leading up to the Crimean War in 1854 seemed to show. Russia was transformed into an enemy, France into an ally.

The Crimean War has become almost synonymous with 'incompetence', and thus it is easy to forget that it was the only successful invasion of Russia in modern times. Britain achieved her basic aims: the Ottoman empire remained independent and relied more heavily on the advice of Britain than Russia; and the Habsburg empire was saved from declining to the level of a Russian satellite. The balance of power in Europe was maintained, but at the price of deeply rooted Russian animosity. For the next half-century everyone expected a great Anglo-Russian war, particularly as the Russians undertook to counter the neutralization of the Black Sea that had been forced on them in 1856 by the Treaty of Paris by posing a counter threat to the British empire in India. British foreign and defence policies for the next thirty years were devoted primarily to forestalling this Russian threat.

Because the British had been concerned for more than a century with the threats posed by the French and the Russians, they were inclined to welcome the rise of Prussia and even the creation of the German empire. A strong Germany seemed to be just what Britain needed: situated as it was between France and Russia, it was perfectly suited to act as the fulcrum in the European balance of power. Moreover, unlike France and Russia, Germany had neither overseas interests nor a navy and therefore was unlikely to challenge either Britain's empire or her maritime supremacy. As long as Bismarck was satisfied with the post-1871 status quo in Europe, Germany was regarded as a 'natural' ally. The only undercurrent of concern emerged as a result of Germany's stunning victory over France in 1871: for Germany to be somewhat stronger than France suited British designs, but for the Germans to be able to overpower the French so quickly might cause complications. The British began to worry that German power might be so great as to render France subordinate in the future: another Franco-German war could even bring about the end of France as an independent state. This thinking led London to warn Berlin during the 'Is War in Sight?' crisis of 1875 that Britain would not remain indifferent if such a war were to take place.

But after 1875 these worries began to recede as growing Anglo-Russian antagonism and the revival of French imperialism combined in such a way as to draw Britain closer to Germany and the Triple Alliance. In the 1880s and the 1890s, a possible German bid for hegemony in Europe seemed a much more unlikely threat than a Franco-Russian assault on the British empire. The Great Eastern crisis of 1878 and the Penjdeh crisis of 1885 convinced the British that the Russians still aimed to dominate the middle east and to place themselves in a position to threaten an invasion of India. Britain's occupation of Egypt in 1881 struck a blow to French pride and led to a series of bitter quarrels in Asia and Africa. As long as France and Russia faced the combined strength of the Triple Alliance in Europe, however, they were not likely to risk a conflict with Britain. In this way the balance of power contributed significantly to the defence of the British empire. And, as Russia and France appeared to be the restless, aggressive powers, determined to expand beyond Europe and to alter the balance within it, the British contributed to the stability of the Triple Alliance by assuring Italy and Austria-Hungary of their co-operation in the Mediterranean agreements of 1887.

This state of affairs became less straightforward when Wilhelm II initiated his 'new course' in foreign policy. Now Germany also appeared to have an interest in overseas expansion, and a series of minor Anglo-German disputes arose over places like Samoa, Togoland and the Cameroons. The British government never took these disputes very seriously, but the kaiser's highly publicised support for the Boers in South Africa, along with the German government's decision in 1898 to build a fleet began to stimulate some opposition in Britain to the policy of co-operation with Germany. Throughout the 1890s, Germany had attempted to draw Britain into becoming a member of the Triple Alliance – a policy which seemed close to fruition with the Mediterranean agreements – but Britain had consistently refused to go any farther. German entreaties had always been rejected, not because of Germanophobia or the German bid for colonies, but because the British feared being drawn into a war in Europe for the sake of Germany's position in Alsace-Lorraine or Poland. Thus, when the war broke out in South Africa, the Germans began to promote the idea of a 'continental league' aimed at the British empire.

By 1900, therefore, the British found themselves isolated. Their traditional enemies, France and Russia, were allied with one another and had recently altered the terms of the alliance to provide for mutual action against the British. Their 'natural' ally, Germany, was increasingly antagonistic and apparently determined to cause them trouble wherever and whenever possible. The Anglo-Boer war demonstrated that this isolation posed little danger to the empire. The continental league amounted to nothing, and no joint action of the European powers was carried out; in fact, no action of any kind was taken against the British, who were able to fight the war in South Africa without worrying about the consequences in the far east, central Asia and the Mediterranean. The empire was never in any serious danger after 1900; Fashoda proved to be the last crisis in which the British contemplated the possibility of a war with a European power arising from her imperial interests. The revolution in British diplomacy that took place after 1900 was sparked not by any immediate fear of a threat to the empire, but by concern for the European balance of power.

3

The European Crisis

THE DIPLOMATIC REVOLUTION

The condition of European international relations was unusually simple and stable by 1900. The continent was clearly divided into two rival alliances: Germany, Austria-Hungary and Italy in the Triple Alliance; France and Russia in the Dual Alliance. Of the great powers, only Britain was unaccounted for. Everyone who engaged in diplomatic and military affairs regarded the alliance system as the primary characteristic of international relations, and every question that arose between 1900 and 1914 was assessed for its possible influence upon this system. After war broke out in 1914 many critics argued that the rival alliances made war inevitable, that sooner or later a crisis was certain to arise that would lead to a general European conflict, that it became increasingly difficult to minimize any friction or localize any controversy that arose in these years. The July crisis seemed the perfect illustration of this argument: what conceivable interest did Germany, Britain and France have in the fate of the Bosnian Serbs, other than the impact of the assassination on the alliance system?

But other observers saw the alliances as providing stability and predictability to the European system. Moreover, as the alliances were fundamentally defensive in nature, they reduced the likelihood of aggressive behaviour. The alliances also appeared to bolster the principle of the balance of power, which many still believed to be the best guarantee of peace: as long as neither side enjoyed a clear superiority over the other, they argued, no statesman would risk the destruction of modern war and possible social upheaval. This was an unpopular point of view after 1919, but the experience of the Cold War after 1945, when most of the world seemed divided into the rival alliances of NATO and the Warsaw Pact – in which localized conflicts became the norm – has given this perspective renewed strength.

Neither argument, that the alliances made war inevitable, nor that they made the chances of it remote, can be tested. And the experience of the decade before the First World War demonstrates that simplistic assumptions about their impact are almost certainly false. To understand the alliance system, it must be located carefully within the context of the times.

The apparent stability of the system is deceptive. We know now that it endured, and that the pattern of the central European powers opposed by France and Russia that emerged in the 1890s was fundamentally the same as the conflict that broke out in 1914. Yet there were some significant changes. Italy, a member of the Triple Alliance for more than thirty years, went to war in 1915 against her former allies; Britain, independent of the alliance system in 1900 (and, if anything, enjoying better relations with Germany and Austria-Hungary than she did with France and Russia) joined the Dual Alliance against the Triple in 1914.

There were also noticeable differences within the alliances themselves, differences that led many to doubt whether the alliances would remain intact. French interests and ambitions in north Africa were never supported by Russia, which was unlikely to support France in a war against Italy, Britain or Germany that began over Tunis, Egypt or Morocco; it was equally doubtful whether France would fight to support Russia in Manchuria or Korea. The Triple Alliance sometimes appeared to be coming apart at the seams: Italy could always be tempted to turn against Austria-Hungary if France offered her concessions; Austria-Hungary had no interest in supporting Germany's *Weltpolitik* ('world policy') in central and southern Africa, in China and the Pacific; some Germans argued that it was a mistake to support Austria-Hungary in the Balkans, that it was preferable to restore good relations with Russia and thereby disrupt the Franco-Russian alliance.

The alliance system appears in retrospect to have been more stable than it actually was. Significant changes took place between 1900 and 1914; diplomats frequently questioned the usefulness of the arrangements; each side worked to dismantle the foundations upon which the rival alliance had been built. Nevertheless, the broad outlines of the system remained intact because the basic preoccupations of the great powers – their ambitions and their fears – survived the criticisms and the crises of the period from 1900 to 1914. It is as important to understand how the alliances withstood these challenges as it is to comprehend the differences that divided the partners.

As the Triple Alliance and the Dual Alliance alike had been constructed entirely for European reasons, it should come as no surprise that complications beyond the frontiers of western and eastern Europe made it difficult for them to operate cohesively. This was certainly true in the far east, where, in the summer of 1900, troubles that had been simmering in China for two years broke out in open rebellion. The 'League of Righteous and Harmonious Fists' (commonly referred to in the west as the '**Boxers**'), with the tacit support of China's dowager empress, murdered Christian missionaries in an

Boxers: Term used to describe those Chinese who violently opposed foreign influence in China, 1899–1900. They attacked Christian missionaries, destroyed European property and besieged foreign legations in Peking for two months in June–August 1900.

anti-European campaign, marched on Peking and besieged the foreign legation there. On 21 June 1900 the Chinese government declared war on the
foreign powers, and it looked for a moment as if a great war would be waged
in China that might result in her dismemberment.

Germany in particular feared the possible consequences of the Boxer
rebellion. Wilhelm II had committed himself to an active role in the far east
in 1897 when, declaring that Germany was now a 'world power', he had
seized the port of Tsingtao in Shantung province. If the rising led to the
partitioning of China among the European powers, Germany's ambitious
designs for the future were likely to be thwarted, as Russia, Britain and Japan
had much stronger forces in the area. The Germans therefore proposed to the
British that they should uphold the principle of the '**Open Door**' in China
and maintain the integrity of the Chinese empire. The British, who did not
wish to transform their sphere of influence in the Yangtze valley into a protectorate unless they had no other choice, agreed, hoping that co-operation
with Germany would prevent the Russians from seizing Manchuria, which
they had occupied during the Boxer crisis. The Anglo-German agreement on
China was duly signed on 16 October 1900.

British hopes of using Germany's friendship to forestall Russian expansion
in China soon vanished. When the Russians refused to evacuate Manchuria,
the German chancellor, Bernhard von Bülow, announced that the agreement
with Britain was not intended to apply to Manchuria. What this really meant
was that the Germans were not prepared to risk a crisis with Russia in Europe
for the sake of their ambitions in the far east. The British, who were currently
embroiled in a colonial war with the Afrikaners (Dutch settlers) of south
Africa, had already committed the bulk of their naval power and were in no
position to forestall Russia on their own. They showed some interest, therefore, when, in March 1901, the Japanese approached them with the suggestion that they would be prepared to oppose the Russians in Manchuria if the
British, in exchange, could keep the French neutral. The Japanese, who were
determined to have Korea for themselves, believed that they could defeat the
Russians if they did not have to face the combined fleets of Russia and France
when attempting to land troops on the Chinese mainland.

An alliance with Japan offered some advantages to Britain, although these
were not as obvious as they later appeared to be. The British, in 1901, did
not believe that Japan was strong enough to defeat Russia, even if France
were neutralized. In November and December of 1901 therefore, the British
foreign secretary, **Lord Lansdowne**, revived the idea of an alliance with
Germany; but the Germans demanded too high a price: Britain must join the
Triple Alliance. The Germans were not going to run risks for the sake of the
British empire without receiving some guarantees of support in Europe in
exchange. Simultaneously, the Japanese were negotiating with the Russians

Open Door: The phrase
that US secretary of state
John Hay gave to his
policy in China in 1899.
Fearing the partition of
China or that European
empires would erect bar-
riers to trade in their
spheres of influence, Hay
issued notes calling for
all states to receive equal
treatment.

**Lansdowne, 5th Marquis
of** *(Henry Charles Keith
Petty-Fitzmaurice, 1845–
1927)*: British statesman
and administrator; sec-
retary of war, 1895–1900;
foreign secretary, 1900–
05.

on the basis of 'Man-Kan Kokan' – Japan to take Korea, Russia to take Manchuria. These negotiations created a new scare for the British: a Russo-Japanese partition of China. Therefore, because the British could not prevent Russian expansion on their own, because German assistance depended on the British committing themselves to fighting France and Russia in Europe, and because a Russo-Japanese partition of China was the least desirable outcome of the crisis in the far east, the British chose to sign, on 30 January 1902, an alliance with Japan [**Doc. 12, p. 100**]. Salisbury feared the consequences: it involved a British pledge 'to defend Japanese action in Corea and in all China against France and Russia . . . There is no limit: and no escape. We are pledged to war . . .' (Howard, 1967: 91).

The Anglo-Japanese alliance did not make war more likely: the Japanese believed that it would strengthen their bargaining position by making it clear to Russia that she would be forced to fight without an ally, should it come to war. But the men making the decisions in Russia were not in a cautious mood. Military adventurers, admirals and some speculators, arguing that Russia's future lay in far eastern expansion, caught the ear of the tsar and stiffened his resolve not to compromise. Racism played a part in this decision, as the Japanese were thought to be racially inferior to the Europeans, and their surprising victory over the Chinese in 1895 was discounted accordingly. Moderates like the foreign minister, **Count Lambsdorff**, and the finance minister, **Count Witte**, were neglected in favour of the 'Korean' extremists, **Bezobrazov**, who was made a secretary of state, and Admiral Alexeiev, who was made viceroy of the far east.

Russia responded to the Anglo-Japanese alliance by signing a new version of their alliance with France. On 20 March 1902 a joint declaration was issued announcing, in effect, that the two would co-operate if a third party (Japan) threatened their interests by endangering the integrity of China. It was apparent to everyone that Russia was not going to back down without a fight. It also seemed apparent that the Franco-Russian alliance was in the process of being transformed from a limited arrangement, which was designed to meet the German challenge in Europe, into something more ambitious: an imperial design to establish Franco-Russian co-operation in Asia and, perhaps, in Africa.

The prospect of being drawn into a war against Britain for the sake of Russian interests in Manchuria and Korea was not a pleasant one for the French to contemplate. Their view of the alliance with Russia had originally been 'European' but, ironically, after the Fashoda crisis demonstrated the failure of the alliance to operate outside Europe – Russia refusing any support against Britain – the French had proposed an expansion of its terms, and these had been incorporated into the alliance in 1899. The new terms, which provided for the possibility of a war with Britain, were in fact designed to

Lambsdorff, Count V.N. *(1844–1907)*: Russian statesman; foreign minister, 1900–06.

Witte, Serge *(1849–1915)*: Russian statesman; minister of finance, 1892–1903; prime minister, 1905.

Bezobrazov, Alexander Mikhailovich *(1866–1933)*: Russian statesman; state secretary and member of Special Committee for the Affairs of the Far East, 1903–05.

Delcassé, Théophile
(1852–1923): French
statesman; elected de-
puty, 1889; minister of
colonies, 1893–95; for-
eign minister, 1898–
1905; naval minister,
1911–13; foreign min-
ister, 1914–15.

avoid one. The French foreign minister, **Delcassé**, wished to expand the alliance in order to encourage the British to negotiate over Egypt and Morocco; they were not intended to draw France into a war.

Nevertheless, Delcassé had no choice but to agree when the Russians insisted that they issue the joint declaration of March 1902. France needed the alliance with Russia in order to avoid being reduced to the level of a German subordinate in Europe and in the hope of coercing the British into an agreement on north Africa. While French foreign policy was guided skil-fully by Delcassé from 1898 to 1905, it was coherent and consistent – in stark contrast with the period between 1871 and 1890, when thirteen dif-ferent foreign ministers had presided over policy. Delcassé believed that French power and prestige could be re-established only by creating the great north African empire envisioned by the **Comité de l'Afrique Française**, and

Comité de l'Afrique
Française: A political
association formed to
promote French colonial-
ism in Africa. It was a
highly influential group,
and one of its presi-
dents, Charles Jonnart,
became French foreign
minister in 1912.

he at first attempted to achieve this by seeking the assistance of Germany, then by expanding the terms of the alliance with Russia. But while he was conducting these diplomatic manoeuvres Delcassé was aware of another option: perhaps the British would agree to settle their differences with France in Africa without the threat of war.

Delcassé's awareness of these options proved to be significant when, in the midst of the Russo-Japanese crisis in the far east, Morocco suddenly appeared ready to disintegrate. Tribes hostile to the sultan of Morocco revolted against his authority in late 1902 and he seemed powerless to stop them. Britain and France were equally fearful of the possible consequences of an uncon-trolled revolt: Britain because it might threaten Gibraltar, France because it might threaten Algeria. Ironically, both turned to Germany for diplomatic support. But the Germans, who believed that Anglo-French quarrels would always work to their advantage, turned them both down. Hoping to exploit the Moroccan crisis, the Germans unwittingly encouraged an Anglo-French entente.

Edward VII *(1841–1910)*:
Son of Queen Victoria;
succeeded her as king of
Great Britain and Ireland
and emperor of India in
1901.

Loubet, Émile *(1838–
1929)*: French statesman;
president, 1899–1906.

The first visible sign of an improvement in Anglo-French relations was the visit of **King Edward VII** to Paris in May 1903, which was a tremend-ous popular success. This was reciprocated when **President Loubet** and Delcassé travelled to London in July. The negotiations for a settlement of colonial differences, which began in earnest in the summer of 1903, were thus conducted in an atmosphere of public support. The displays of good-will in both countries, while they were not responsible for the settlement that eventually emerged, certainly made the endeavours of the diplomats easier than had been expected.

The French would have found it more difficult to pursue a settlement with the British if the Russians had objected to the negotiations, but they did not. In part, Russia's attitude was the result of misplaced confidence in her strength in the far east: the 'Koreans' in the Russian government argued that they could defeat the Japanese without French assistance, as long as the British did not intervene. Plehve, minister of the interior and a bitter opponent of Witte and the moderates, declared in May 1903 that 'Russia has been made by bayonets not diplomacy . . . we must decide the questions at issue with China and Japan with bayonets and not with diplomatic pens' (Jelavich, 1964: 243). This argument was strengthened when the trans-Siberian railway was completed in August 1903, which made it seem that Russia would, for the first time, be able to transport troops and supplies quickly and efficiently to the far east.

But Russian strategy was not entirely 'Asiatic' or expansionist. The tsar and his military advisors had recently concluded that the existence of France as a great power was now vital to Russian security in Europe. In March 1901 Russian strategists predicted that France could not survive a war with Germany unless Russia mobilized rapidly and attacked Germany in the east. This thinking led to a new Russian mobilisation scheme, which was formally approved in November 1902. The Russian commitment to France remained firm. The Dual Alliance, which both parties had unsuccessfully attempted to utilise for purposes outside of Europe – Russia in the far east, France in north Africa – nevertheless remained the most essential element in the European policy of each power.

Thus, when Japan attacked Russia at Port Arthur on 8 February 1904, it had little immediate impact upon power politics in Europe. **Nicholas II** dismissed the attack as 'a flea-bite' (Rogger, 1983: 177). Neither the Dual Alliance nor the Anglo-French colonial discussions were disrupted. If anything, the Japanese attack only encouraged France and Britain to reach an agreement. In spite of Japan's initial victory at Port Arthur, no one was predicting that the Japanese could win the war – even though they enjoyed a naval superiority and their army outnumbered the Russian army of the far east by 330,000 to 100,000.

Nicholas II *(1869–1918)*: Son of Alexander III of Russia, became tsar in 1894; abdicated in 1917; shot by revolutionaries in 1918.

The discussions between Britain and France not only continued but accelerated. The agreement, which was signed on 8 April 1904, resolved a wide range of Anglo-French differences in Newfoundland, Gambia, Nigeria, Madagascar, Siam and the New Hebrides. But the essence of the agreement lay in the provisions pertaining to Egypt and Morocco. What the British wanted in Egypt was an end to the troublesome opposition of the French, both on Egypt's frontiers and within the committee of bondholders that was responsible for Egypt's financial affairs. Such a promise from France would reduce the expense involved in safeguarding Egypt and make it possible to continue with financial reform more quickly and more easily. In return, the French wanted the British to acknowledge their primacy in Morocco. In a secret protocol to the agreement, Britain promised that, should the sultan's authority in Morocco disappear, she would give France a free hand there – providing that the coastline opposite Gibraltar went to Spain and that this strip of territory would remain unfortified. The French, in other words, finally recognized the permanence of the British occupation of Egypt in exchange for the opportunity to establish a French occupation of Morocco. 'England gains the assurance that we shall no longer trouble her' in Egypt, declared Delcassé, and he believed that she had given France 'a good price for this peace of mind' (Andrew, 1968: 214).

The Anglo-French 'entente' was not an alliance. No enemy was singled out. No contingencies were provided for. No co-ordinated activities were planned. The entente was simply a settlement of colonial disputes that had been simmering for the last quarter-century. Such a scheme had surfaced repeatedly during these years, but had never emerged successfully because of French intransigence on the Egyptian question. France, in fact, conceded little in Egypt: the British occupation had become stable and, under the guid-

Cromer, 1st Earl of *(Evelyn Baring, 1841–1917)*: British colonial administrator; British agent and consul-general in Egypt, 1883–1907.

ing hand of **Lord Cromer**, progressive. What the French gave up was a dream, and this was the true significance of the entente. Anglo-French antagonism had been one of the steady factors upon which European diplomats and strategists had come to rely. The end of the antagonism was bound to cause reverberations throughout the international system. But in 1904 no one imagined that this would end with millions of British troops fighting alongside their French allies in a continental European war.

The Anglo-French entente did not signify a diplomatic revolution; it did no more than suggest that one might be possible. But there were other signs of important changes going on at the same time. In the midst of the Anglo-French negotiations, Russian and Austro-Hungarian representatives met at Murzsteg in October 1903, where they agreed to co-operate in preventing disturbances in Macedonia from undermining the peace of the Balkans. The likelihood that the crisis in the far east might cause fundamental shifts in Russia's European policy began to be considered: perhaps the commitment to expansion in Asia and the possibility of war with Japan would lead the Russians to welcome a revived *Dreikaiserbund*; perhaps the failure of the French to support their ally would lead the Russians to abandon the alliance. The Germans encouraged these ideas and pushed them further along when, with the Russo-Japanese war raging in the far east, they signed a new commercial treaty with the Russians in July 1904.

The stage seemed set for a major shift in European diplomacy when ships in Russia's Baltic fleet, which had set out to make its way around Europe and Africa to join the fighting against Japan, fired on some British fishing boats off the Dogger Bank in the North Sea. The Russians had mistaken the trawlers from the Hull fishing fleet for Japanese torpedo-boats; they managed to sink the *Crane*, killing its captain, a crew member and wounding six others. Germany seized the opportunity to propose an alliance to Russia.

They were to promise one another assistance against attack by an unspecified 'European power' – which really meant that Germany would assist Russia against Britain and that Russia would assist Germany against France. The Germans even suggested that the Franco-Russian alliance need not be abandoned, as they imagined that it provided for the contingency of war against Britain, as well as against Germany. The tsar responded positively: 'Germany, Russia and France should at once unite upon an arrangement to abolish the Anglo-Japanese arrogance and insolence . . . This combination has often come to my mind. It will mean peace and rest for the world' (Albertini vol. 1, 1952: 152). However, the tsar's advisors restrained him, and when they insisted that any treaty would have to be submitted first to France, the Germans dropped the idea. There was to be no Russo-German equivalent of the Anglo-French entente.

The Germans, in spite of the apparently cautious terms they had suggested, were asking too high a price and had too little to offer in return. There were no Gambias or Madagascars in Russo-German relations. Even the idea of assistance against Britain could not be taken seriously: the German army was of no use against the empire; the German navy was in no condition to challenge the British. Some Germans even feared that the British would launch a preventive attack against the fleet that they were building, destroying the German warships in harbour before they were strong enough to defend themselves. The Germans could offer the Russians security on their western frontier, but neither Bülow nor Wilhelm II would be satisfied with a simple revival of the old Bismarckian arrangement, because this would have meant admitting that their policy had been a failure – and that Bismarck had been right when he had condemned the new course in German policy.

Any arrangement with Russia had to emphasize Germany's strength and the success of Bülow's 'world policy'. What the Germans were proposing in fact was their old idea of a 'continental league' with Germany at the centre, directing Russia and France. Bülow believed that recent events had shown that neither of them was able to act independently, or even, as the war with Japan had shown, together. But the negotiations conducted in the autumn of 1904 showed that Russia did not feel herself to be so weak as to compel her to join Germany. When the negotiations failed, Bülow, and the head of the political section in the German foreign ministry, **Friedrich von Holstein**, decided that they might be more successful in persuading the weaker member of the Dual Alliance, France, to join Germany. Bülow and Holstein were also anxious to show the French that their entente with the British was of little use to them when it came to a contest with Germany.

An opportunity almost exactly designed to fit German specifications came in January 1905 when a French mission arrived at Fez, the capital of Morocco. The aim of the mission was to institute a programme of internal

Holstein, Friedrich von (1837–1909): German administrator; served in foreign ministry, 1876–1906; although his highest post was as Director of the Political Section, he was very influential in the period 1890–1906.

reforms, and thus make it clear to the Moroccans the French were in control. The Germans knew how deeply the French were committed to their ambitions in Morocco, for practically the entire French foreign ministry, and especially the bureaucrats of the Quai d'Orsay, aspired to establish a French empire there. 'Morocco constitutes the last imperial chance which can remain for us' declared the Deputy and president of both the foreign affairs commission in the Chamber and the *groupe coloniale*, Eugène Etienne (quoted in Fieldhouse, 1973: 297). When the sultan appealed to the Germans for assistance, therefore, they readily agreed. On 31 March a somewhat reluctant Wilhelm II – who was about to embark upon a Mediterranean cruise – landed at Tangier with his entourage and rode through the streets in military uniform on a magnificent horse, with a band playing. When he reached the German legation he declared that he would support the continued independence of the Moroccan state. Germany, he announced, knew how to safeguard her interests.

But it was actually the absence of any significant German interest that gave this, the first Moroccan crisis, its peculiar character. The French had frequently approached the Germans over the previous decade with proposals for an arrangement concerning Morocco; Delcassé in particular believed that German assistance might be useful there in his diplomatic contest with Great Britain. The Germans always replied that they lacked sufficient interests in Morocco to become embroiled in a dispute. Now, with the display of pomp and ceremony at Tangier, the Germans appeared to be suddenly reversing their position.

The point of the first Moroccan crisis, however, was not Morocco, but the nature of the relationship between Germany and France. If the French were forced to give in to German demands in an area where France had a significant interest and great plans for the future while Germany had few, it would make it plain that Germany was so much more powerful in Europe that France could expand their empire overseas only with Germany's consent. It would mean nothing that the French navy was more powerful than the German, that the French army in Africa was more powerful than the German; in the future, all that would really matter would be the ability of Germany to defeat France on the ground in Europe. The Moroccan crisis was tremendously important because it seemed likely to determine whether or not France was still capable of pursuing an independent foreign policy. The 'grey eminence' of the German foreign office understood the stakes involved: if Germany abandoned the position stated earlier by the Kaiser, public opinion everywhere would regard it as a humiliation and as the first great practical success of the entente cordiale. France would not be drawn into Germany's orbit: for the foreseeable future 'she would stand steadfastly and firmly by England' (Rich vol. 4, 1963: 356–7).

It was this question of the future of France as a great power that drew Britain into the crisis. During the past decade, and especially since the kaiser's highly publicized telegram to Kruger in support of the Afrikaners at the outbreak of the Boer War [**Doc. 8, p. 96**], a group of young men had arisen within the British foreign office who were convinced that Germany posed a greater threat to the empire than did either Russia or France. This potential threat began to turn into something real with Germany's decision to construct an ocean-going navy. The 'Germanophobes' of the foreign office argued that it was only the existence of France and Russia that kept German ambitions in check. These men, led by **Francis Bertie**, **Arthur Nicolson**, **Charles Hardinge** and **Eyre Crowe**, had, by the time of the first Moroccan crisis, achieved positions of authority. They were now convinced that if the French were forced to back down it would mean that France had been transformed into a satellite of Germany. In order to prevent this they argued that Britain must find some way to steady French nerves. They did not suggest that the entente had imposed this necessity on Britain; rather, it was precisely because the entente was not an alliance that they had to find, in the midst of the Moroccan crisis, some new way of assuring the French of British support.

Such assurance was forthcoming in May 1905, when the British foreign secretary, Lord Lansdowne, told the French ambassador in London, **Paul Cambon**, that Britain was prepared to transform the entente into an alliance. Lansdowne's words were vague but encouraging, as he suggested that Britain and France should 'discuss in advance any contingencies by which they might in the course of events find themselves confronted'. In Paris, Delcassé argued that these words ought to be interpreted as the prelude to an alliance. But the French prime minister, **Rouvier**, believed that the Moroccan crisis might lead to war with Germany and that this would almost certainly end in another disastrous defeat for France. Hints of British assistance were not enough: even if it were forthcoming, how would it be made real? After all, the British navy 'does not run on wheels'.

When the Germans discovered what Delcassé was up to, they demanded that he be forced to resign. Rouvier agreed. The Germans thereby scored a great diplomatic victory: the architect of the Anglo-French entente had been forced out of office due to German pressure, and it appeared that France would no longer be capable of pursuing a foreign policy that did not meet with Germany's approval. But the German ambassador in London anticipated trouble: the British, though not wishing to fight Germany, would not abandon France [**Doc. 13, p. 100**]. The kaiser was nevertheless triumphant; he made Bülow a prince, and Rouvier consented to Germany's insistence that an international conference be convened to settle the Moroccan dispute.

In the summer of 1905 everything seemed to be going Germany's way. Her success in Morocco was followed by the defeat of Russia in the far east. After

Bertie, Francis *(1st Viscount Bertie of Thame, 1844–1919)*: British diplomat; assistant under-secretary of state for foreign affairs, 1894–1903; ambassador in Rome, 1903–05; ambassador in Paris, 1905–18.

Nicolson, Sir Arthur *(1849–1928)*: British diplomat and administrator; minister in Tangier, 1901–04; in Madrid, 1904–06; in St Petersburg, 1906–10; undersecretary of state for foreign affairs, 1910–16.

Hardinge, Charles *(1st Baron Hardinge of Penshurst, 1858–1944)*: British diplomat and administrator; ambassador in St Petersburg, 1904–06; under-secretary of state for foreign affairs, 1906–10; viceroy of India, 1910–16.

Crowe, Sir Eyre *(1864–1925)*: British administrator; assistant undersecretary of state for foreign affairs, 1912–20.

Cambon, Paul *(1843–1924)*: French diplomat; ambassador to Britain, 1898–1921.

Rouvier, Maurice *(1842–1911)*: French statesman; elected deputy, 1871; minister of foreign affairs, 1902–05; prime minister, 1905–06, 1906–11.

a long and slow voyage from Europe, the Russian Baltic fleet had finally arrived off the coast of Japan in May 1905, where it was almost immediately destroyed. The Battle of Tsushima on 27 May 1905 left Japan in absolute control of the sea. The Germans quickly renewed their efforts of the previous November to disengage Russia from her alliance with France. On 24 July the kaiser met the tsar at Björkö and persuaded him to sign a defensive alliance with Germany. The success of the new course and world policy seemed guaranteed: French ambitions had been checked in Morocco, Russian strength sapped in the far east; both would now be forced to submit to German-directed alliances; Britain would be left in isolation.

Within three months of the meeting at Björkö, however, it began to appear that Germany's success was less than complete. First, the tsar's closest advisors, the **Grand Duke Nicholas Nikolayevich**, Count Witte and Count Lambsdorff (the foreign minister), all joined in advising against an alliance with Germany, insisting that it would mean abandoning France, the end of the balance of power in Europe, and the encouragement of German expansion into the middle east. It was apparent to his advisors, if not to Nicholas II, that the 'defensive' arrangement proposed by the kaiser would reduce Russia to dependence on Germany. The proposed treaty of Bjökö was therefore rejected in November. Secondly, the British decided that they would have to go further than Lansdowne's vague indications of support if the French will to resist German demands was to be bolstered. Accordingly, secret discussions with the French general staff were initiated in December 1905 in order to consider joint operations in the event of war. The British had implicitly recognised the validity of Rouvier's point concerning the uselessness of the Royal Navy to France: they would have to hold out the prospect of military assistance on the continent if critics of co-operation with Britain were to be satisfied.

By the time the Morocco conference met at Algeciras in southern Spain on 16 January 1906, Germany's position had weakened considerably. Russia had chosen her alliance with France over the Björkö agreement; France had agreed to divide Morocco with Spain; and the new British foreign secretary, Sir Edward Grey, quickly showed that he was more suspicious of Germany – and therefore more inclined to support France – than his predecessor had been. The conference showed that Germany could not even count on her allies.

The Italians, in December 1900, had secretly pledged to recognise the special interests of France in Morocco in exchange for a similar recognition of their rights in Libya. Two days after the Triple Alliance had been renewed in June 1902, the Italian foreign minister, **Giulio Prinetti**, signed a secret agreement with the French ambassador, **Camille Barrère**, which gave an assurance of Italian neutrality in any conflict into which France had been provoked. The German ambassador in Rome complained that the 'pseudo-

Nicholas Nikolayevich, Grand-Duke *(1856–1929)*: Russian soldier and administrator, nephew of tsar Alexander II. Commander-in-chief, 1914–17.

Prinetti, Giulio *(1851–1908)*: Italian statesman; minister of foreign affairs, 1901–03.

Barrère, Camille *(1851–1940)*: French diplomat; ambassador to Italy, 1897–1924.

Great Power, Italy, is nothing but a deadweight which our policy has to drag along behind it' (Bosworth, 1983: 65). Prince Bülow recognised, shortly after the conference convened, that Germany could not hope for a successful outcome: the only power sympathetic to her was Austria-Hungary – and even she counselled moderation. The final act of the conference, signed on 7 April 1906, although it affirmed Morocco's independence and integrity, left the policing of the country to France and Spain and gave the control of the *Banque d'État* to France, thereby placing her in a position to control Morocco's economic development.

The debacle of the Algeciras Conference had immediate repercussions within Germany. Holstein, the grey eminence of the foreign office who had done much to engineer the new course in German policy, was forced to resign. General von Moltke ('the younger'), who had succeeded Schlieffen as chief of the general staff in January, proposed to alter his predecessor's plan for a war against France by providing for a pre-emptive strike through Belgium. German navalists had their own reasons for approving such a strike: eight years earlier one official had argued that 'the possession of Antwerp and the mouth of the Schelde would be enormously valuable for the German naval operations, whether in a war against England or against France or against both' (Lambi, 1984: 125). Admiral von Tirpitz, whose fleet-building scheme had been challenged in the autumn of 1905 by the British decision to begin constructing the huge new '**dreadnought**' class of battleship, was now able to get the approval of the **Reichstag** for an accelerated building programme of bigger ships in the Third Navy Law, which was ratified on 5 June 1906. A more general effect of the Moroccan crisis inside Germany was the widespread impression that she was being 'encircled', that the other European states resented her growing power and prosperity and would do everything they could to prevent her from assuming her rightful place as a world power. Germany, her leaders concluded, must rely less on diplomacy and more on her own military and naval strength.

There certainly seemed to be evidence to support the German belief that the ring around them was drawing tighter. Barely two weeks after the Algeciras Act was signed, the Russians agreed to a French proposal that the clauses in the Dual Alliance providing for military co-operation in a war against Great Britain should now be dropped. The French themselves had proposed these clauses in the aftermath of the Fashoda crisis of 1898; to drop them now indicated that they no longer regarded Britain as a possible enemy. Although there was still no Anglo-French alliance, these changes were significant because German policy since the accession of Wilhelm II had been predicated upon the assumption that Anglo-French and Anglo-Russian rivalry overseas would become increasingly bitter, and that this would work to Germany's advantage. Instead, the three powers showed signs that they

Dreadnought A new class of battleship launched in Britain in 1906, which were faster and more powerful (and much more expensive). Earlier battleships were rendered obsolete and the Anglo-German naval race was intensified.

Reichstag The German parliament that was established in Berlin by the constitution of 1871. It was based on universal manhood suffrage and it could block certain measures, but it could not initiate legislation. Ministers did not need to be appointed from it, nor were they responsible to it.

might draw closer together: on 17 April France provided a huge new loan of 2,250,000,000 francs to Russia to shore up her disintegrating finances in the wake of the war against Japan; in 1905 the British government decided to transfer ships from the Mediterranean – where they had been deployed to guard against France and Russia – to the North Sea. The only possible interpretation of this move was that Britain was preparing for a challenge from the new German fleet. The question that remained unanswered was whether or not Britain and Russia would also find a way to resolve their differences.

In the midst of the Moroccan crisis an Anglo-Russian reconciliation seemed most unlikely. On 12 August 1905 Britain and Japan had agreed upon a revision of their alliance that extended its terms considerably and in a way highly unfavourable to Russia. First, it was extended geographically to include India and adjacent territories: the Japanese now promised to assist Britain if Russia attacked in central Asia. Secondly, the alliance would now operate if Russia attacked on her own: the provision for a two-power attack was dropped, so Russia, even without French assistance, would face combined British and Japanese forces should she become embroiled in a war with either of them.

The Russian failure in the far east, however, might render the revised Anglo-Japanese alliance insignificant. If Russia now decided to pursue a policy of caution in her relations with Britain and Japan, the new terms might never come into operation; and caution was made more likely by the moderate conditions of the Treaty of Portsmouth, which ended the Russo-Japanese war on 5 September 1905. In essence, all the treaty provided for was a Russian recognition of Japanese predominance in Korea and the withdrawal of Russian forces from southern Manchuria and south Sakhalin. These were hardly oppressive terms: there was no indemnity, and the Japanese public was far more disappointed than the Russian with the conditions of peace. There was no popular cry for revenge in Russia, no stimulus to further adventure. The 'Koreans', those in Russian governing circles who had argued that Russia's future lay in the far east, had been discredited by the disasters of the Russo-Japanese war. And, as the men in these circles had been generally 'pro-German', arguing that good relations with Germany on the western frontier gave Russia the safety necessary to expand in the far east and central Asia, the pro-German line of policy also suffered a setback.

Duma: The Russian parliament established after the revolution of 1905. Although this represented a significant concession on the part of the Russian monarchy, it was a weak and unrepresentative institution, with strictly limited powers.

But perhaps the most important lessons of the war were its repercussions on the Russian political system. The war generated chaos and rebellion at home. The most famous incident occurred on 'Bloody Sunday' (22 January 1905), when the troops of the tsar opened fire on demonstrators, killing hundreds. Not only did this discontent provide further impetus for a policy of restraint in foreign policy, it led to the signing of the October Manifesto on 30 October 1905, in which the tsar promised new civil rights, a **Duma** (representative assembly) and a constitution. These promises were enacted in the 'Fundamental Laws' of 6 May 1905. Although the new system was still far from a parliamentary democracy, it did encourage the formation and circulation of public opinion; and most of this opinion, in the decade that followed, was unhappy with the idea of further imperialist adventures in Asia.

A new Russian foreign minister, **A.P. Izvolsky**, came into office in May 1906 eager to limit Russian commitments and to put relations with all the great powers on a more equable footing. Over the next seventeen months he managed to reach a political agreement with Japan (recognizing her authority in Korea and southern Manchuria in exchange for her recognition of Russian authority in northern Manchuria and outer Mongolia), an agreement with Germany to maintain the status quo in the Baltic, and an agreement with Britain on Persia and Afghanistan. Izvolsky was seeking neither an alliance with Britain nor the encirclement of Germany. Rather, his policy aimed to provide stability and calm in Russia's foreign relations while the new political system took root and time healed the damage done by the war with Japan.

> **Izvolsky, Alexander (1856–1919)**: Russian diplomat and statesman; entered Russian diplomatic service in 1875; foreign minister, 1905–10; ambassador to France, 1910–16.

The Anglo-Russian agreement, which was signed on 31 August 1907, was even less of an alliance than the Anglo-French entente had been. The two powers agreed that Tibet should act as a neutral buffer between their empires and that Russia should have no direct contact with Afghanistan. Thus, the British seemed to have achieved the security for their north-west frontier that they had long sought. Most difficult, and most important, was the agreement on Persia, which created a Russian sphere of influence in the more populous and richer north, and a British sphere in the south, bordering on Afghanistan and the Persian Gulf; a neutral sphere in the centre was to separate the two.

Like the Anglo-French entente, the Anglo-Russian version provided for no political action, no military planning and suggested no possible contingencies that might lead the two powers to consult on these matters in the future. It was simply a resolution – and by no means a complete one – of long-standing differences that had made for troubled relations in central Asia. Like the Anglo-French entente, however, even this cautious arrangement threatened to undermine the foundations of German strategy, which had assumed that Britain and Russia would remain enemies and that this would eventually take one or the other of them into the German camp as a subordinate ally.

THE VORTEX OF SOUTH-EASTERN EUROPE

With the Anglo-Japanese alliance and the end of the Russo-Japanese war in the far east, with the Anglo-French entente resolving differences in the Pacific, in North America, south-east Asia and Africa, and with the Anglo-Russian entente resolving differences in central Asia, it is not surprising that most diplomatic disputes in the following years were located in, or near, Europe itself. This is not to suggest that Great Britain had carefully crafted a series of arrangements with old rivals in order to enable her to prepare for the inevitable conflict with imperial Germany. While it is true that some British officials felt threatened by German pretensions to world power, it is also true that practically nothing was done to transform the colonial ententes into European alliances. Moreover, the Russians, while they believed that the continued existence of France as an independent great power was essential to the balance of power and thus vital to their own security, did not believe that Germany posed any immediate danger to them. The 'diplomatic revolution' that took place between 1904 and 1907 thus represented a shift in mood and a change in emphasis; it did not represent the forging of a coalition that made war inevitable, or even predictable.

Many of those who participated in the diplomatic process believed the balance of power to be the best guarantee of peace, and that the rival alliance systems – with Britain remaining free to throw its weight onto either side – had established a better balance than had existed at any time since 1815. It was certainly arguable that the alliances had provided stability within Europe, where there had not been a significant crisis since the Russo-Turkish war of 1878. As important as the alliance system was to the maintenance of stability, south-eastern Europe remained one area where everyone continued to anticipate trouble; since 1897 however, the agreement between Russia and Austria-Hungary to put the Balkans 'on ice' had kept things quiet. The co-operation between the two powers had been extended in 1903 when, with a crisis brewing in Macedonia, their representatives had met at Murzsteg and agreed upon a programme of reforms that would preserve peace in the Balkans.

Ironically, it was this Austro-Russian co-operation in the Balkans that laid the groundwork for the first European crisis in thirty years. First, a new

Aehrenthal, Count Alois von *(1854–1912)*: Austrian diplomat and statesman; ambassador in St Petersburg, 1899–1906; Austro-Hungarian minister of foreign affairs, 1906–12.

Austro-Hungarian foreign minister, **Count Aehrenthal**, came into office in 1906 determined to demonstrate that the differences between Vienna and Budapest did not mean that the Habsburg empire was finished as a great power. A recent political crisis had led some observers to argue that the empire was no longer capable of conducting a coherent foreign policy because of the differences between the Germans and the Magyars. Aehrenthal decided that some of the problems that plagued the Dual Monarchy, especially those arising from questions of nationality, could be alleviated by a vigorous foreign policy. The new chief of the general staff, **Count Conrad**,

Conrad von Hötzendorf, Count *(1852–1925)*: Austrian soldier; chief of Austro-Hungarian general staff, 1906–11, 1912–17.

supported Aehrenthal's view that the troublesome Serbs of southern Hungary could be silenced by reducing the independence and the pretensions of Serbia. The first step in this design would be to annex Bosnia and Herzegovina, the two autonomous provinces of the Ottoman empire, inhabited mainly by

Serbs that had been administered by Austria-Hungary since 1878. The annexation of the provinces would make it impossible for the Serbs to achieve their ambition of creating a large Serbian state that would incorporate all Serbs. The idea that nationalist agitation could be subdued by such a strategy was not particularly new; what was surprising was that the Russian foreign minister consented to it.

Izvolsky was anxious to maintain the spirit of co-operation with the Austrians, but he also saw the possibility of achieving a diplomatic triumph that would bolster Russia's flagging prestige without putting her in any danger. When he met Aehrenthal at Büchlau, in Moravia, on 16 September 1908, he quickly became convinced that the Austrians were determined to occupy Bosnia and Herzegovina regardless of what the Russians might do. He concluded that to oppose the annexation would be dangerous, and, after the recent misadventure in the far east, to embark on such a dangerous course would be foolhardy. He proposed, instead, that in exchange for his acquiescence, Austria-Hungary should support Russia's long-standing ambition of having the Straits of the Bosporus and the Dardanelles opened to the passage of warships in peacetime. In exchange, Austria might pursue the ambition of its navalists summed up in their slogan, 'Supremacy in the Adriatic' which would provide further insurance against Serbian expansionism.

If the bargain had worked, Austro-Russian co-operation in the Balkans might have been maintained. But the Russian government refused to support Izvolsky, partly because public opinion – which was now more important under the new constitutional process – would be enraged by the abandonment of Slav brothers to Germanic rule. Izvolsky himself insisted that the Austrians, when they announced the annexation of the two provinces, had violated a number of the promises they had given him at Büchlau. On the other hand, the Austrians, led by the bellicose Conrad, were prepared to fight for the provinces, while the Russians were not. The German government supported Austria's policy, whereas France and Britain proved unwilling to join Russia in opposing it. When, in February 1909, the Austrians threatened to invade Serbia unless Russia and Serbia formally recognised the annexation, the Russians felt that they had no choice but to comply. One leading Russian liberal criticized the weakness he saw in the government's foreign policy: the Black Sea and Balkans represented natural and legitimate objectives of Russian expansion. Russia's failure in the Bosnian crisis was a 'national disgrace' (Pipes, 1980: 182). Negotiations to resolve the Bosnian situation in a spirit of co-operation ended in bitterness, suspicion and a renewed sense of rivalry.

The annexation crisis proved to be a turning-point in a number of significant ways. First, it killed the Austro-Russian co-operation that had kept the Balkans relatively quiet for the previous thirty years; from this point on the Balkans were in an almost constant state of turmoil. Moltke, the chief of the German general staff, was convinced that the moment would come when Serbian provocations would force Austria to act: 'The Monarchy will have no other choice but to invade Serbia' (Geiss, 1976: 115). Secondly, it convinced Serbia that Austria-Hungary was aiming at her destruction as an independent state; from now on Serbian nationalists believed that they must rely on Russia for support and that, ultimately, only the break-up of the Dual Monarchy could save them. Thirdly, it convinced many Austrians that a bold policy in the Balkans could reduce the danger posed by Serbia; after 1909 they launched a dreadnought-building campaign, believing that naval strength in the Adriatic would enable them to form an alliance with Albania against Serbia. Finally, and most important, the Russians concluded that the unity between the Austrians and the Germans that had been demonstrated during the crisis posed a direct threat to them. Unlike their decision to proceed cautiously in the far east following the war with Japan, the Russians neither abandoned the Balkans nor came to an agreement with their antagonist. The Balkans and the Straits continued to be perceived as vital to Russia's security, to her reputation as a great power, and to her internal harmony. Accordingly, Russian ties with Serbia were tightened, mobilization plans were refurbished, and a new programme of battleship building in the Black Sea was launched.

Sazonov, Serge Dmitrievich *(1861–1927)*: Russian statesman; minister of foreign affairs, 1910–16.

The unfortunate Izvolsky was replaced in September 1910 by **S.D. Sazonov**. The new foreign minister apparently decided that, apart from strengthening the Russian presence in the Balkans, the best method of countering Austria-Hungary was to drive a wedge between her and Germany. His first visit was to Potsdam where he agreed to drop Russian objections to German enterprises in the Ottoman empire and Persia in exchange for a promise that Germany would not support any form of Austrian aggression in the Balkans.

The Germans regarded the Bosnian crisis as convincing proof that neither the alliance with France nor the entente with Britain would provide Russia with any meaningful assistance in the Balkans. Perhaps the ententes would prove equally useless to France in north Africa, where another crisis began to emerge in Morocco. When demonstrators rioted in Fez against the rule of the sultan in the spring of 1911, French colonialists were encouraged to believe that the opportunity to impose direct French rule had come at last. In the foreign ministry the colonial party was firmly in control of policy: a weak

Cruppi, Jean *(1855–1933)*: French statesman; minister of foreign affairs, 1911; minister of justice, 1911–12.

minister, **Jean Cruppi**, who was ignorant of foreign affairs and incapable of countering arguments for intervention, ordered troops to Morocco on 17 April. By 21 May a joint Franco-Moroccan force of 20,000 had occupied Fez.

The French move violated both the Algeciras Act of 1906, which had left the Germans with some privileges in Morocco, and a Franco-German agreement of 1909 that recognized France's special political interests in Morocco in exchange for a promise that Germany's economic interests would not be damaged. These legal niceties counted for little, but they did provide the Germans with a legitimate excuse for responding to the French move. On the other hand, the German foreign minister, **Alfred von Kiderlen-Wächter**, whose ultimatum to Russia in the Bosnian crisis had proven to be such a dramatic success, privately believed that Morocco was bound to fall to the French sooner or later. He decided to act not in order to protect German interests there but to demonstrate to the French that they were in no position to act unilaterally or to violate their agreements with Germany. The French would have to offer concessions before he would recognize their authority in Morocco; precisely what these were mattered little and Kiderlen had not defined them. On 1 July 1911 a German gunboat, the *Panther*, steamed into the Moroccan port of Agadir, and the second Moroccan crisis began.

Kiderlen-Wächter, Alfred von *(1852–1912)*: German administrator; foreign minister, 1910–13.

The British had not been pleased with the French decision to occupy Fez, which they interpreted as a triumph for the troublesome colonialists at the Quai d'Orsay. When the Germans sent their gunboat to Agadir however, the British quickly forgot their irritation with the French. The officials of the foreign office concluded that the Germans were not attempting to protect their interests in Morocco but were attempting to disrupt the entente by showing the French that they were too weak to resist German demands. This calculation seemed accurate: the Russian foreign minister warned the French president that their alliance was 'purely defensive' and could not be used to act aggressively against German claims in Morocco (Lieven, 1983: 38). The British feared that an isolated France would be thrown into the 'teuton embrace'. Sir Edward Grey behaved more cautiously than the officials who advised him. He was prepared to countenance French concessions to Germany in the Congo in return for French control of Morocco; but even he began to worry when it appeared that the Germans were demanding almost all of the French Congo in exchange. Nevertheless, the cabinet, fearing that a strong line might lead to war, instructed Grey to inform the French that they would not regard as a legitimate cause of war a French decision to resist German territorial gains that might result from a settlement of the Moroccan crisis.

British actions during the crisis demonstrated that they, like the Germans, were not really concerned with territorial issues or economic privileges in either Morocco or the Congo. What worried them was that German power in Europe could be used to control French behaviour overseas; if this proved to be the result of the crisis, then France would be reduced to subordinate status and the balance of power in Europe would have shifted clearly in Germany's favour. In other words, Britain had no immediate fear of German imperialism, but she did regard the balance of power as essential to her security and she was increasingly concerned that this was being endangered by Germany. This thinking was quite different from that which had led to the entente with France in 1904 and explains why, on 21 July 1911, the chancellor of the exchequer, **David Lloyd George**, gave a strong speech at the Mansion House warning that Britain was not to be ignored in such matters [**Doc. 18, p. 105**]. The Germans were offended by these strong words, and the British fleet was placed on alert.

Lloyd George, David
(1863–1945): British
statesman; elected to
the British parliament in
1890; entered the cabi-
net in 1905, chancellor
of the exchequer, 1908–
15; prime minister,
1916–22.

Nevertheless, the crisis was resolved in October and November when the French conceded to the Germans two strips of territory in the Congo (amounting to some 100,000 square miles) in exchange for a recognition of the French protectorate in Morocco. This outcome pleased no one. The French colonialists, who had initiated the crisis, felt they had been abandoned by the British and by their own politicians; but they were themselves soon discredited. A parliamentary inquiry into the handling of the crisis was instituted, which condemned the power of the officials at the Quai d'Orsay in its report. Within a few months the chairman of the inquiry, Raymond Poincaré, had become premier and foreign minister. He was resolved to avoid any more colonial adventures and to work more closely with Russia and Britain. Grey, and his less moderate officials, felt that French impetuosity had brought them to the brink of war; although he believed that France must be supported in the event of a conflict with Germany, he was determined to restrain French adventurism. In Germany, Kiderlen had succeeded neither in subordinating France nor in driving a wedge into the entente. Even the Congo concessions – which consisted of practically worthless territory – did not help him to save face. Moltke wanted to press home German's military advantage and attack France, but he failed to convince the politicians. The military began to refer to Wilhelm as 'the peace kaiser', and the chief of the military cabinet complained that Wilhelm was 'big in words and weak in deeds' (Hull, 1982: 259). The popular right-wing German press joined in the chorus of criticism: 'Have we become a generation of women?' asked the *Berlin Post* 'What is the matter with the *Hohenzollerns*?' (Cecil vol. 2, 1996: 165). Kiderlen's strategy had succeeded in the Balkans but failed in Morocco, and the general impression in Germany after 1911 was that the wicked British were pulling the strings of their French puppet, that they were seeking to encircle Germany and prevent her natural and rightful development into a world power.

The only ones truly satisfied by the outcome of the Agadir crisis were the Italians. In a secret agreement signed in December 1900, they had recognized the special interests of France in Morocco in return for recognition of their special interests in the Ottoman provinces of Tripolitania and Cyrenaica (Libya). When the French moved into Fez, the Italians began to consider a

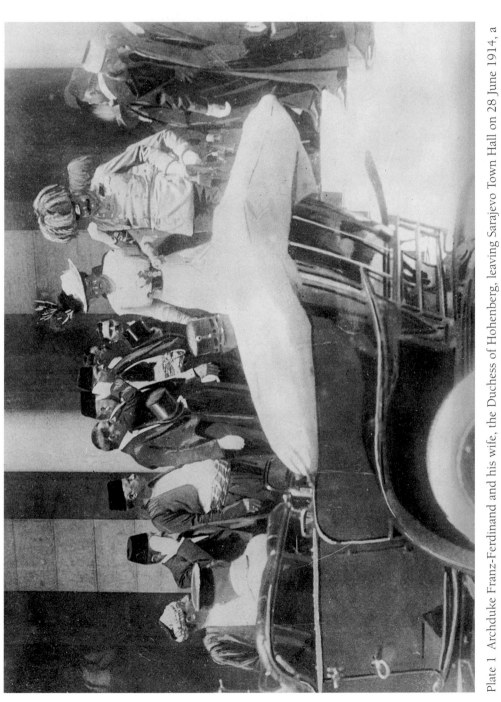

Plate 1 Archduke Franz-Ferdinand and his wife, the Duchess of Hohenberg, leaving Sarajevo Town Hall on 28 June 1914, a few moments before they were assassinated

Source: popperfoto.com

Plate 2 Russian troops in action during the Russo-Japanese War
Source: popperfoto.com

Plate 3 HMS Dreadnought
Source: popperfoto.com

Plate 4 Kaiser Wilhelm II instructing a group of generals during the last manoeuvers before the outbreak of the First World War
Source: popperfoto.com

similar move into Tripoli. Public support for such a move was widespread and enthusiastic; the government, in fact, was more cautious than the people. But the Italians had also prepared the diplomatic ground more carefully than the French: in March 1902 Britain had recognized Italy's special interests in Libya, and in October 1909 Russia had been persuaded to do the same; the Italians assumed that they could also count on the support of Germany and Austria-Hungary, their partners in the Triple Alliance. In September 1911 the Italian government decided to invade Libya, believing that the war would be short and simple; but, as so often proved to be the case, this forecast was unduly optimistic. The Libyan campaign lasted more than a year and formal recognition of the Italian annexation did not come until after the First World War.

Although no power opposed Italy's invasion of Libya neither did anyone give them their enthusiastic support, least of all her partners in the Triple Alliance. Conrad, the chief of the Austrian general staff, went so far as to propose to take advantage of Italy's commitment in Africa by attacking her in the north: 'Austria's opportunity has come and it would be suicidal not to use it' (Rothenberg, 1976: 163). But this daring plan was rejected by the politicians. Once again, none of the European powers were really concerned with Libya itself; what concerned them were the repercussions that the Italian invasion might have throughout the rest of the Ottoman empire. There was a growing belief in all the European capitals that the empire was in danger of dissolution, which would raise a series of extremely complicated questions, as the near east was the one area where all six great powers had interests and ambitions.

The British in particular worried that this succession of crises in the Mediterranean would lead to war, if current trends continued. One of the factors that seemed to be pointing to war by 1911 was the Anglo-German naval race. It would be quite wrong to assume, however, that the British immediately interpreted the German decision to build a navy as a threat to the empire. In spite of the German naval bills of 1898 and 1900, the British government continued to calculate its naval requirements on the basis of the two-power standard of France and Russia. Only when the Russian fleet was destroyed by the Japanese did the British admiralty propose to substitute Germany for Russia in their calculations. Even then the change did not signify a political decision to view Germany as the emerging enemy. Rather, the change simply continued the long-standing policy of the admiralty to prepare to fight simultaneously Britain's two strongest rivals in case they should combine with one another. At the time of the first Moroccan crisis no one believed that Germany, on her own, would be able to match the British navy, and no one believed in the possibility of a Franco-German alliance. The decisive change came when the British concluded that Germany was aiming to establish her hegemony in Europe – the first stage of which would be the domination of France. Only then did Germany begin to be seen as Britain's principal rival, and this for continental political reasons, not imperial and naval ones.

In 1905, British planners began to construct contingency plans for war against Germany – long before the German fleet was seen as a serious threat to British security. The plans were designed to provide France with assistance in the event of a German attack, which explains why the **Committee of Imperial Defence** decided, during the Moroccan crisis, that an expeditionary force should be created that would be capable of fighting on the continent itself. British strategists over the next few years came to regard the force as an essential diplomatic device. The Director of Military Operations (Colonel Spencer Ewart) concluded in 1908 that if it were cut back 'then "goodbye" to the *Entente Cordiale*'. The alternative for Britain was an isolation which would produce 'a combination of all Europe against us under the dictatorship of Germany' (Michael Howard, 1972: 36). From 1905 on, additional changes in strategy were instituted in order to meet the German threat: more of the fleet was concentrated in home waters and new battleship building paralleled that of Germany. By 1911 everyone spoke of the Anglo-German naval 'race' and some believed that it was the real cause of the antagonism between the two countries that brought them close to war during the Agadir crisis.

When the minister of war, **Viscount Haldane**, was sent on a special mission to Germany in February 1912, therefore, some members of the government hoped that an end to the naval race could be negotiated and that this would diminish the growing sense of an impending conflict. But the mission failed. On the eve of his arrival, new and more ambitious navy and army bills were announced in the Reichstag; and, in the negotiations that followed, the Germans insisted that the first step in any naval agreement must be a British promise of neutrality in the event of war. The German moves merely served to convince Sir Edward Grey that his fears were justified, that Germany was indeed aiming to neutralise Britain in order to dominate France. He concluded that only strong British support would enable France to remain independent, but he also steadfastly refused to turn this support into an alliance. Grey feared that, if Britain went too far in her assurances, it would encourage French adventurism.

His fear was probably no longer justified after Poincaré, who aimed to subdue the adventurers in the Quai d'Orsay, became premier of France in January 1912. Poincaré believed that the colonialists had taken France to the brink of disaster in the Agadir crisis; he preferred a policy of caution and stability, and the best guarantee of stability, he believed, was to be found in the balance of power that had been established with the alliance system. France,

Committee of Imperial Defence: Established by the British government at the end of the South African war in an effort to improve strategic planning and overcome the traditional rivalry between the army and the navy. It proved largely ineffective in accomplishing its goals.

Haldane, Viscount Richard Burdon *(1856–1928):* Elected to British parliament, 1885; secretary of war, 1905–12; lord chancellor, 1912–15 and 1924.

he said, should be a firm and loyal ally of Russia, draw as close as possible to Britain and avoid the temptation of working to disrupt the Triple Alliance, either by an agreement with Italy or with Germany.

This policy, which was apparently safer and more straightforward, was potentially more dangerous than that of Poincaré's predecessors. No longer would France fail to support Russia in the Balkans. In September 1912, he assured the Russians that, if a crisis in the Balkans led to war with the Central Powers, they could count on the French fulfilling their obligations to assist them. In giving this commitment to the Russians, Poincaré was relying largely upon Izvolsky's personal reputation for caution and moderation.

But there were other, less cautious, forces at work within Russia and in the Balkans. The Italian war with Turkey had encouraged the Balkan states in general, and Serbia and Bulgaria in particular, to anticipate the final dissolution of the Ottoman empire in Europe. This would at last make it possible for them to incorporate into their states the Serbs and Bulgars who remained in the Turkish province of Macedonia. Although Serbia and Bulgaria had long been bitter rivals, two Russian ambassadors, Hartwig in Serbia and Neklyudov in Bulgaria, succeeded in encouraging them to overcome their differences and to come together in the spirit of Slavic brotherhood. A Serbo-Bulgarian alliance was signed in March 1912. Within a few months a complicated network of alliances and alignments had been constructed linking Greece and Montenegro with Serbia and Bulgaria in a 'Balkan League'. In spite of the efforts of both Russia and Austria-Hungary to restrain them, the Montenegrins declared war on Turkey on 8 October 1912 and the other Balkan states quickly followed them. The Turks were defeated rather easily in the Balkans, although the Bulgarian attack on Constantinople became bogged down in the mud.

The defeat of the Turks suited neither the Austrians nor the Russians. An expanded Serbia, with a coastline on the Adriatic, would prove an even more troublesome neighbour for Austria-Hungary, encouraging the growth of Serb nationalism within the Dual Monarchy. A big Bulgarian state in possession of Constantinople would be in a position to inflict serious damage on Russia, especially if the Bulgarians continued to co-operate with the Austrians. The two great powers informed the Balkan states, therefore, that no change in the status quo would be permitted without their consent, and a conference of ambassadors met in London in December 1912 to sort things out.

The general principle adopted at the London conference was that the Turks should lose their remaining possessions in Europe, except for a rump of land around the Dardanelles and Bosporus Straits stretching from Enos to Midia. This satisfied Russia because it kept the Bulgarians away from this strategically sensitive area. The conference also agreed that an independent state should be created in Albania. This satisfied Austria-Hungary because it limited Serbian gains to a restricted area in the interior. Both great powers had feared that the war would upset the balance in the Balkans and that their potential enemies would be placed in a better position to threaten them than they had been previously. But diplomacy, in this instance, had triumphed. Russia and Austria-Hungary had proved reluctant to champion the cause of their satellites, Serbia and Bulgaria; the continuing rivalry among the Balkan states themselves enabled the great powers to impose a settlement upon them. The 'preliminaries of peace' were signed in London on 30 May 1913.

War broke out again in less than a month. The Bulgarians felt that they had been cheated of a proper victory in the First Balkan War because the Serbs and Greeks had occupied, and retained, territories that ought to have gone to them. At the end of June, therefore, Bulgaria attacked Serbia, and the Second Balkan War was underway. The Greeks immediately joined in against the Bulgarians; so too did the Rumanians and the Turks. Faced with this coalition, Bulgaria was easily defeated and, by the end of July, she was ready to come to terms. The Treaty of Bucharest, signed on 10 August 1913, expanded the territories of Serbia, Greece and Romania; a further Treaty of Constantinople, signed on 30 September 1913, permitted Turkey to recover some of the territory she had earlier lost to Bulgaria.

The Balkan wars left a dangerous legacy in the Balkans. The victors, now bigger and more powerful, remained dissatisfied nevertheless: Serbia, which had doubled in size, was still landlocked and made plain its sympathy with the Serbs of Austria-Hungary whom it regarded as oppressed brethren; Greece, which had expanded to take in almost all territories where Greek was the language of the majority, looked beyond her frontiers to a 'greater Greece' that included Constantinople and substantial portions of Asia Minor. Austria-Hungary and Turkey had good reason to believe that new dangers lay ahead. And Bulgaria, not surprisingly, was embittered by the disasters of the previous year – she had lost 25,000 men and been brought to the verge of revolution; she would eagerly grasp any opportunity that offered her an opportunity to reverse the outcome of 1913.

In spite of the success of Serbia and the failure of Bulgaria, Russia too was dissatisfied with the experience of the Balkan wars. First, at decisive moments of crisis, the Austrians had managed to impose their views by threatening war against Serbia and Montenegro. Secondly, the Germans showed increasing signs of committing themselves to an ambitious policy in the middle east both by supporting Austria-Hungary in the Balkans and by turning Turkey into a satellite. One of the most consistent elements in the policy of Wilhelm II had been the encouragement of German interests in the middle east, and by 1914 Germany was the most important foreign component in the Turkish economy. Even more worrying in Russian eyes was the appointment of a German general, **Liman von Sanders**, to command the

Liman von Sanders, Otto *(1855–1929)*: German soldier; led German military commission to Constantinople in 1913; appointed inspector-general of Turkish army, 1914.

Turkish garrison at Constantinople. If this permitted Germany to control the Straits in a moment of crisis it could place Russia in a very difficult position, as more than one-third of her trade moved between the Black Sea and the Mediterranean. By 1914 it had become an axiom of Russia's policy that, although there was no compelling need for her to seize Constantinople for herself, she would fight rather than allow a foreign power to do so [**Doc. 17, p. 105**].

Russia's fears of German ambitions in the middle east were not unjustified. In the autumn of 1913 Wilhelm II had assured both the chief of the general staff and the foreign minister of Austria-Hungary that the time for decisive military action in the Balkans was drawing near and that Germany could be relied upon for support. In February 1914 Russian military intelligence intercepted two German memoranda that expressed determination to capture Constantinople should the Ottoman empire collapse, and that suggested ways to prepare German public opinion for the coming war with Russia and France. These revelations convinced the Russians that a combined Austro-German effort would soon be made to establish predominance in the Balkans and at the Straits. They replied to this threat by consolidating their relationship with France and Britain and by relying upon Serbia – with her army of 200,000 men and 200,000 reservists – to act as the bastion against further Austrian expansion.

Ironically, considering these Russian fears, the Austrians and the Germans had reason to believe that their situation was deteriorating. The success of the Schlieffen plan, and Moltke's revision of it in 1911, depended upon the ability of Austro-German forces to keep Russia at bay in the east while the Germans knocked out the French in the west; the German strategists believed that this was the only method by which they could hope to win a two-front war. The role that had been assigned to Austria-Hungary was an offensive one: she was to launch an attack through Galicia, which would force a significant part of the Russian army to stand on the defensive. But this scheme had been designed before the Balkan wars and before the growing size and power of Serbia placed in doubt some of the strategic assumptions on which it was based. The latest estimates were that Austria-Hungary would have to commit half of her forces to the south if a crisis began there. At the same time as the threat of Serbia was growing in the south, Russian military strength appeared to be expanding rapidly. A 'Great Military Programme' had been adopted in November 1913 that provided for a 40 per cent increase in the size of the standing army over the next four years. The expansion in the number of troops available to Russia was to be supplemented by continuing with the rapid expansion of the railway network, an expansion that was made possible by a combination of French loans and by the industrial revolution that was going on in the Ukraine.

Wilhelm II's apparently wild encouragement to the Austrians to settle the Serbian question once and for all was, therefore, not as irrational as it might appear. If the danger in the south were removed, Austria-Hungary could again concentrate her forces against Russia, and the foundations of the Schlieffen plan would be restored. Thus, on 28 June 1914, when a Serb nationalist in Sarajevo assassinated the Austrian successor to the throne during his visit to Bosnia, a situation seemed to have presented itself that was tailor-made to suit German requirements: Austria-Hungary could 'settle' the Serbs, who were unlikely to receive much support, given the facts of the assassination. Neither France nor Britain had ever demonstrated an inclination to support Russia's Balkan policy in the past [**Doc. 24, p. 112**].

When, on 4 July, the emperor Franz Joseph wrote to Wilhelm II that he proposed to 'eliminate Serbia as a power factor in the Balkans' he received a sympathetic response. After consulting his chancellor, **Bethmann Hollweg**, the kaiser urged Austria-Hungary to make war on Serbia, issuing what has long been referred to as the 'blank cheque' in assuring the Austrians of support – even if this meant going to war with Russia [**Doc. 23, p. 112**]. Wilhelm was eager to prove his mettle following the criticisms of weakness and vacillation during the Moroccan crises: on 6 July he repeated three times that 'this time I shall not chicken out' (Hull, 1982: 238). But the kaiser did not believe that Russia would intervene, for this would require the tsar to come out in support of assassins, which seemed a most unlikely position for any monarch to take. The situation had all the makings of a great diplomatic and political triumph; he therefore saw no need to alter his summer vacation plans and proceeded to leave on a cruise. No preparations for war were made. Bethmann Hollweg foresaw the disintegration of the Triple Entente. The Germans believed that they had a great diplomatic victory in their grasp.

Speed was essential to such a victory. Austria-Hungary would have to act quickly and decisively to present Serbia with a *fait accompli* while the memory of the assassination was still vivid. But the Austrians did not move quickly, as the politicians proved to be badly divided on the next step to be taken: the foreign minister, Berchtold, proposed to launch a surprise attack, while the Hungarian prime minister, **Count Tisza**, insisted that some diplomatic preparation was necessary if Austria-Hungary were not to be branded the aggressor. All agreed with the governor of Bosnia that the assassination would have been 'wholly impossible' unless 'known and tolerated' by the Serbian government itself (Fay, 1966 II: 239). Tisza proposed to issue a list of stiff, but not impossible, demands, which, if accepted, would give Austria-Hungary almost everything she needed without resorting to war. The rest of the ministers agreed on 7 July to the idea of presenting Serbia with a series of demands; they also agreed that there should be no mobilization until these demands had been rejected and an ultimatum issued. On the other hand,

Bethmann Hollweg, Theobald von *(1856–1921)*: Prussian minister of the interior, 1905–07; German minister of the interior, 1907–09; German chancellor, 1909–17.

Tisza, Count István *(1861–1918)*: Hungarian statesman; prime minister of Hungary, 1904–05, 1913–17; murdered in 1918.

they also agreed that the demands should be so extreme as to make it practically impossible for the Serbs to agree to them. The Austrian strategy slowed down the process so much that it practically negated the original German plan. The note containing the demands and the ultimatum was not presented until 23 July – almost three weeks after the blank cheque had been issued [**Doc. 27, p. 115**].

When the Russian foreign minister, Sazonov, received a copy of the demands on the following day he immediately concluded that the Austrians knew they would be unacceptable and that they must therefore have been designed as a prelude to war with Serbia. He also believed that the Austrians would not have gone this far had they not been certain of German support. At a council of ministers on 24 July Sazonov maintained that, if Serbia were abandoned to Austria-Hungary, Russia's position in the Balkans would 'collapse utterly'. Furthermore, as the crisis was being used by the Germans to increase their power in central Europe and in the middle east, Russia would, if she failed to take a strong stand, come to be seen as a decadent state and slip into the ranks of the second-rate powers. The defence ministers, although they could not guarantee a military victory over Germany and Austria-Hungary, argued that there was no military reason why Russia should not display firmness in diplomatic negotiations. That evening Serbia was given an assurance of Russia's continuing support.

It is questionable whether Russia would have responded so decisively had she not been confident of French support. Poincaré, however, had insisted upon the closest possible connection with Russia as the most vital ingredient of his foreign policy. He had decided, in contrast with the Bosnian crisis of 1908, that France could not jeopardise that alliance with Russia by once again failing to support her in the Balkans; if Russia were forced to yield in the Balkans it would encourage the pro-German group at St Petersburg to insist on reconciliation with Germany. If Russia were reconciled to Germany, if the French alliance with Russia were dissolved, the balance of power in Europe would be destroyed and France would no longer be capable of acting as an independent great power.

Because the Russians hoped to avoid a confrontation with Germany they attempted to limit the escalation of the crisis to a contest between themselves and the Austrians. When, on 24–25 July, they undertook military measures preliminary to a mobilization, therefore, they attempted to localize the crisis by preparing to mobilize only in the military districts of Odessa, Kiev, Kazan and Moscow. In this way they hoped to demonstrate their determination to intervene if Austria-Hungary attacked Serbia, but at the same time to avoid the appearance of a challenge to Germany.

Any lingering doubts there may have been in Russia concerning Austria's intentions disappeared when the Austrians rejected the Serbian reply to their demands. The Serbs had gone much further in their attempt to accommodate Austria-Hungary than the Russians, the French and the British had believed possible [**Doc. 29, p. 118**]. On 28 July Austria-Hungary declared war on Serbia; the next day Belgrade was shelled. On 30 July the Russian government, convinced by the military authorities that a partial mobilization was impossible, ordered a general mobilization [**Doc. 32, p. 123**]. Still, Tsar Nicholas desperately hoped to convince the Kaiser that this need not lead to war: 'I hope from all my heart that these measures won't interfere with your part as mediator' (Kennedy, 1979: 263).

The Kaiser did believe that the Austrians had triumphed and that the Serbs had conceded all the vital points [**Doc. 31, p. 121**]. The German military authorities had by this time come round to the view that, as war seemed likely, and as Austria-Hungary could not be abandoned if she were to fight Russia, this was likely to be the best opportunity they would have for a contest with the entente. The French, they argued, were not prepared for a fight, while the Russians would only continue to grow stronger with each passing year. Moltke was convinced that, even if the British did enter the war (and it was far from certain that they would), the French could still be beaten quickly and decisively; the 150,000 men of the British expeditionary force would make no difference. The Russian mobilization played directly into the hands of the militarists: they were now able to argue that if Germany failed to respond to it immediately her long-standing strategic plans would be negated. Moreover, because Russia had taken the initiative, the German people as a whole would support the war effort. On the morning of 31 July, therefore, Germany mobilized and insisted that Russia cease all military measures aimed at Germany and Austria-Hungary within twelve hours. No reply came. Germany declared war on Russia at 6 p.m. on 1 August. Three days later Bethmann Hollweg assured the Reichstag that 'The feeling that animated everyone from the Kaiser down to the youngest soldier was this: Only in defence of a just cause shall our sword fly from its scabbard. The day has now come when we must draw it against our wish and in spite of our sincere endeavours. Russia has set fire to the building' (Albertini vol. 3, 1952: 219).

The most fateful step had been taken. Once Germany declared war on Russia, France had little choice but to join in. Not to have done so would have signalled that she was finished as a great power. This was made abundantly clear on 1 August when the Germans asked what the French attitude would be in the event of a Russo-German war – while telling the French that, should they choose to remain neutral, they would have to surrender the fortresses on their eastern frontier. The Germans were determined to be the winners, and to be seen to win, whether or not they met the French on the field of battle. The French replied to these demands by announcing their mobilization. Two days later Germany declared war on France; on 4 August she invaded Belgium.

An awful sense of predetermination surrounds the events of the first days of August: each step along the road to war from the Austrian ultimatum onwards appears, in hindsight, to have been logical and irreversible. But this could not be foreseen prior to the events. Italy, for example, was not drawn into the abyss as a result of her prior commitments. On 3 August she declared her neutrality [**Doc. 28, p. 117**]. Her partners in the Triple Alliance had practically ignored her during the crisis, mainly because they distrusted her, but also because they had a low opinion of her abilities as a great power. They offered her nothing in exchange for honouring her commitments. Thus, if Italy had chosen to side with Germany and Austria-Hungary in spite of these snubs, she would have confirmed her role as a weak and subordinate member of the alliance, and could expect to be treated as such in the future. The Italians, calmly and rationally, chose to remain on the sidelines and wait upon events. 'The ideal for us,' remarked the Italian Foreign Minister, 'is that Austria should be beaten on the one hand and France on the other' (Bosworth, 1979: 10).

Although the British reached a different conclusion, they too refused to be drawn into the war as if their participation had been predetermined. As the crisis unfolded, Grey made it clear to Russia and France that Britain was entirely free from commitments. In spite of repeated efforts to include Britain in a demonstration of entente solidarity, Grey feared that such a demonstration would alarm the Germans and deepen the crisis; he counselled moderation and direct negotiations between Russia and Austria-Hungary and was encouraged when the Serbs responded to the Austrian ultimatum [**Doc. 30, p. 120**]. Even when the Austrians presented their ultimatum – the seriousness of which Grey fully recognized – and then spurned the Serbian reply, Grey refused to take any dramatic steps. His advisors at the foreign office were distressed: from the time of the ultimatum onward they were convinced that the crisis was being used by Germany to achieve her ambition of political domination in Europe. On the other hand, the foreign secretary kept those members of the cabinet who were known to be opposed to any British armed intervention in the dark concerning the details of the crisis and the expectations of support in France and Russia.

Grey was determined to avoid a conflict if at all possible, but he also believed that Britain would have to assist France if she went to war with Germany. In the last days of July he began to prepare the cabinet for the worst. Germany, he warned, did not seem interested in mediation and appeared to be doing nothing to restrain Austria-Hungary. On 29 July the majority of the cabinet refused to agree to his proposal that they should promise to support France; they even refused to promise to uphold the neutrality of Belgium that had been guaranteed by treaty in 1839; if Belgian neutrality were violated, they decided, the British decision would be 'one of policy rather than legal obligation'. On 1 August Grey was forced to tell the French ambassador that a British expeditionary force might not be sent to France, even if Britain were to enter the war. On the next day, following a plea from the French government, the cabinet did agree to warn the Germans that Britain would not tolerate any naval action by them in the English Channel or on the French coast; but the Germans readily assented to this provision.

The British decision to present this ultimatum to the Germans was significant nevertheless, because a large majority of the cabinet had finally agreed that they had to support the entente. The only question that remained after 2 August was what form this support ought to take. One minister, **John Burns**, resigned; the others who had earlier opposed intervention now realized that if they forced the issue, the government would fall, probably to be replaced by a coalition that would intervene anyway.

The violation of Belgian neutrality by Germany on 4 August provided a convenient justification for those in the British cabinet who had already reluctantly decided that intervention was inevitable. They could now claim to have supported war for reasons of morality and law. Britain's entry into the war had little to do with Belgium. If Germany had not violated Belgian neutrality there might have been a few more resignations, but nothing more. Britain would have intervened in any case, believing that this was essential to preserve the balance of power and prevent the German domination of Europe [**Doc. 26, p. 114**]. On 6 August it was agreed to send the expeditionary force to France. Within a week the five great powers were at war.

Burns, John *(1858–1943)*: British statesman; elected to House of Commons in 1892; president of local government board, 1905–14; president of the board of trade, 1914; resigned during July crisis.

4

Assessment

The most persistent assumption underlying the decisions of July 1914 was the illusion that the war would be short. The thinking behind this was relatively simple: modern methods of transportation and communication created unprecedented opportunities for speed and mobility in attack. This lesson had been learned in the Franco-Prussian war of 1870. The Prussian use of railways had been decisive; the French, after all, had had as many men under arms and were, in every measurable military category, as powerful as the Germans. The difference, it was believed, was to be found in the Prussian ability to harness the new possibilities for warfare to be found in industrial society. The lessons that might have been learned by the Russo-Japanese war and by the Balkan wars had been discounted accordingly: they had not been fought by peoples or in regions to which the new technology applied. The 'only true defence is offence,' insisted one British strategist (Colonel Ewart); the belief in home defence was 'the most poisonous strategic fallacy ever propounded by man' (Gooch, 1974: 289). The war plans of the great powers before 1914 hinged on railway timetables and the rapid deployment of men in the field.

The belief in speed was crucial. The most famous stratagem, the Schlieffen plan, called for a lightning attack on France's western flank – but this was not exceptional; in France, **Joffre** proposed a quick strike through Alsace in his **Plan 17**; in Russia, **Plan B** called for Russia to seize the offensive and attack through Poland; in Austria-Hungary, the alliance with Germany provided for an attack on Russia to be launched from Galicia; in Great Britain, the planning for the British Expeditionary Force assumed that it must land in France within days of a war being declared in order for it to be effective. These plans showed the extent to which strategists committed themselves to the view that standing on the defensive would lead to ruin. In spite of advancing firepower, few strategists believed that it meant changing their assumptions. One French general (Bazaine-Hayter) insisted that a defensive battle 'will seldom bring victory'; no matter how powerful weapons became victory would

Joffre, Joseph Jacques Césaire *(1852–1931)*: French soldier and administrator; vice-president of the higher war council, 1911–14; commander-in-chief, 1914–16.

Plan 17: The French war plan of 1911 inspired by General Joffre's belief that the 'spirit of the offensive' was a key to victory. Rather than standing on the defensive and resisting a German attack, the French army was to seize the initiative and attack Germany.

Plan B: The Russian strategic plan for responding to a war with Germany. Based on the Franco-Russian alliance, the Russians were to go onto the offensive in the east, attacking through Poland in order to relieve pressure on the French.

go to the offensive 'which stimulates moral force, disconcerts the enemy and deprives him of his freedom of action' (Porch, 1981: 226). The Germans believed that they had to defeat France quickly to enable them to concentrate their full attention on Russia, and that an Austrian offensive against Russia would be vital in allowing them time to defeat France; the Russians believed that only an overwhelming attack in the east could prevent the Germans from overrunning France in the west.

Although most of these strategic calculations turned out to be mistaken, they were essential to the decisions made at the end of July and the beginning of August. Once the first steps towards mobilization were taken, everyone assumed that it would be fatal to stand still while their potential enemies moved forward. The most important steps were the Russian mobilization and the German response to it. When the Russians attempted to mobilize against Austria-Hungary alone, they discovered that this was practically impossible as they had made no plans for such a contingency and lacked the logistical support to carry it out; moreover, beginning with a partial mobilization would make a general one extremely difficult should it prove impossible to localize the war in the Balkans. If the Germans had permitted the Russian mobilization to be carried through without responding in kind, it would have jeopardized what was regarded as their only feasible plan for fighting a major war. By 28–30 July the generals had taken over from the politicians and the nature of their plans made a general war among the great powers a virtual certainty.

It is also true that Germany had really decided to force a war before Russia mobilised. Although the war plans are important in understanding why the crisis unfolded in the way that it did, they provide only a partial answer to the question, 'why did the war begin?' Ultimately, the German decision to force a war with Russia was not determined so much by railway timetables as by their belief that they could not permit Austria-Hungary to be defeated and that, if a war for the future of the Balkans and the middle east had to be fought some time, the best time was now. It is tempting, given this Austro-German connection on the one hand, and the Franco-Russian on the other, to regard the alliance 'system' as the real cause of the war.

The system, however, worked far from systematically in July 1914. First, Italy refused to come to the assistance of her allies. Germany and Austria-Hungary alike distrusted her and kept her in the dark when critical decisions were being made. The Triple Alliance turned out not to be a Triplice after all. Nor did the 'Triple Entente' operate as an alliance. No one, not the Russians, not the French, not the Central Powers, knew what Britain's response to the crisis would be. The Russian decision to mobilize was taken in spite of the absence of any guarantee of support from the British; the German decision to force a war with Russia was taken when the attitude of the British was still uncertain. The British case shows that not all of the great powers were committed to act; the Italian case shows that even when commitments had been made they could be ignored if it seemed to be in someone's interest to ignore them. It was not the alliance 'system' that drew the great powers into war in 1914, but the belief that it was more dangerous to stay out of a war than enter into one.

Each of the great powers decided in 1914 that they had vital interests at stake – interests for which it was worth risking defeat, dismemberment, impoverishment and social revolution. Had they anticipated the extent of the carnage, the duration of the war, the political and social chaos that it caused, they might have made different decisions. But even this is doubtful. By and large the men who made the decisions, drawn mainly from the traditional ruling classes of Europe, believed it better to die honourably than to survive in disgrace – and this applied to their states as well as to themselves [Doc. 25, p. 113]. This was especially true of the eastern powers, Austria-Hungary, Russia and Germany, who felt they were already teetering on the brink of a disaster, and that war (which they hoped and assumed would be successful) was the only alternative to a humiliating diplomatic defeat.

A more difficult question is why, when the great powers had survived a succession of crises over the previous decade, this one led to a general war. What distinguished the July crisis from the first and second Moroccan crises, or from the first and second Balkan Wars? The war plans and the system of alliances had not differed in any fundamental way; the real difference was the fact that in these earlier crises one or more of the leading participants took the view that the interests at stake did not justify the risk of war. Nor would it have been easy to persuade people to take up arms on behalf of some of the issues involved in these crises: few Germans were convinced that the economic stake in Morocco was worth a war with France; few Russians could have been persuaded that the change from an Austrian occupation of Bosnia and Herzegovina to a protectorate was worth fighting to stop. The crisis of July 1914 was exceptional in that the issues at stake made it possible for each of the great powers to mobilize public support – without which war would have been impossible.

The first fateful step along the road to war was taken by Austria-Hungary when her government decided that the assassination at Sarajevo at last gave her the opportunity she had been looking for to 'solve' the problem of Slav nationalism – a problem that was seen to threaten her continued existence. As Conrad wrote to Archduke Ferdinand in 1912: 'there must be a trial of strength between the monarchy and Serbia' (Rothenberg, 1976: 168). Such an opportunity was not likely to come again. Although the actual extent of complicity on the part of Serbian officials was not known at the time, all of the great powers expected Austria-Hungary to take some action against Serbia, and they accepted this as justified; each of the 'entente' powers urged

Serbia to be as accommodating as possible when she replied to the Austrian ultimatum – and they would have accepted the considerable limitations on her independence that her reply involved. Moreover, the assassination provided more than a pretext: it offered a possibility of mobilizing public sentiment throughout the Dual Monarchy in favour of vigorous action; any future attempt to 'solve' the South Slav problem was unlikely to occur in such favourable circumstances. Finally, Germany's strong encouragement to act decisively and crush the Serbian threat once and for all was decisive: her support had been essential in the Bosnian crisis of 1909, and without it Austria-Hungary would not have dared to risk war with Russia. Thus, it may be legitimately argued that a substantial underlying cause of the war was nationalism in general, and in particular the demand for unified, independent states in the Balkans and the threat this posed to the socio-political structure of Austria-Hungary.

But there would not have been a war in 1914 if Russia had declined to support Serbia. Her fateful decision to mobilize on Serbia's behalf (even if only partially at first) was made at several different levels. First, the strategic calculation was that Russia could not permit the transformation of Serbia into a satellite of Austria-Hungary because this would lead to an Austrian domination of the Balkans which, when combined with Germany's expanding role in Turkey, might allow the Central Powers to dominate most of the middle east. If Austria-Hungary and Germany dominated the Balkans and the Straits it would make the defence of Russia extremely difficult and endanger vital Russian trade. Secondly, support for the Slavic peoples of south-eastern Europe was the one programme that tied together almost all sections of influential Russian society. Whereas the war against Japan had been popular with only a few, and whereas a war against Britain in central Asia would have stirred up little emotional support, almost all sectors of the Russian political community believed that Russia was destined to perform a great cultural and religious task in south-eastern Europe. In fact, the Russian government would have been severely shaken by opposition had it failed to respond forcefully to Austria-Hungary's ultimatum. Thirdly, in contrast with 1909, the French had assured the Russians that they would support them in the Balkans, and it was highly unlikely that, if the Russians now backed down and allowed the Central Powers to prevail, such support would again be available in the future. Thus, it may be argued that the Russian version of Slav nationalism was an underlying cause of the war because, had the government abandoned what was widely perceived to be its historical mission, the cultural foundations of the tsarist state might have been shaken too badly for it to survive.

The July crisis was, in essence, an Austro-Russian one, but the transformation of that crisis into a world war was the responsibility of Germany.

The German government decided immediately following the assassination that the perfect opportunity had arisen by which Austria-Hungary could eradicate much of the internal unrest that plagued her while simultaneously reducing the Balkans to an order that suited Austro-German interests. This was not a decision calculated to precipitate a war but rather one which looked forward to a diplomatic triumph even more dramatic than that of 1909. The triumph that the Germans envisioned in the summer of 1914 would strengthen Austria-Hungary while attaching her to Germany even more closely in the future. The fateful moment came when Russia undertook a partial mobilization, which made it clear that she would not back down this time. Faced with this determined Russian response, Germany had either to go backward, by restraining her ally and admitting to another defeat in diplomacy, or go forward by threatening Russia with a general war. She chose to go forward.

The thinking behind Germany's decision was both strategic and political. Her military leaders advised that her position relative to Russia would deteriorate over the next few years: the Russian army would be expanded at a rate that Germany could not hope to match; the Russian economy appeared to have passed through the first stages of an industrial revolution; plans for railway construction, if they were realized, would allow the Russians to maximize the advantage they enjoyed in their numbers of fighting men. As Moltke told Conrad in 1912, 'a European war must come sooner or later in which ultimately the struggle will be one between Germanism and Slavism' (Taylor, 1954: 496) – an attitude that laid the foundation for the famous, and controversial, 'war conference' of December 1912 [**Doc. 19, p. 106**]. By 1914 German leaders concluded that they had been 'encircled' by Russia, France and Great Britain, and that the decade-long series of diplomatic crises had demonstrated that it was impossible to break this combination by peaceful means. The German landowners and the bourgeoisie were also generally inclined to believe that a great victorious war would enable them to triumph over those elements in German society, particularly the socialists of the industrial cities, who were opposed to their continuing domination of the German state. The most significant of the underlying causes of the war was the dynamic growth of German power in the decades that preceded it, and the fact that the management of that power resided with an élite who had come to believe that war was an attractive policy because it usually brought them social, political and economic rewards.

The German, Russian and Austrian decisions were the momentous ones. Given Moltke's revision of the Schlieffen plan, France was bound to be attacked, no matter what she did. Her only alternative to fighting was to concede defeat in advance. But the role of France was significant nevertheless. Had Russia not been repeatedly assured by Poincaré, since he came into power in 1912, of French assistance in any future Balkan crisis, she might have been more reluctant to support Serbia to the point of war with Austria-Hungary. Furthermore, without the Russian alliance, which almost all France's statesmen regarded as indispensable to her foreign policy, it is possible that the Schlieffen plan would not have been formulated. But the French believed that without the Russian alliance there would be no balance of power and France would inevitably succumb to the domination of Germany. Although the French decision to go to war, therefore, was not made on the basis of *revanche* for the 'lost provinces' of Alsace and Lorraine, national pride was significant in encouraging French politicians to fight for France's survival as an independent great power.

Of the five great powers that went to war in August 1914, Britain played the least significant part. Her support, or lack of it, neither encouraged nor restrained Russia and France. While some have argued that war might have been averted if she had made it evident early in the crisis that she would assist Russia and France in the event of a general European war, this seems doubtful. The German military – as well as the French – took little account of Britain's ability to contribute substantially to the fighting; their plans hinged on a quick knock-out blow of France, and they assumed that this would have been achieved before Britain could do much about it. Had the Germans anticipated a four-year-long war of attrition they would perhaps have rated British power more highly. It might just as easily be argued that if Britain had taken a strong and committed line from the start she would simply have confirmed the argument of those Germans who believed that she was behind the policy of encirclement, and that an armed conflict was the only way whereby Germany could break up the coalition that had been organized to contain her.

The British, who had done their best in the decade before 1914 to show the French that they would stand by them if they were threatened by Germany, consistently refused to commit themselves in advance of events. Neither Liberal fuzzy-mindedness nor adherence to tradition was responsible for this refusal; it was based on a realistic appraisal of the situation on the continent. The British rated themselves more highly than the Germans did; consequently, they believed that if the French and/or the Russians were guaranteed British support in a war they would be more intransigent in times of crisis and might even provoke a conflict. The British were nevertheless drawn reluctantly into the war in August 1914 because they believed that a victorious Germany would inevitably dominate the continent. The British empire was in no immediate danger; Britain did not go to war in order to crush the German fleet, but to save France. The naval race had helped to embitter the British public against Germany, to turn their animosity away from the traditional enemies, France and Russia; and the German invasion of Belgium was instrumental in confirming the British in the righteousness of their cause. Strategists had anticipated such a manoeuvre for some time; as early as 1905 a British war game envisioned that Germany would violate Belgian neutrality. The men making the decisions would have led Britain into war regardless of the invasion; the real threat to Britain was the creation of a German hegemony in Europe – and it did not matter much how this was achieved.

The First World War was not inevitable. Although it is essential to understand the underlying factors that formed the background to the July crisis, it is equally essential to see how the immediate circumstances of the crisis fit into this background in a particular, and perhaps unique, way. Europe was not a powder-keg waiting to explode; one crisis did not lead necessarily to another in an escalating series of confrontations that made war more and more difficult to avoid. Europe had successfully weathered a number of storms in the recent past; the alliances were not rigidly fixed; the war plans were always being revised and need not necessarily have come into play. It is difficult to imagine a crisis in the far east, in north Africa or the Mediterranean that would have unleashed the series of events that arose from the assassination in Sarajevo. The First World War was, in the final analysis, fought to determine who would control the future of the middle east; whoever won this struggle would, it was believed, be in a position to dominate all of Europe. Germany and her ally made the bid for control; Russia and her allies resolved to stop them.

Most difficult to answer is the question of what part popular attitudes, cultural assumptions and competing versions of 'historical destiny' played in the coming of war. In spite of the position taken by the organized working-class movements of pre-war Europe that wars were caused by capitalist competition and that they were fought for the interests of the bourgeoisie, they seem to have had little influence on working-class opinion. In the French elections of 1898 a socialist politician (Viviani) told constituents that although socialists stood for international understanding of the workers they did not deny the duties of patriotism and were ready to defend France because she was 'the material *patrie*, the glorious cradle of our race' (Tint, 1964: 109). Although it was principally the lives of workers which would be lost, or whose bodies would be ruined, there was no popular resistance to the declarations of war. Some socialists stood up for their beliefs when war broke out, but they soon proved to represent only a small minority, and 'resisters' were mainly middle-class intellectuals who formed the basis of the pacifist movement before the war. Organized pacifism had been growing before 1914, particularly when the movement focused on disarmament or on international law as the means of preventing conflicts. Occasionally, these ideas even received official sanction. But even many pacifists abandoned their beliefs when war was declared.

More influential than socialism and pacifism were militarism, nationalism and racism. Decades of drilling, marching, and flag-waving fused with popular nationalism and xenophobia to create a lethal combination. Most Europeans – high, low and middling – placed themselves according to national and racial categories, assumptions and stereotypes. Those who made the fateful decisions of July frequently revealed how pervasive and deep-seated these views were. Kaiser Wilhelm, who regarded Serbia's submission to most of Austria's ultimatum as a triumph for Austro-German policy, warned that they must not assume too much: 'The Serbs are Orientals, therefore liars, tricksters, and masters of evasion' (Cecil vol. 2, 1996: 203). Assumptions that nations and races behaved according to predetermined characteristics were widespread. Before the Anglo-French entente, and before the first Moroccan crisis, Delcassé had declared that the question had to be solved quickly, before the German race 'with its tendency to expand and overrun' succeeded in finding 'a historic and nationalist justification' for doing so (Andrew, 1968: 211). Fred Jane, the founder of the naval publishing house, who had pleaded in his 1899 *The Imperial Russian Navy* for an Anglo-Russian alliance, had changed his mind by 1904. With the formation of the Anglo-Japanese alliance, he said, 'the first step of the great coming struggle between the Anglo-Saxon and the Slav has been taken' (Jane, 1904: 11).

Young nations and old behaved differently. The old were tired, falling apart, dying; the young were energetic, ambitious, expanding. An advisor to Bethmann in 1913 described Germany as 'A young nation of enormous energy and capacity.' This recognition determined the course of her policy: now awakened to activity, 'its interests enlarge and reach overseas . . . External necessity and inner vitality force it to engage in Weltpolitik' (Jarausch, 1973: 143). Many were steeped in the ideas of Darwin and Nietzsche. Conrad insisted that 'the only real and rational basis for policy making' was found in the recognition that 'the struggle for existence' formed the basic principle 'of all events on this earth' (Deak, 1990: 74).

Those who made the decisions and those who followed them down the road to war shared the impression that the states of Europe had reached a turning-point. 'A new era in world history begins' declared a leading Russian liberal upon hearing of Germany's declaration of war on Russia (Pipes, 1980: 203). 'Serbia has passed only through the first stage of her historical career' declared Sazonov in 1913. 'To reach her goal she must endure another frightful struggle, in which her very existence will be staked . . . Time is working for Serbia and for the destruction of her enemies' (Stieve, 1926: 180). The enemies of Serbia, he argued, already showed obvious signs of dissolution. Others saw Russia as the problem: Pilsudski, a most prominent member of the Polish Socialist Party, declared a decade before the war that 'The historical role of socialism in Poland is the role of a defender of the West against reactionary tsardom' (Rogger, 1983: 189). Words that evoked destiny, mission and sacrifice were to be heard everywhere. General von der Goltz, in his *Volk in Waffen* warned that German children had to be taught 'that a time of rest has not yet come, that the prediction of a final struggle for the existence and greatness of Germany is not a mere fancy of ambitious fools, but that it will come one day, inevitably, with full fury' (Kitchen, 1968: 100). The Italian nationalist, Corradini (who was converted to the cause by the 'shame of Adua') founded *Il Regno* in 1903 to preach ideas of mission and sacrifice to all those 'who are for an intense and heroic life against a narrow and vulgar life'. Death in a righteous cause was noble: 'When lives have to be sacrificed we are not saddened if before our minds shines the magnificent harvest of a superior life that will rise from those deaths' (Whittam, 1977: 170).

Although the scenery has shifted, notions that different ways of life are engaged in a life-and-death struggle, that it is the destiny and the duty of the young and the heroic to kill or be killed in this struggle are still very much with us at the beginning of the twenty-first century.

Part 2

DOCUMENTS

Document 1   THE DUAL ALLIANCE

This alliance between Germany and Austria was signed on 7 October 1879, and consisted of four articles. Articles III and IV provided for a five-year renewable term for the treaty and that the treaty should be kept secret – but the tsar was to be informed that an attack on either of the signatories would be regarded as an attack on both of them.

ART. I. Should, contrary to their hope, and against the loyal desire of the two High Contracting Parties, one of the two Empires be attacked by Russia, the High Contracting Parties are bound to come to the assistance one of the other with the whole war strength of their Empires, and accordingly only to conclude peace together and upon mutual agreement.

ART. II. Should one of the High Contracting Parties be attacked by another Power, the other High Contracting Party binds itself hereby, not only not to support the aggressor against its high Ally, but to observe at least a benevolent neutral attitude towards its fellow Contracting Party.

Should, however, the attacking party in such a case be supported by Russia, either by an active co-operation or by military measures which constitute a menace to the Party attacked, then the obligation stipulated in Article I of this Treaty, for reciprocal assistance with the whole fighting force, becomes equally operative, and the conduct of the war by the two High Contracting Parties shall in this case also be in common until the conclusion of a common peace.

Source: Michael Hurst (ed.) (1974), *Key Treaties for the Great Powers 1814–1914*, Vol. 2: *1871–1914* (London: David and Charles), p. 590.

Document 2   THE TRIPLE ALLIANCE

This treaty between Austria-Hungary, Germany and Italy was signed on 20 May 1882. Further articles provided for a term of five years and that the treaty should remain secret.

ART. I. The High Contracting Parties mutually promise peace and friendship, and will enter into no alliance or engagement directed against any one of their States.

They engage to proceed to an exchange of ideas on political and economic questions of a general nature which may arise, and they further promise one another mutual support within the limits of their own interests.

ART. II. In case Italy, without direct provocation on her part, should be attacked by France for any reason whatsoever, the two other Contracting

Parties shall be bound to lend help and assistance with all their forces to the Party attacked.

This same obligation shall devolve upon Italy in case of any aggression without direct provocation by France against Germany.

ART. III. If one, or two, of the High Contracting Parties, without direct provocation on their part, should chance to be attacked and to be engaged in a war with two or more Great Powers nonsignatory to the present Treaty, the *casus foederis* will arise simultaneously for all the High Contracting Parties.

ART. IV. In case a Great Power nonsignatory to the present Treaty should threaten the security of the states of one of the High Contracting Parties, and the threatened Party should find itself forced on that account to make war against it, the two others bind themselves to observe towards their Ally a benevolent neutrality. Each of them reserves to itself, in this case, the right to take part in the war, if it should see fit, to make common cause with its Ally.

ART. V. If the peace of any of the High Contracting Parties should chance to be threatened under the circumstances foreseen by the preceding Articles, the High Contracting Parties shall take counsel together in ample time as to the military measures to be taken with a view to eventual co-operation.

They engage henceforward, in all cases of common participation in a war, to conclude neither armistice, nor peace, nor treaty, except by common agreement among themselves.

Source: Key Treaties, pp. 611–12.

BISMARCK'S EASTERN POLICY   **Document 3**

After Bismarck's resignation in 1890 he was anxious to clarify the difference between his conservative policy in the East, and the apparently adventurous one of Wilhelm II.

. . . in the future not only military equipment but also a correct political eye will be required to guide the German ship of state through the currents of coalitions to which we are exposed in consequence of our geographical position and our previous history. We shall not avoid the dangers which lie in the bosom of the future by amiability and commercial *pourboires* to friendly Powers. We should only increase the greed of our former friends and teach them to reckon on our anxieties and necessities. . . . Our reputation and our security will develop all the more permanently, the more, in all conflicts which do not immediately touch us, we hold ourselves in reserve and do not show ourselves sensitive to every attempt to stir up and utilise our vanity . . . Germany would be guilty of a great folly if in Eastern struggles which did not affect her interests she were to take a side sooner than the other Powers who were more directly concerned . . . in future Eastern negotiations Germany, by holding back, will be able to turn to its advantage the fact that it is the Power which has least interest in Oriental questions . . .

If Germany has the advantage that her policy is free from direct interests in the East, on the other side is the disadvantage of the central and exposed position of the German Empire, with its extended frontier which has to be defended on every side, and the ease with which anti-German coalitions are made. At the same time Germany is perhaps the single Great Power in Europe which is not tempted by any objects which can only be attained by a successful war. It is our interest to maintain peace, while without exception our continental neighbours have wishes, either secret or officially avowed, which cannot be fulfilled except by war . . . we must do our best to prevent war or limit it.

Source: Otto, Fürst von Bismarck (1898), *Bismarck, the man & the statesman: being the reflections and reminiscences of Otto, Prince von Bismarck, written and dictated by himself after his retirement from office*, trans. under supervision of A. J. Butler (London: Smith, Elder), pp. 287–9.

Document 4   THE KAISER AND BISMARCK'S DEPARTURE

The difference in views between the kaiser and Bismarck marked a turning-point in German policy. Wilhelm II, as indicated in this diary entry, was quite clear that his attitude to Russia and Austria-Hungary was going to differ from Bismarck's.

The Emperor said it was better that they should part now, when they could do so amicably, than that a serious conflict should arise. He then told the generals that Russia wished to begin a military occupation of Bulgaria, and to assure herself, of the neutrality of Germany in the meantime. The Emperor said that he had promised the Emperor of Austria to be a loyal ally, and he would keep his word. The occupation of Bulgaria by the Russians would mean war with Austria, and he could not leave Austria in the lurch. It looks more and more as if the breach between the Emperor and Bismarck had been caused by a difference of opinion concerning the plans of Russia. Bismarck was ready to abandon Austria. The Emperor declines to leave Austria, even at the risk of being involved in war with Russia and France.

From this point of view I understand Bismarck's statement when he said that the Emperor was conducting his policy in the manner of Friedrich Wilhelm IV. This is the black cloud on the horizon.

Source: F. Curtius (ed.) (1906), *Memoirs of Prince Chlodwig of Hohenlohe Schillingsfuerst*, trans. George W. Chrystal, Vol. 2 (London: William Heinemann), p. 413.

THE 'WILLY–NICKY' CORRESPONDENCE **Document 5**

Wilhelm II hoped, by means of a friendly personal correspondence with Nicholas II (which, ironically, was conducted in English), to deflect Russia's ambitions from Europe to Asia, and to arouse the tsar's fears of too close a relationship with revolutionary France.

26 April 1895 . . . I shall certainly do all in my power to keep Europe quiet, and also guard the rear of Russia so that nobody shall hamper your action towards the Far East!

For that is clearly the great task of the future for Russia to cultivate the Asian Continent and to defend Europe from the inroads of the Great Yellow race. In this you will always find me on your side, ready to help you as best I can . . .

26 September 1895 . . . The proposed new Corps would increase the already overwhelming French forces to 5 Corps, and constitutes a threat as well as a serious danger to my country . . . [it] has made people uneasy here and given affairs an ugly look, as if Russia would like France to be offensive against Germany with the hopes of help from the first named . . . I perfectly know that you personally do not dream of attacking us, but still you cannot be astonished that the European Powers get alarmed seeing how the presence of your officers and high officials in *official way* in France fans the inflamable [*sic*] Frenchman into a white heated passion and strengthens the cause of Chauvinism and Revanche! . . . if France goes on openly or secretly encouraged like this to violate all rules of international courtesy and Peace in peace times, one fine day my dearest Nicky you will find yourself *nolens volens* suddenly embroiled in the most horrible of wars Europe ever saw! . . .

25 October 1895 . . . it is not a *fact* of the *Rapport* or friendship between Russia and France that makes one uneasy . . . but the danger which is brought to our Principle of Monarchism through the lifting up [of] the Republic on a pedestal by the form under which the friendship is shown. The constant appearance of Princes, Grand-dukes, statesmen, Generals in 'full fig' at reviews, burials, dinners, races, with the head of the Republic or in his

entourage makes Republicains [*sic*] . . . believe that they are quite honest excellent people with whom Princes can consort and feel at home! . . . Don't forget that Jaurès . . . sits on the throne of the King and Queen of France 'by the Grace of God' whose heads Frenchmen Republicans cut off. The Blood of their Majesties is still on that country! Look at it, has it since then ever been happy or quiet again? Has it not staggered from bloodshed to bloodshed? And in its great moments did it not go from war to war? Till it soused all Europe and Russia in streams of blood? Till at last it had the Commune over again? Nicky take my word on it the curse of God has stricken that people forever!

Source: N.F. Grant (ed. and trans.) (1920), *The Kaiser's Letters to the Tsar* (London: Hodder & Stoughton), pp. 10–11, 20–1, 23–5.

Document 6   THE FRANCO-RUSSIAN ALLIANCE

The alliance between France and Russia was created in an exchange of letters between their foreign ministers in August 1891; the alliance was not formally ratified by the two governments until the following year.

Letter of M. de Giers, Minister of Foreign Affairs of Russia, to M. de Mohrenheim, Ambassador of Russia at Paris. Petersburg, August 9/21, 1891.

The situation created in Europe by the open renewal of the Triple Alliance and the more or less probable adhesion of Great Britain to the political aims which that alliance pursues, has, during the recent sojourn here of M. de Laboulaye, prompted an exchange of ideas between the former Ambassador of France and myself, tending to define the attitude which, as things now stand and in the presence of certain eventualities, might best suit our respective Governments, which, having kept out of any league, are none the less sincerely desirous of surrounding the maintenance of peace with the most efficacious guarantees.

It is thus that we have been led to formulate the two points below:

1. In order to define and consecrate the cordial understanding which unites them, and desirous of contributing in common agreement to the maintenance of the peace which forms the object of their sincerest aspirations, the two Governments declare that they will take counsel together upon every question of a nature to jeopardize the general peace;

2. In case that peace should be actually in danger, and especially if one of the two parties should be threatened with an aggression, the two parties undertake to reach an understanding on the measures whose immediate and

simultaneous adoption would be imposed upon the two Governments by the realization of this eventuality . . .

Source: Key Treaties, p. 663.

FRANCO-RUSSIAN MILITARY CONVENTION   **Document 7**

The military co-operation provided for in document 6 was outlined in this 1892 draft agreement, which was ratified by the two governments in December 1893 and January 1894.

France and Russia, being animated by an equal desire to preserve peace, and having no other object than to meet the necessities of a defensive war, provoked by an attack of the forces of the Triple Alliance against the one or the other of them, have agreed upon the following provisions:

1. If France is attacked by Germany, or by Italy supported by Germany, Russia shall employ all her available forces to attack Germany.

If Russia is attacked by Germany, or by Austria supported by Germany, France shall employ all her available forces to fight Germany.

2. In case the forces of the Triple Alliance, or of one of the Powers composing it, should mobilize, France and Russia, at the first news of the event and without the necessity of any previous concert, shall mobilize immediately and simultaneously the whole of their forces and shall move them as close as possible to their frontiers.

3. The available forces to be employed against Germany shall be, on the part of France, 1,300,000 men, on the part of Russia, 700,000 or 800,000 men.

These forces shall engage to the full, with all speed, in order that Germany may have to fight at the same time on the East and on the West.

4. The General Staffs of the Armies of the two countries shall co-operate with each other at all times in the preparation and facilitation of the execution of the measures above foreseen.

They shall communicate to each other, while there is still peace, all information relative to the armies of the Triple Alliance which is or shall be within their knowledge.

Ways and means of corresponding in times of war shall be studied and arranged in advance.

5. France and Russia shall not conclude peace separately.

6. The present Convention shall have the same duration as the Triple Alliance.

7. All the clauses above enumerated shall be kept rigorously secret.

Source: Key Treaties, pp. 668–9.

Document 8   THE 'KRUGER TELEGRAM'

The prime minister of the Cape Colony in South Africa, Cecil Rhodes, con-spired with his friend, the South African Company's administrator for Rhodesia, Dr Leander Starr Jameson, to attack the Boer republic of the Transvaal. The attack was planned to coincide with a 'spontaneous' rising of the (English) 'Uitlanders' in the Transvaal. Although the rising failed to materialize, Jameson launched his famous raid on 29 December 1895. His force was captured by the Boers and forced to surrender on 2 January 1896. The kaiser the next day despatched a telegram congratulating Kruger on his victory which infuriated both the British government and public opinion.

I express to you my sincerest congratulations that you and your people have succeeded by your own energy, without appealing to the aid of friendly Powers, in defeating the armed forces which, as disturbers of the peace, invaded your country, in re-establishing order, and in protecting the inde-pendence of the country against attacks from without.

Source: Louis Elkind (ed. and trans.) (1904), The German Emperor's Speeches: being a selection from the speeches, edicts, letters, and telegrams of the Emperor William II (London: Longmans, Green), p. 104.

Document 9   THE TIRPITZ MEMORANDUM OF JUNE 1897

In this memorandum Admiral von Tirpitz laid down the principle design of German naval policy: that the greatest naval danger came from Britain, that Germany could not effectively threaten the British Empire and thus should aim at threatening Britain itself, and that battleship building was essential to this design.

Very Secret

General Considerations on the Constitution of our Fleet according to Ship Classes and Designs

    1. In the distinctions between one class of ship and another, and in the choice among ship designs within the various classes, the most difficult situation in war into which our fleet can come must be used as a basis. For

that constitution of our naval force which meets the most difficult situation will be seen to be sufficient for all other situations. The limits of our resources prevent any attempt to meet every conceivable eventuality on its own in an ideal manner.

2. For Germany the most dangerous naval enemy at the present time is England. It is also the enemy against which we most urgently require a certain measure of naval force as a political power factor.

3. Commerce raiding and transatlantic war against England is so hopeless, because of the shortage of bases on our side and the superfluity on England's side, that we must ignore this type of war against England in our plans for the constitution of our fleet.

4. Our fleet must be so constructed that it can unfold its greatest military potential between Heligoland and the Thames.

5. A fleet constructed on this basis corresponds so well to our requirements, both against France as far as Brest or Cherbourg and against Russia as far as Kronstadt, that for the moment we need not pay attention to those enemies in the determination of our ship classes and in the selection of designs. The precondition here is that the coal capacity of the individual ship designs should be sufficiently large to permit a radius of action as far as Brest or Cherbourg.

6. The military situation against England demands battleships in as great a number as possible. Given the measure of our powers of development, which are limited by the capacity of our shipbuilding, armour and armament industries, by the expansion of our military harbours and shipyards, by the possibility of training the necessary personnel and making available the necessary funds, and by our organisation which has been developed and tested in the last few years, we cannot create in the near future, that is up to 1905, more than two full squadrons of eight battleships each. Reserve material is vital in order to be able to count on these squadrons at full strength in case of mobilisation. . . .

Source: Jonathan Steinberg (1965), *Yesterday's Deterrent: Tirpitz and the birth of the German battlefleet* (London: Macdonald), pp. 209–10.

GERMANY AND 'WORLD POLICY'   **Document 10**

The expenditure necessary to build the fleet proposed by Tirpitz (above) had to be justified politically. The German Chancellor, Prince Bernhard von Bülow, explained in a speech to the Reichstag on 11 December 1899 why deputies must support both a large army and navy.

. . . recent decades have brought to Germany great good fortune and power and prosperity. Good fortune and growing prosperity in one quarter are not always greeted in others with pure satisfaction; they may awaken envy. Envy plays a great part in the life of individuals and in the life of nations. There is a great deal of envy of us in the world, political envy and economic envy . . . [the] times of political impotence and economic and political insignificance must not return. We do not intend again to be . . . the bondmen of humanity. The one condition, however, on which alone we shall maintain our position is that we realize that without power, without a strong army and a strong navy, there can be no welfare for us. The means of fighting the battle for existence in this world without strong armaments on land and water, for a nation soon to count sixty millions, living in the centre of Europe and at the same time stretching out its economic feelers in all directions, have not yet been found. In the coming century the German nation will be either the hammer or the anvil.

Source: Franz von Stockhammern (ed.), Bernhard, Fürst von Bülow (1931), *Memoirs* (trans. F.A. Voigt and Geoffrey Dunlop) (London: Putnam), vol. 1, p. 353.

Document 11   ECONOMIC PARASITES OF IMPERIALISM

'Imperialism' as a cause of the First World War was one of the earliest interpretations and has proved to be one of the most enduring. In this selection one of the earliest 'theorists' of the phenomenon outlines his position and draws the connection between empire and international conflict.

Seeing that the Imperialism of the last six decades is clearly condemned as a business policy, in that at enormous expense it has procured a small, bad, unsafe increase of markets, and has jeopardised the entire wealth of the nation in rousing the strong resentment of other nations, we may ask, 'How is the British nation induced to embark upon such unsound business?' The only possible answer is that the business interests of the nation as a whole are subordinated to those of certain sectional interests that usurp control of the national resources and use them for their private gain. This is no strange or monstrous charge to bring; it is the commonest disease of all forms of government. The famous words of Sir Thomas More are as true now as when he wrote them: 'Everywhere do I perceive a certain conspiracy of rich men seeking their own advantage under the name and pretext of the commonwealth.'

Although the new Imperialism has been bad business for the nation, it has been good business for certain classes and certain trades within the nation.

The vast expenditure on armaments, the costly wars, the grave risks and embarrassments of foreign policy, the checks upon political and social reforms within Great Britain, though fraught with great injury to the nation, have served well the present business interests of certain industries and professions.

It is idle to meddle with politics unless we clearly recognise this central fact and understand what these sectional interests are which are the enemies of national safety and the commonwealth. We must put aside the merely sentimental diagnosis which explains wars or other national blunders by outbursts of patriotic animosity or errors of statecraft. Doubtless at every outbreak of war not only the man in the street but the man at the helm is often duped by the cunning with which aggressive motives and greedy purposes dress themselves in defensive clothing. There is, it may be safely asserted, no war within memory, however nakedly aggressive it may seem to the dispassionate historian, which has not been presented to the people who were called upon to fight as a necessary defensive policy, in which the honour, perhaps the very existence, of the State was involved.

The disastrous folly of these wars, the material and moral damage inflicted even on the victor, appear so plain to the disinterested spectator that he is apt to despair of any State attaining years of discretion, and inclines to regard these natural cataclysms as implying some ultimate irrationalism in politics. But careful analysis of the existing relations between business and politics shows that the aggressive Imperialism which we seek to understand is not in the main the product of blind passions of races or of the mixed folly and ambition of politicians. It is far more rational than at first sight appears. Irrational from the standpoint of the whole nation, it is rational enough from the standpoint of certain classes in the nation. A completely socialist State which kept good books and presented regular balance-sheets of expenditure and assets would soon discard Imperialism; an intelligent *laissez-faire* democracy which gave duly proportionate weight in its policy to all economic interests alike would do the same. But a State in which certain well-organised business interests are able to outweigh the weak, diffused interest of the community is bound to pursue a policy which accords with the pressure of the former interests . . .

Certain definite business and professional interests feeding upon imperialistic expenditure, or upon the results of that expenditure, are thus set up in opposition to the common good, and, instinctively feeling their way to one another, are found united in strong sympathy to support every new imperialist exploit . . .

Source: J.A. Hobson (1905), *Imperialism: A Study* (rev. edn, London: Archibald Constable), pp. 42–4.

Document 12   THE ANGLO-JAPANESE ALLIANCE

This agreement was made on 30 January 1902; further articles provided for consultation in case the interests of either signatory were jeopardized, and for a renewable term of five years.

ART. I. The High Contracting Parties, having mutually recognised the independence of China and Korea, declare themselves to be entirely uninfluenced by any aggressive tendencies in either country. Having in view, however, their special interests of which those of Great Britain relate principally to China, while Japan, in addition to the interests which she possesses in China, is interested in a peculiar degree politically as well as commercially and industrially in Korea, the High Contracting Parties recognise that it will be admissible for either of them to take such measures as may be indispensable in order to safeguard those interests if threatened either by the aggressive action of any other Power, or by disturbances arising in China or Korea, and necessitating the intervention of either of the High Contracting Parties for the protection of the lives and property of its subjects.

ART. II. If either Great Britain or Japan, in the defence of their respective interests as above described, should become involved in war with another Power, the other High Contracting Party will maintain a strict neutrality, and use its efforts to prevent other Powers from joining in hostilities against its ally.

ART. III. If, in the above event, any other Power or Powers should join in hostilities against that ally, the other High Contracting Party will come to its assistance, and will conduct the war in common, and make peace in mutual agreement with it.

Source: Key Treaties, pp. 726–7.

Document 13   GERMANY, BRITAIN AND MOROCCO

Near the height of the Moroccan crisis, at a time (22 July 1905) when German diplomacy appeared triumphant, the German ambassador in London warned the Chancellor (Bülow) that they could end up by driving Britain and France closer together.

. . . There is no doubt that at the moment King Edward is strongly aroused against us and, unfortunately, against the person of the Emperor in particular. I imagine that he talked several times to Delcassé, a fact which his Ministers do not know. Nothing can have angered him so much as our

Moroccan policy, which ignores the Agreement with France, the great event of his reign. When at one moment it looked as if M. Rouvier, driven by fear, was ready to sacrifice the Entente, King Edward must have done his best to appear as France's firm support. As far as can be ascertained here, the French seem to have lost their first fear and to have assumed a distinctly Anglophil attitude. Since they feel surer than before of British help, our negotiations with France may have to go slower and be more difficult to complete. Nevertheless, if this assumption is correct, I think quiet, continuous pressure on the French will be the best way to attain our wishes in Morocco. The prospect of reaching a general agreement with France about Morocco seems unfortunately to be becoming more remote. The increase of self-confidence on the subject, which is inspired in them by England, may give rise to a serious situation before or during the Conference. A trial of strength to the point of bending or breaking would involve a greater danger to peace than the first time. But it may be assumed that fear would again grip them in Paris; but if the French go mad and allow it to come to a war, they will, even without a treaty, find England's armed power on their side. In England the Morocco question has come to mean a fight for the friendship of France, and in order to keep this and also to prevent a predominant German hegemony over Europe they would venture on a war.

Nevertheless, I insist that neither King Edward nor his Government, nor even the British people, who are aroused against us, wish for a war with Germany. But there are causes which might lead to it. The Morocco question has brought us a step nearer to war with England.

Source: E.T.S. Dugdale (trans.) (1930), *German Diplomatic Documents 1871–1914*, vol. III *The Growing Antagonism 1898–1910* (London: Methuen), pp. 232–3.

MANIFESTO OF FUTURISM   Document 14

Various groups, societies and movements before the First World War viewed conflict and violence as not only natural but desirable. Among these was the 'modernist' movement known as 'Futurism' founded by the Italian poet, F. T. Marinetti.

1. We want to sing the love of danger, the habit of energy and rashness.

2. The essential elements of our poetry will be courage, audacity and revolt.

3. Literature has up to now magnified pensive immobility, ecstasy and slumber. We want to exalt movements of aggression, feverish sleeplessness, the double march, the perilous leap, the slap and the blow with the fist.

4. We declare that the splendor of the world has been enriched by a new beauty: the beauty of speed. A racing automobile with its bonnet adorned with great tubes like serpents with explosive breath . . . a roaring motor car which seems to run on machine-gun fire, is more beautiful than the Victory of Samothrace.

5. We want to sing the man at the wheel, the ideal axis of which crosses the earth, itself hurled along its orbit.

6. The poet must spend himself with warmth, glamour and prodigality to increase the enthusiastic fervor of the primordial elements.

7. Beauty exists only in struggle. There is no masterpiece that has not an aggressive character. Poetry must be a violent assault on the forces of the unknown, to force them to bow before man.

8. We are on the extreme promontory of the centuries! What is the use of looking behind at the moment when we must open the mysterious shutters of the impossible? Time and Space died yesterday. We are already living in the absolute, since we have already created eternal, omnipresent speed.

9. We want to glorify war – the only cure for the world – militarism, patriotism, the destructive gesture of the anarchists, the beautiful ideas which kill, and contempt for woman . . .

Source: Released in Milan in 1909, first published in *Le Figaro* (Paris) on 20 February 1909.

Document 15   THE BLACK HAND

In Belgrade on 9 May 1911 a secret organisation was formed with a constitution that laid down the purposes, principles and procedures of the group. It called itself Ujedinjenje ili Smrt – 'Unification or Death'. In addition to the selections below, other articles made it clear that it was to proceed with complete secrecy and laid down punishments – including death – for members that violated any of its provisions.

Article 1. For the purpose of realising the national ideals – the Unification of Serbdom – an organisation is hereby created, whose members may be any Serbian irrespective of sex, religion, place or birth, as well as anybody else who will sincerely serve this idea.

Article 2. The organisation gives priority to the revolutionary struggle rather than relies on cultural striving, therefore its institution is an absolutely secret one for wider circles.

Article 4. In order to carry into effect its task the organization will do the following things:

1. Following the character of its raison d'être it will exercise its influence over all the official factors in Serbia – which is the Piedmont of Serbdom – as also over all the strata of the State and over the entire social life in it.
2. It will carry out a revolutionary organisation in all the territories where Serbians are living.
3. Beyond the frontiers, it will fight with all means against all enemies of this idea.
4. It will maintain friendly relations with all the States, nations, organisations, and individual persons who sympathise with Serbia and the Serbian race.
5. It will give every assistance to those nations and organisations who are fighting for their own national liberation and unification.

Article 35. On entering into the organisation the joining member must pronounce the following oath of allegiance:

'I (the Christian name and surname of the joining member), by entering into the organisation "Unification or Death", do hereby swear by the Sun which shineth upon me, by the Earth which feedeth me, by God, by the blood of my forefathers, by my honour and by my life, that from this moment onward and until my death, I shall faithfully serve the task of this organisation and that I shall at all times be prepared to bear for it any sacrifice. I further swear by God, by my honour and by my life, that I shall unconditionally carry into effect all its orders and commands. I further swear by my God, by my honour and by my life, that I shall keep within myself all the secrets of this organisation and carry them with me into my grave. May God and my comrades in this organisation be my judges if at any time I should wittingly fail or break this oath!'

Source: Henri Pozzi (1935), *Black Hand Over Europe, consisting of War is coming again* (Francis J. Mott, trans.) (London: Francis Mott), pp. 268–73.

CAPITALISM IN THE BALKANS   **Document 16**

Marxist commentators interpreted most international conflicts as arising from the imperialist ambitions of the bourgeoisie. Here, one of the leading journalist–theorists of pre-war Marxism, Leon Trotsky, explains the cause of – and the solution to – 'the eastern question' in an article which appeared in Pravda *in August 1910.*

Two aspects need to be distinguished in what is known as the Eastern Question: first, it is a question of the relations between the Nations and States of the Balkan Peninsula; second, it is a question of the conflicting interests and intrigues of the European capitalist powers in the Balkans. These two questions are not at all identical. On the contrary: the real solution of the purely Balkan Question runs entirely counter to the interests of the European dynasties and stock exchanges. . . .

The frontiers between the dwarf states of the Balkan Peninsula were drawn not in accordance with national conditions or national demands, but as a result of wars, diplomatic intrigues, and dynastic interests. The Great Powers – in the first place, Russia and Austria – have always had a direct interest in setting the Balkan peoples and states against each other and then, when they have weakened one another, subjecting them to their economic and political influence. The petty dynasties ruling in these 'broken pieces' of the Balkan Peninsula have served and continue to serve as levers for European diplomatic intrigues. And this entire mechanism, founded on violence and perfidy, constitutes a huge burden weighing upon the Balkan peoples, holding back their economic and cultural development . . . This peninsula, richly endowed by nature, is senselessly split up into little bits; people and goods moving about in it constantly come up against the prickly hedges of state frontiers, and this cutting of nations and states into many strips renders impossible the formation of a single Balkan market, which could provide the basis for a great development of Balkan industry and culture. On top of all this is the exhausting militarism that has come into being in order to keep the Balkans divided, and which has given rise to the danger of wars fatal to the peninsula's economic progress – wars between Greece and Turkey, Turkey and Bulgaria, Romania and Greece, Bulgaria and Serbia . . .

The only way out of the national and state chaos and the bloody confusion of Balkan life is a union of all the peoples of the peninsula in a single economic and political entity, on the basis of national autonomy of the constituent parts. Only within the framework of a single Balkan state can the Serbs of Macedonia, the sanjak, Serbia and Montenegro be united in a single national–cultural community, enjoying at the same time the advantages of a Balkan common market. Only the united Balkan peoples can give a real rebuff to the shameless pretensions of tsarism and European imperialism . . .

Source: George Weissman and Duncan Williams (eds) (1980), *The Balkan Wars, 1912–13: the war correspondence of Leon Trotsky* (trans. Brian Pearce) (New York: Monad Press), pp. 38–41.

RUSSIA'S BALKAN POLICY   **Document 17**

Although the memoirs and autobiographies of the leading participants in the events of 1914 are invariably self-serving, they are still useful and interesting. Here the Russian Foreign Minister, Serge Sazonov, explains both the idealist and the practical components of Russian policy.

. . . Russia's historical mission – the emancipation of the Christian peoples of the Balkan peninsula from the Turkish yoke – was almost fulfilled by the beginning of the twentieth century; its completion could be left to the efforts of the liberated peoples themselves . . . Although these younger countries no longer needed the guardianship of Russia, they were not yet strong enough to dispense with her help in the event of any attempt upon their national existence by warlike Teutonism. Serbia in particular was exposed to this danger, having become the object of the decorously concealed covetousness of Austrian diplomacy . . . [Russia's] sole and unchanging object was to see that those Balkan peoples who had been freed by her age-long efforts and sacrifices should not fall under the influence of Powers hostile to her, or become the obedient tools of their political intrigues. The ultimate aim of Russian policy was to obtain free access to the Mediterranean, and to be in a position to defend her Black Sea coasts against the constant threat of the irruption of hostile naval forces through the Bosphorous . . .

Russia proclaimed and defended the principle of the independence of the Balkan States as fundamentally just, in view of their inalienable right to an independent political existence. In our eyes this principle, in addition to its moral significance, had also a practical value; for not only was it not detrimental to any of Russia's vital interests, but it indirectly furthered their maintenance. 'The Balkan Peninsula for the Balkan peoples' was the formula which comprised the aspirations and aims of Russian policy; it precluded the possibility of the political predominance, and still more of the sovereignty in the Balkans, of a foreign Power hostile to Balkan Slavdom and to Russia.

Source: Serge Dmitrievich Sazonov (1928), *Fateful Years 1909–16: the reminiscences of Serge Sazonov* (London: Jonathan Cape), pp. 49–51.

LLOYD GEORGE'S MANSION HOUSE SPEECH   **Document 18**

On 1 July 1911 the German gunboat Panther *arrived in Agadir, precipitating the second Moroccan crisis. The British Chancellor of the Exchequer, David Lloyd George, on 21 July warned Germany that Britain was not prepared to ignore threats to their interests. The speech was effective and became famous because Lloyd George was thought to be on 'the left' in the cabinet and not aggressively inclined in international affairs.*

Personally I am a sincere advocate of all means which would lead to the settlement of international disputes by methods such as those which civilization has so successfully set up for the adjustment of differences between individuals, and I rejoice in my heart at the prospect of a happy issue to Sir Edward Grey's negotiations with the United States of America for the settlement of disputes which may occur in future between ourselves and our kinsmen across the Atlantic by some more merciful, more rational, and by a more just arbitrament than that of the sword.

But I am also bound to say this – that I believe it is essential in the highest interests, not merely of this country, but of the world, that Britain should at all hazards maintain her place and her prestige amongst the Great Powers of the world. Her potent influence has many a time been in the past, and may yet be in the future, invaluable to the cause of human liberty. It has more than once in the past redeemed Continental nations, who are sometimes too apt to forget that service, from overwhelming disaster and even from national extinction. I would make great sacrifices to preserve peace. I conceive that nothing would justify a disturbance of international good will except questions of the greatest national moment. But if a situation were to be forced upon us in which peace could only be preserved by the surrender of the great and beneficent position Britain has won by centuries of heroism and achievement, by allowing Britain to be treated where her interests were vitally affected as if she were of no account in the Cabinet of nations, then I say emphatically that peace at that price would be a humiliation intolerable for a great country like ours to endure. National honour is no party question. The security of our great international trade is no party question; the peace of the world is much more likely to be secured if all nations realize fairly what the conditions of peace must be . . .

Source: The Times, 22 July 1911.

————◄●►————

Document 19   THE 'WAR CONFERENCE' OF DECEMBER 1912

The following excerpt from the diary of the Chief of the Kaiser's Naval Cabinet, Admiral Georg Alexander von Müller records a meeting that became one of the most hotly contested issues in the 'Fischer debate': did it indicate a predisposition to war in Germany? Was it only a matter of timing from December 1912 onwards?

Sunday. Ordered to see His Maj. at the Schloss at 11 a.m. with Tirpitz, Heeringen (Vice Admiral) and General von Moltke. H.M. speaks to a telegraphic report from the Ambassador in London, Prince Lichnowsky, concerning the political situation. Haldane, speaking for Grey, has told Lichnowsky that England, if we attacked France, would unconditionally spring to France's aid, for England could not allow the balance of power in Europe to be disturbed. H.M. greeted this information as a desirable clarification of the situation for the benefit of those who had felt sure of England as a result of the recent friendliness of the press.

H.M. envisaged the following:

Austria must deal energetically with the foreign Slavs (the Serbs), otherwise she will lose control of the Slavs in the Austria-Hungarian monarchy. If Russia supports the Serbs, which she evidently does (Sasonoff's declaration that Russia will immediately move into Galicia if Austria moves into Serbia) then war would be unavoidable for us too. We could hope, however, to have Bulgaria and Rumania and also Albania, and perhaps also Turkey on our side. An offer of alliance by Bulgaria has already been sent to Turkey. We have exerted great pressure on the Turks. Recently H.M. has also pressed the Crown Prince of Rumania, who was passing through on his way back from Brussels, to come to an understanding with Bulgaria. If these powers join Austria then we shall be free to fight the war with full fury against France. The fleet must naturally prepare itself for the war against England. The possibility mentioned by the Chief of the Admiralty Staff in his last audience of a war with Russia alone cannot now, after Haldane's statement, be taken into account. Therefore immediate submarine warfare against English troop transports in the Scheldt or by Dunkirk, mine warfare in the Thames. To Tirpitz: speedy build-up of U-boats, etc. Recommendation of a conference of all naval authorities concerned.

General von Moltke: 'I believe a war is unavoidable and the sooner the better. But we ought to do more through the press to prepare the popularity of a war against Russia, as suggested in the Kaiser's discussion.'

H.M. supported this and told the State Secretary [Tirpitz] to use his press contacts, too, to work in this direction. T[irpitz] made the observation that the navy would prefer to see the postponement of the great fight for one and a half years. Moltke says the navy would not be ready even then and the army would get into an increasingly unfavourable position, for the enemies were arming more strongly than we, as we were very short of money.

That was the end of the conference. The result amounted to almost 0.

The Chief of the Great General Staff says: War the sooner the better, but he does not draw the logical conclusion from this, which is to present Russia or France or both with an ultimatum which would unleash the war with right on our side.

In the afternoon I wrote to the Reich Chancellor about the influencing of the press.

Source: John C.G. Röhl (1994), *The Kaiser and his Court: Wilhelm II and the Government of Germany* (Cambridge: Cambridge University Press), pp. 162–3.

Document 20   GERMANY, SIR EDWARD GREY AND FOREIGN POLICY

The German ambassador in London, Lichnowsky, was one of those German diplomats who tried to persuade the officials and politicians in Berlin that the British in general – and Grey in particular – were peacefully inclined and that there was no need to fear an attack on Germany. On the contrary, he suggested to the Chancellor, Bethmann Hollweg on 20 December 1912, that there was a real opportunity for an Anglo-German rapprochement if Germany avoided a direct threat to British naval power.

Great Britain as a world-power stands and falls with her predominance at sea. If we ourselves were responsible for the safeguarding of an empire like that of Great Britain, we should without doubt strive to maintain our sea-power with the same solicitude as that now shown by the British Ministers.

As for the so-called Entente policy, I am of opinion that its solidarity varies in inverse ratio to the cordiality of England's relations with Germany and that the only way of loosening this friendship is in all our dealings with the English to ignore their Entente friendships as far as possible, at the same time avoiding anything that might possibly give rise to distrust and uneasiness. England will never formally break off her engagement with France and Russia and penitently fall into the arms of Germany, unless we have first been defeated. The powerful of this earth have at all times regarded each other askance, and throughout the course of her history England has never willingly tolerated any very powerful nation on the Continent, and when any such Power threatened to establish a hegemony, England has invariably gone to war with it. To guard her security and influence in the rest of Europe, England will therefore continue to insist on a certain 'balance of power', a counterpoise to this or that powerful group, and *under all circumstances will hold a protecting hand over France*. We are respected here; we are highly esteemed, perhaps even overrated, and from this feeling, that some people have been inclined to regard as fear, proceeds England's endeavour to hem us in, which is quite a different thing from a wish to go to war with us. Our common interests are too colossal, our economic ties too close and too important and the material losses involved, even in a victorious war, too vast for that. And people in Great Britain have grown too comfort-loving to want a war. The nation loves peace and does not care to be disturbed in the routine of its daily life. A war with us would therefore not be popular, but in spite of all this *the English would wage such a war if France were threatened* by us, for the opinion is general here that France would not be able to stand up against the superior might of Germany without British help . . .

Source: Karl Max, Fürst von Lichnowsky (1928), *Heading for the Abyss* (trans. Sefton Delmer) (New York: Payson & Clarke), pp. 188–90.

ENGLISH OPINION AND THE TRIPLE ENTENTE   **Document 21**

Months before shots were fired in Sarajevo, Britain's most famous debating club, the Oxford Union, welcomed visitors for a special debate on international affairs. The motion placed before the debaters on 29 May 1914 was 'That this House condemns the Triple Entente as embodying both an unnecessary and an unnatural policy'.

Mr J.H.B. Nihill (Emmanuel College, Cambridge), Vice-President of the Cambridge Union Society, opened with a humorous sketch of Oxford's weaker spots and a happy reference to the inter-University Entente. Our Foreign Office, he said, was blind to two vital axioms: first, that publicity was necessary, and next that we should not dabble promiscuously in problems that were remote from us. Following on an able historical summary, he denied that the Triple Entente could balance the Triple Alliance – its ostens-ible object. We must be careful, for Ententes, like matrimony, were easier to enter into than to recede from. Our present misguided policy was making a *rapprochement* with Germany impossible. Mr Nihill relieved a weighty manner by flashes of humour, and succeeded in stimulating interest in an intricate question. The best speech.

Mr H.D. Barnard (Jesus College, Cambridge), Secretary of the Cambridge Union Society, opposed with a debating speech. He refused to accept any facts on the Hon. Mover's authority alone. The Entente was a very different thing from an Alliance, and a time of peace was the ideal opportunity for making connexions. Germany was evidently an obsession with the Hon. Mover; and as to Great Britain receiving no benefit from the Entente, if it con-tributed to European peace, that was ample justification. The Opposer was perhaps a little too scornful of his honourable friend's intelligence, and his speech was rather rambling and disconnected; but, judging it as a debating speech, it was a clear and direct criticism, and was well received. . . .

Mr A.H.M. Wedderburn (Balliol), President [of the Oxford Union] . . . criticized a policy which divided the European powers into two armed camps, and so encouraged rivalry in armaments and strained relations between the opposing factors.

Mr V.A.L. Mallet (Balliol), Secretary, gave the historical reasons for the birth ten years ago of the French Entente, at a time when an understanding with Germany was out of the question. Germany and France were in any case irreconcilable, and we were bound to choose between them. He welcomed the end of our traditional enmity with France, because of his intense admiration for that nation. His eulogy of the French people left us cold, but the speech was backed by sound knowledge and was of considerable merit.

Mr J.S. Lithiby (Wadham) attacked the secrecy of the Entente. No one knew exactly what it was; but if it was not an alliance, it fulfilled no useful function; and if it was, it was highly dangerous. The crux of foreign policy was Germany's attitude towards us, and the Entente was a challenge well calculated to provoke her, and so produce a European conflagration. An effective speech.

Mr W.G. Woodroffe (Pembroke College, Cambridge) said that a true insight into the character and aims of the European powers found full justification for the Entente. For Germany the one necessary policy was expansion. To meet that and other dangers the Entente was essential, and without it war would be inevitable . . .

Mr C.T. Chevallier (Worcester) anticipated some startling changes in European history, and welcomed Alliance and Entente as about to amalgamate into a second Holy Alliance . . .

Baron von Richthofen (Lincoln) gave, to those who could follow him, an interesting defence of German policy . . .

On a division there voted – for the motion, 96; against it, 60.

Source: The Oxford Magazine, 4 June 1914; XXXII/22.

Document 22   GERMANY AND THE ASSASSINATION

On 30 June 1914 the German Ambassador at Vienna, von Tschirschky, reported on the emerging Austro-Hungarian response to the assassination, and his efforts to restrain them from precipitate action. The marginal notes by the kaiser indicate the extent of his disagreement with a policy of caution.

	Count Berchtold told me today that *everything pointed to the fact that the threads of the conspiracy to which the Archduke fell a sacrifice, ran together at Belgrade.* The affair was so well thought out that very young men were intentionally selected for the perpetration of the crime, against whom *only a mild punishment*
I hope not.	*could be decreed.* The Minister spoke very bitterly about the Serbian plots.
	I frequently hear expressed here, even among serious people, the wish that *at last a final and fundamental reckoning should be had*
Now or never.	*with the Serbs.* The Serbs should first be
Who authorized him to act that way? That is very stupid! It is none of his business, as it is solely the affair of Austria, what she plans to do in this case. Later, if plans go wrong, it will be said that Germany did not want it! Let Tschirschky be good enough to drop this nonsense! The Serbs must be disposed of, and that right soon! Goes without saying; nothing but truisms.	presented with a number of demands, and in case they should not accept these, energetic measures should be taken. *I take opportunity of every such occasion to advise quietly but very impressively and seriously against too hasty steps.* First of all, they must make sure what they want to do, for so far I have heard only indefinite expressions of opinion. Then the chances of every kind of action should be carefully weighed, and it should be kept in mind that Austria-Hungary does not stand alone in the world, that it is her duty to think not only of her allies, but to take into consideration the entire European situation, and especially to bear in mind the attitude of Italy and Roumania on all questions that concern Serbia.

von Tschirschky |

Source: Max Montgelas and Walther Schücking (eds) (1924), *Outbreak of the World War: German Documents Collected by Karl Kautsky* (trans. Carnegie Endowment for International Peace) (New York: Oxford University Press), p. 61.

Document 23   THE KAISER'S 'BLANK CHEQUE' TO AUSTRIA

This is the report of the famous conversation between Wilhelm II and the Austrian ambassador in Berlin, Count von Szögyény-Marich, in which the kaiser seemed to promise his support for Austria under any conditions.

5 July 1914

Count Szögyény to Count Berchtold (tel. 237; Strictly Private)

. . . the Emperor authorised me to inform our gracious Majesty that we might in this case, as in all others, rely upon Germany's full support . . . he did not doubt in the least that Herr von Bethmann Hollweg would agree with him. Especially as far as our action against Servia was concerned. But it was his (Emperor William's) opinion that this action must not be delayed. Russia's attitude will no doubt be hostile, but for this he had for years prepared, and should a war between Austria-Hungary and Russia be unavoidable, we might be convinced that Germany, our old faithful ally, would stand at our side. Russia at the present time was in no way prepared for war, and would think twice before it appealed to arms . . . if we had really recognised the necessity of warlike action against Servia, he (Emperor William) would regret if we did not make use of the present moment, which is all in our favour . . .

Source: Austrian Red Book: Official Files Pertaining to Pre-War History, Part 1 (London: George Allen & Unwin), pp. 18–19.

Document 24   GERMANY'S BALKAN POLICY

The German secretary for foreign affairs, von Jagow, explained (on 18 July) to the ambassador in London the reasons for Germany's policy in the July crisis. Lichnowsky had been critical of Germany's policy of supporting Austria-Hungary.

Austria no longer intends to tolerate the sapping activities of the Serbians, and just as little does she intend to tolerate longer the continuously provocative attitude of her small neighbour at Belgrade . . . She fully realizes that she has neglected many opportunities, and that she is still able to act, though in a few years she may no longer be able to do so. Austria is now going to force a showdown with Serbia, and has told us so. During the whole Balkan crisis we mediated successfully in the interest of peace, without forcing Austria to passivity at any of the critical moments. The fact that notwithstanding that we have often, with injustice, been accused of trimming and shuffling, makes no difference to me. Nor have we at the present time forced Austria to her decision. But we neither could nor should attempt to stay her hand. If we should do that, Austria would have the right to reproach us (and we ourselves) with having deprived her of her last chance of political rehabilitation. And then the process of her wasting away and of her internal decay would be still further accelerated. Her standing in the Balkans would be gone forever. You will undoubtedly agree with me that the absolute establishment of the Russian hegemony in the Balkans is, indirectly, not permissible, even for us. The maintenance of Austria, and, in fact, of the most powerful Austria possible, is a necessity for us both for internal and external reasons. That she cannot be maintained forever, I will willingly admit. But in the meantime we may perhaps be able to arrange other combinations.

We must attempt to localise the conflict between Austria and Serbia. Whether we shall succeed in this will depend first on Russia, and secondly on the moderating influence of Russia's allies. The more determined Austria shows herself, the more energetically we support her, so much the more quiet will Russia remain. To be sure, there will be some agitation in St Petersburg, but, on the whole, Russia is not ready to strike at present. Nor will France or England be anxious for war at the present time. According to all competent observation, Russia will be prepared to fight in a few years. Then she will crush us by the number of her soldiers; then she will have built her Baltic Sea fleet and her strategic railroads. Our group, in the meantime, will have become weaker right along.

Source: Max Montgelas and Walther Schücking (eds) (1924), *Outbreak of the World War: German Documents Collected by Karl Kautsky* (trans. Carnegie Endowment for International Peace) (New York: Oxford University Press), pp. 131–2.

RUSSIA AND THE THREAT OF REVOLUTION   **Document 25**

Although some Russians feared that war would result in revolution, most of those in government, as this recollection by Nicolas de Basily (of the Ministry of Foreign Affairs) of a conversation with Hohenloe (the Austrian military attaché in St Petersburg) shows, felt confident or preferred the risk over humiliation.

One evening in July 1914 . . . [Hohenloe and I] took the road out of St. Petersburg toward Finland. The huge forests of black pine were immersed in absolute silence, undisturbed by the slightest breath of air. It was the time of the marvelous white nights of the northern summer. The sun had scarcely disappeared beneath the horizon only to rise again about an hour later. A faint, pale light illuminated the landscape, sad and austere, and increased in us a certain state of anxiety inspired by the recent political news . . .

[We] could not turn our thoughts from the tension growing day by day between our two countries. We could already foresee some of the possible consequences of the Sarajevo murder. Taking me by the arm, Hohenloe said, 'Do you understand that you cannot go to war? If you do, you will expose yourself to revolution and to the ruin of your power.' I replied to my friend that while some changes within Russia and perhaps even a serious internal crisis were probable in the future, at present there was no indication of internal trouble. Public opinion was clamoring for an intervention in support of Serbia, and the Russian government would have the approval of the entire nation if it judged itself obliged to act. I added forcefully, 'You commit a serious error of calculation in supposing that fear of a revolution will prevent Russia from fulfilling its national duty now. As for the future, who can predict that with certainty?'

Source: Nicolai A. Bazili (1973), *Nicolas de Basily, Diplomat of Imperial Russia, 1903–1917: Memoirs* (Stanford, CA: Hoover Institution Press), pp. 89–90.

Document 26   THE POLICY OF SIR EDWARD GREY

In the 1920s Sir Edward Grey tried to defend himself against charges that he had contributed to the outbreak of war by following a weak and vacillating policy at the time of the July crisis.

What was said or done by me will be most clearly explained and best understood by stating the considerations and convictions that were dominant in my mind throughout that week . . .

1. A conviction that a great European war under modern conditions would be a catastrophe for which previous wars afforded no precedent . . . I thought this must be obvious to everyone else, as it seemed obvious to me; and that, if once it became apparent that we were on the edge, all the Great Powers would call a halt and recoil from the abyss.

2. That Germany was so immensely strong and Austria so dependent upon German strength that the word and will of Germany would at the critical moment be decisive with Austria. It was therefore to Germany that we must address ourselves.

3. That, if war came, the interest of Britain required that we should not stand aside, while France fought alone in the West, but must support her. I knew it to be very doubtful whether the Cabinet, Parliament and the country would take this view on the outbreak of war, and through the whole of this week I had in view the probable contingency that we should not decide at the critical moment to support France. In that event I should have to resign . . .

4. A clear view that no pledge must be given, no hope even held out to France and Russia, which it was doubtful whether this country would fulfil. One danger I saw so hideous that it must be avoided and guarded against at every word. It was that France and Russia might face the ordeal of war with Germany relying upon our support; that this support might not be forthcoming, and that we might then, when it was too late, be held responsible by them for having let them in for a disastrous war . . .

The notion of being involved in war about a Balkan quarrel was repugnant . . . there was no sentiment urging us to go into a war on Serbia's behalf. If France were involved, it would not be in any quarrel in which we owed her good-will. . . . It would indeed not be in any quarrel of her own at all; it would be because she, as Russia's Ally, had the misfortune to be involved in a Russian quarrel. . . . What, it was asked, was the good of keeping so carefully clear of alliances and obligations if we were to be drawn into European war in such a quarrel as this? . . . Some of us felt that the considerations stated above did not touch the true issue. We felt that to stand aside would mean the domination of Germany; the subordination of France and Russia; the isolation of Britain, the hatred of her by both those who had feared and those who had wished for her intervention in the war; and ultimately that Germany would wield the whole power of the Continent. How would she use it as regards Britain? Could anyone feel comfortable about that question? Could anyone give to it truthfully in his heart any but a sinister and foreboding answer?

Source: Edward, Viscount Grey of Fallodon (1925), *Twenty-five Years 1892–1916* (New York: Frederick A. Stokes), pp. 302–3, 325–6.

THE AUSTRIAN ULTIMATUM   **Document 27**

The preamble to the ultimatum of 23 July asserted that the Serbian government was culpable in the assassination because it had tolerated the rise of a subversive movement within its territory and had done nothing to prevent its criminal activities.

. . . the Imp[erial]. and Roy[al]. government find itself obliged to demand from the Servian government an official assurance that it condemns the propaganda directed against Austria-Hungary and in their entirety the dealings whose ultimate aim it is to disjoin parts of the territory belonging to the monarchy and that it pledges itself to suppress with all the means in its power this criminal and terrorist propaganda.

With a view to giving these assurances a solemn character, the Royal Servian Government will publish the following declaration on the first page of its official press-organ of 26th/13th July:

'The Royal Servian government condemns the propaganda directed against Austria-Hungary, that is the entirety of the ambitions, whose ultimate aim it is to disjoin parts of the territory belonging to the Austrian-Hungarian monarchy and regrets sincerely the horrible consequences of these criminal ambitions.

The Royal Servian government regrets that Servian officers and officials have taken part in the propaganda above-mentioned and thereby imperilled the friendly and neighbourly relations, which the Royal government had solemnly promised to cultivate in its declaration of the 31st March 1909.

The Royal government, which condemns and rejects every thought and every attempt to interfere on behalf of the inhabitants of any part of Austria-Hungary, considers it a duty to warn officers, officials and indeed all the inhabitants of the kingdom, that it will in future use great severity against such persons, as will be found guilty of similar doings, which the government will make every effort to suppress.'

This declaration will at the same time be communicated to the Royal army by an order of His Majesty the King, and will besides be published in the official organ of the army.

The Royal Servian government will overmore pledge itself to the following:

1. To suppress every publication likely to inspire hatred and contempt against the monarchy or whose general tendencies are directed against the integrity of the latter;
2. to begin immediately dissolving the society called *Narodna odbrana*; to seize all its means of propaganda and to act in the same way against all the societies and associations in Servia, which are busy with the propaganda against Austria-Hungary; the Royal government will take the necessary measures to prevent these societies continuing their efforts under another name or in another form;
3. to eliminate without delay from public instruction everything that serves or might serve the propaganda against Austria-Hungary, both where teachers or books are concerned;
4. to remove from military service and from the administration all officers and officials who are guilty of having taken part in the propaganda against Austria-Hungary, whose names and the proofs of whose guilt the Imp. and Roy. government will communicate to the Royal government;
5. to consent that Imp. and Roy. officials assist in Servia in the suppressing of the subversive movement directed against the territorial integrity of the monarchy;
6. to have a judicial enquiry instituted against all those who took part in the plot of 28th June, if they are to be found on Servian territory; the

Imp. and Roy. Government will delegate organs who will take an active part in these enquiries;

7. to arrest without delay Major Voija Tankosić and a certain Milan Ciganović, a Servian government official, both compromised by the results of the enquiry;

8. to take effective measures so as to prevent the Servian authorities from taking part in the smuggling of weapons and explosives across the frontier;

    to dismiss from service and severely punish those organs of the frontier service at Schabatz and Loznica, who helped the perpetrators of the crime of Sarajevo to reach Bosnia in safety;

9. to give the Imp. and Roy. government an explanation of the unjustified remarks of high Servian functionaries in Servia as well as in foreign countries, who, notwithstanding their official positions, did not hesitate to speak in hostile terms of Austria-Hungary in interviews given just after the event of 28th June;

10. to inform the Imp. and Roy. government without delay that the measures summed up in the above points have been carried out.

Source: *Austrian Red Book: Official Files Pertaining to Pre-War History*, Part 1 (London: George Allen & Unwin), pp. 60–2.

ITALY AND THE BREAKDOWN OF THE TRIPLE ALLIANCE   **Document 28**

The German ambassador at Rome (von Flotow) reported on 24 July the Italian decision not to support the Austrian demands on Serbia.

During a more or less excited conference lasting several hours with Premier Salandra and Marquis di San Giuliano, the latter argued that the spirit of the Triple Alliance compact demanded that Austria come to an understanding with her allies, before entering upon a move so portentously aggressive. As she had not done so, so far as Italy was concerned, Italy could not consider herself bound in connection with the further consequences of this move.

Furthermore, Article 7 of the Triple Alliance compact . . . required that the contracting parties should come to an agreement previous to any alteration of the *status quo* in the Balkans, and that if either of the contracting parties should bring about a territorial change, the other should be compensated . . .

Source: Max Montgelas and Walther Schücking (eds) (1924), *Outbreak of the World War: German Documents Collected by Karl Kautsky* (trans. Carnegie Endowment for International Peace) (New York: Oxford University Press), p. 183.

Document 29   SERBIA'S REPLY TO THE ULTIMATUM

The Serbian government communicated its reply to the Austro-Hungarian ultimatum on 25 July, asserting that its reply should be sufficient to maintain the peace. Furthermore, while denying responsibility for private acts such as the publication of articles in the newspaper, it agreed to hand over to trial anyone who appeared guilty of complicity in the assassination and to make public the following declaration:

The Royal Government of Serbia condemns all propaganda which may be directed against Austria-Hungary, that is to say, all such tendencies as aim at ultimately detaching from the Austro-Hungarian Monarchy territories which form part thereof, and it sincerely deplores the baneful consequences of these criminal movements. The Royal Government regrets that, according to the communication from the Imperial and Royal Government, certain Serbian officers and officials should have taken part in the above-mentioned propaganda, and thus compromised the good-neighborly relations to which the Royal Serbian Government was solemnly engaged by the declaration of the 18th (31st) March, 1909, which declaration disapproves and repudiates all idea or attempt at interference with the destiny of the inhabitants of any part whatsoever of Austria-Hungary, and it considers it a duty formally to warn officers, officials and entire population of the Kingdom that henceforth it will take the most rigorous steps against all such persons as are guilty of such acts, to prevent and to repress which it will use its utmost endeavor . . .

The Royal Government further undertake:

1. To introduce at the first regular convocation of the Skuptchina a provision into the press law providing for the most severe punishment of incitement to hatred or contempt of the Austro-Hungarian Monarchy, and for taking action against any publication the general tendency of which is directed against the territorial integrity of Austria-Hungary. The Government engages at the approaching revision of the Constitution to cause an amendment to be introduced into Article 22 of the Constitution of such a nature that such publication may be confiscated, a proceeding at present impossible under the categorical terms of Article 22 of the Constitution.

2. The Government possesses no proof, nor does the note of the Imperial and Royal Government furnish it with any, that the *Narodna Odbrana* and other similar societies have committed up to the present any criminal act of this nature through the proceedings of any of their members. Nevertheless, the Royal Government will accept the demand of the Imperial and Royal Government and will dissolve the *Narodna Odbrana* society and every other society which may be directing its efforts against Austria-Hungary.

3. The Royal Serbian Government undertakes to remove without delay from its public educational establishments in Serbia all that serves or

could serve to foment propaganda against Austria-Hungary, whenever the Imperial and Royal Government furnishes them with facts and proofs of this propaganda.

4. The Royal Government also agrees to remove from military service all such persons as the judicial inquiry may have proved to be guilty of acts directed against the integrity of the territory of the Austro-Hungarian Monarchy, and it expects the Imperial and Royal Government to communicate to it at a later date the names and the acts of these officers and officials for the purposes of the proceedings which are to be taken against them.

5. The Royal Government must confess that it does not clearly grasp the meaning or the scope of the demand made by the Imperial and Royal Government that Serbia shall undertake to accept the collaboration of the organs of the Imperial and Royal Government upon its territory, but it declares that it will admit such collaboration as agrees with the principle of international law, with criminal procedure, and with good-neighborly relations.

6. It goes without saying that the Royal Government considers it its duty to open an inquiry against all such persons as are, or eventually may be, implicated in the plot of the 15th (28th) June, and who happen to be within the territory of the Kingdom. As regards the participation in this inquiry of Austro-Hungarian agents or authorities appointed for this purpose by the Imperial and Royal Government, the Royal Government cannot accept such an arrangement, as it would be a violation of the Constitution and of the law of criminal procedure; nevertheless, in concrete cases communications as to the results of the investigation in question might be given to the Austro-Hungarian agents.

7. The Royal Government proceeded, on the very evening of the delivery of the note, to arrest Commandant Voislav Tankositch. As regards Milan Ciganovitch, who is a subject of the Austro-Hungarian Monarchy and who up to the 15th (28th) June was employed (on probation) by the directorate of railways, it has not yet been possible to arrest him.

The Austro-Hungarian Government is requested to be so good as to supply as soon as possible, in the customary form, the presumptive evidence of guilt, as well as the eventual proofs of guilt which have been collected up to the present, at the inquiry of Serajevo, for the purposes of the latter inquiry.

8. The Serbian Government will reinforce and extend the measures which have been taken for preventing the illicit traffic of arms and explosives across the frontier. It goes without saying that it will immediately order an inquiry and will severely punish the frontier officials on the Schabatz-Loznica line who have failed in their duty and allowed the authors of the crime of Serajevo to pass.

9. The Royal Government will gladly give explanations of the remarks made by its officials, whether in Serbia or abroad, in interviews after the crime, and which, according to the statement of the Imperial and Royal Government, were hostile towards the Monarchy, as soon as the Imperial and Royal Government has communicated to them the passages in question in these remarks, and as soon as they have shown that the remarks were actually made by the said officials, although the Royal Government will itself take steps to collect evidence and proofs.

10. The Royal Government will inform the Imperial and Royal Government of the execution of the measures comprised under the above heads, in so far as this has not already been done by the present note, as soon as each measure has been ordered and carried out.

If the Imperial and Royal Government is not satisfied with this reply, the Serbian Government, considering that it is not to the common interest to precipitate the solution of this question, are ready, as always, to accept a pacific understanding, either by referring this question to the decision of the International Tribunal of The Hague, or to the Great Powers which took part in the drawing up of the declaration made by the Serbian Government on the 18th (31st) March, 1909.

Source: Max Montgelas and Walther Schücking (eds) (1924), *Outbreak of the World War: German Documents Collected by Karl Kautsky* (trans. Carnegie Endowment for International Peace) (New York: Oxford University Press), pp. 251–4.

Document 30   BRITAIN'S RESPONSE TO THE SERBIAN REPLY

Sir Edward Grey believed that the Serbs had acceded to the Austrian demands almost in their entirety, and that this ought to be sufficient to prevent war. On 27 July the German ambassador in London, Lichnowsky, warned of the consequences should Germany now fail to restrain Austria-Hungary from attacking Serbia.

Sir E. Grey had me call on him just now and requested me to inform Your Excellency as follows:

The Serbian Chargé d'Affaires had just transmitted to him the text of the Serbian reply to the Austrian note. It appeared from the reply that Serbia had agreed to the Austrian demands to an extent such as he would never have believed possible; except in one point, the participation of Austrian officials in the judicial investigation, Serbia had actually agreed to everything that had been demanded of her. It was plain that this compliance of Serbia's *was to be attributed solely to the pressure exerted from Petersburg.*

Should Austria fail to be satisfied with this reply, in other words, should this reply not be accepted at Vienna as a foundation for peaceful negotiations, or should Austria proceed even to the occupation of Belgrade, which lay quite defenseless before her, it would then be absolutely evident that Austria was only seeking an excuse for crushing Serbia. And thus that Russia and Russian influence in the Balkans were to be struck at through Serbia. It was plain that Russia could not regard such action with equanimity, and would have to accept it as a direct challenge. The result would be the most frightful war that Europe had ever seen, and no one could tell to what such a war might lead.

We had repeatedly, and even yesterday, stated the Minister, turned to him with the request that he *make a plea for moderation at Petersburg. He had always gladly complied with this request* and during the last crisis had subjected himself to reproaches from Russia to the effect that he was placing himself too much on our side and too little on theirs. Now he was turning to us with the request that we should make use of our influence at Vienna either to get them to accept the reply from Belgrade as satisfactory or as the basis for conferences. He was convinced that it lay in our hands to bring the matter to a settlement by means of the proper representations, and he would regard it as a good augury for the future *if we two should once again succeed in assuring the peace of Europe by means of our mutual influence on our allies.*

I found the Minister irritated for the first time. He spoke with great seriousness and seemed absolutely to expect that we should successfully make use of our influence to settle the matter. He is also going to make a statement in the House of Commons today in which he is to express his point of view. In any event, I am convinced that in case it should come to war after all, we should no longer be able to count on British sympathy or British support, as every evidence of ill-will would be seen in Austria's procedure. Also, everybody here is convinced, and I hear it in the mouths of all my colleagues, that the key to the situation is to be found in Berlin, and that, if peace is seriously desired there, Austria can be restrained from prosecuting, as Sir E. Grey expresses it, a foolhardy policy.

Source: Max Montgelas and Walther Schücking (eds) (1924), *Outbreak of the World War: German Documents Collected by Karl Kautsky* (trans. Carnegie Endowment for International Peace) (New York: Oxford University Press), pp. 243–4.

GERMANY'S RESPONSE TO THE SERBIAN REPLY   **Document 31**

The kaiser's response to the Serbian reply was remarkably similar to Grey's. But he proposes a 'hostage' to assure that the 'Oriental' liars and tricksters live up to their words. At 10 a.m. on 28 July he sent this memorandum to his foreign secretary:

After reading over the Serbian reply, which I received this morning, I am convinced that on the whole the wishes of the Danube Monarchy have been acceded to. The few reservations that Serbia makes in regard to individual points could, according to my opinion, be settled by negotiation. But it contains the announcement *orbe et urbi* of a capitulation of the most humiliating kind, and as a result, *every cause for war* falls to the ground.

Nevertheless, the piece of paper, like its contents, can be considered as of little value so long as it is not translated into *deeds*. The Serbs are Orientals, therefore liars, tricksters, and masters of evasion. In order that these beautiful promises may be turned to truth and facts, a *douce violence* must be exercised. This should be so arranged that Austria would receive a HOSTAGE (Belgrade), as a guaranty for the enforcement and carrying out of the promises, and should occupy it until the *petita* had ACTUALLY been complied with. This is also necessary in order to give the army, now UNNECESSARILY mobilized for the third time, the external *satisfaction d'honneur* of an ostensible success in the eyes of the world, and to make it possible for it to feel that it had at least stood on foreign soil. Unless this were done, the abandonment of the campaign might be the cause of a wave of bad feeling against the Monarchy, which would be dangerous in the highest degree. In case Your Excellency shares my views, I propose that we say to Austria: Serbia has been forced to retreat in a very humiliating manner, and we offer our congratulations. Naturally, as a result, EVERY CAUSE FOR WAR HAS VANISHED. But a GUARANTY that the promises WILL BE CARRIED OUT is unquestionably necessary. That could be secured by means of the TEMPORARY military occupation of a portion of Serbia, similar to the way we kept troops stationed in France in 1871 until the billions were paid. ON THIS BASIS, I am ready to MEDIATE FOR PEACE with Austria. Any proposals or protests to the contrary by other nations I should refuse regardless, especially as all of them have made more or less open appeals to me to assist in maintaining peace. This I will do in my own way, and as sparingly of Austria's NATIONALISTIC FEELING, and of the HONOR OF HER ARMS as possible. For the latter has already been appealed to on the part of the highest War Lord, and is about to respond to the appeal. Consequently it is absolutely necessary that it receive a visible *satisfaction d'honneur*; this is the *prerequisite* of my mediation. Therefore Your Excellency will submit a proposal to me along the lines sketched out; which shall be communicated to Vienna. I have had Plessen write along the lines indicated above to the Chief of the General Staff, who is entirely in accord with my views.

Source: Max Montgelas and Walther Schücking (eds) (1924), *Outbreak of the World War: German Documents Collected by Karl Kautsky* (trans. Carnegie Endowment for International Peace) (New York: Oxford University Press), pp. 273–4.

THE RUSSIAN MOBILIZATION   **Document 32**

The French Ambassador in St Petersburg, Maurice Paléologue, recorded Russia's explanation of her decision to commence a general mobilization.

29 July

At eleven o'clock tonight, Nicholas-Alexandrovitch Basily, Deputy-Director of the chancellery of the Foreign Office, appeared at my embassy. He came to tell me that the imperious language used by the German Ambassador this afternoon has decided the Russian Government (1) to order this very night the mobilization of the thirteen corps earmarked for operations against Austria-Hungary; (2) secretly to commence general mobilization.

These last words made me jump:

'Isn't it possible for them to confine themselves – provisionally at any rate – to a partial mobilization?'

'No. The question has just been gone into thoroughly by a council of our highest military officers. They have come to the conclusion that in existing circumstances the Russian Government has no choice between partial and general mobilization as from the technical point of view a partial mobilization could be carried out only at the price of dislocating the entire machinery of general mobilization. So if to-day we stopped at mobilizing the thirteen corps destined for operations against Austria and tomorrow Germany decided to give her ally military support, we should be powerless to defend ourselves on the frontiers of Poland and East Prussia.'

Source: Maurice Paléologue (1923), *An Ambassador's Memoirs* (trans. F.A. Holt) (London: Hutchinson), vol. 1, p. 32.

GERMANY AND THE NEXT WAR   **Document 33**

Above and beyond diplomacy – or lying below the surface of politics – was the profound and widespread belief that war was natural, necessary and right. Here, the German general Bernhardi expresses the views of many who warned of the debilitating effects of pacifism.

Everyone will, within certain limits, admit that the endeavours to diminish the dangers of war and to mitigate the sufferings which war entails are justifiable. It is an incontestable fact that war temporarily disturbs industrial life, interrupts quiet economic development, brings widespread misery with it, and emphasizes the primitive brutality of man. It is therefore a most desirable consummation if wars for trivial reasons should be rendered impossible, and if efforts are made to restrict the evils which follow necessarily in the train of war, so far as is compatible with the essential nature of war. All that the Hague Peace Congress has accomplished in this limited sphere deserves, like every permissible humanization of war, universal acknowledgment. But it is quite another matter if the object is to abolish war entirely, and to deny its necessary place in historical development.

This aspiration is directly antagonistic to the great universal laws which rule all life. War is a biological necessity of the first importance, a regulative element in the life of mankind which cannot be dispensed with, since without it an unhealthy development will follow, which excludes every advancement of the race, and therefore all real civilisation. 'War is the father of all things.' [Heraclitus of Ephesus] The sages of antiquity recognized this long before Darwin.

The struggle for existence is, in the life of Nature, the basis of all healthy development. All existing things show themselves to be the result of contesting forces. So in the life of man the struggle is not merely the destructive, but the life-giving principle. 'To supplant or to be supplanted is the essence of life,' says Goethe, and the strong life gains the upper hand. The law of the stronger holds good everywhere. Those forms survive which are able to procure themselves the most favourable conditions of life, and to assert themselves in the universal economy of Nature. The weaker succumb. This struggle is regulated and restrained by the unconscious sway of biological laws and by the interplay of opposite forces. In the plant world and the animal world this process is worked out in unconscious tragedy. In the human race it is consciously carried out, and regulated by social ordinances. The man of strong will and strong intellect tries by every means to assert himself, the ambitious strive to rise . . . In the extrasocial struggle, in war, that nation will conquer which can throw into the scale the greatest physical, mental, moral, material, and political power, and is therefore the best able to defend itself. War will furnish such a nation with favourable vital conditions, enlarged possibilities of expansion and widened influence, and thus promote the progress of mankind; for it is clear that those intellectual and moral factors which insure superiority in war are also those which render possible a general progressive development. They confer victory because the elements of progress are latent in them. Without war, inferior or decaying races would easily choke the growth of healthy budding elements, and a universal decadence would follow . . .

If we sum up our arguments, we shall see that, from the most opposite aspects, the efforts directed towards the abolition of war must not only be termed foolish, but absolutely immoral, and must be stigmatized as unworthy of the human race . . . The weak nation is to have the same right to live as the powerful and vigorous nation . . .

With the cessation of the unrestricted competition, whose ultimate appeal is to arms, all real progress would soon be checked, and a moral and intellectual stagnation would ensue which must end in degeneration . . . The apostles of peace draw large sections of a nation into the spell of their Utopian efforts, and they thus introduce an element of weakness into the national life; they cripple the justifiable national pride in independence, and support a nerveless opportunity policy by surrounding it with the glamour of a higher humanity, and by offering it specious reasons for disguising its own weakness. They thus play the game of their less scrupulous enemies, just as the Prussian policy, steeped in the ideas of universal peace, did in 1805 and 1806, and brought the State to the brink of destruction . . .

Every means must therefore be employed to oppose these visionary schemes. They must be publicly denounced as what they really are – as an unhealthy and feeble Utopia, or a cloak for political machinations. Our people must learn to see that *the maintenance of peace never can or may be the goal of a policy* . . . The inevitableness, the idealism, and the blessing of war, as an indispensable and stimulating law of development, must be repeatedly emphasized. The apostles of the peace idea must be confronted with Goethe's manly words:

> Dreams of a peaceful day?
> Let him dream who may!
> 'War' is our rallying cry,
> Onward to victory!

Source: General Friedrich von Bernhardi (1914), *Germany and the Next War* (trans. Allien H. Powles) (London: Edward Arnold), pp. 18–20, 34–7.

Further Reading

To describe the literature on the origins of the First World War as 'vast' would be to understate the situation. Simply to list all of the books, articles and essays on the subject would require a book several times longer than this one. What follows, then, is an attempt to identify those works which seem most helpful for English-speaking students to pursue the subject in greater detail. Although it cannot be comprehensive I believe it does include everything worth reading on the subject in English (up to 2003). The place of publication is London, unless otherwise noted.

Sources

Collections of diplomatic documents may be found in: **British Documents on the Origins of the War**, G.P. Gooch and Harold Temperley (eds), 11 vols (1927–38); and the four volumes of **German Diplomatic Documents: 1871–1914**, E.T.S. Dugdale (ed.) (1928). Also helpful is the collection devoted to the July crisis edited by Immanuel Geiss: **July 1914: The Outbreak of the First World War. Selected Documents** (New York, 1968). A new collection of documents, **Soldiers, Statesmen and July 1914** (New York), edited by Van Wyk, Russel Wyk and Samuel R. Williamson is due to appear in 2003. **The Kaiser's Letters to the Tsar** (1920), N.F. Grant (ed.), provides a fascinating insight into the mind of Wilhelm II, while the four volumes of **The Holstein Papers** (Cambridge, 1955–63), edited by Norman Rich and M.H. Fisher, provide equally fascinating material on the inner workings of the German diplomatic system. **The Journals and Letters of Reginald Viscount Esher**, M.V. Brett and Oliver, Viscount Esher (eds) (4 vols, 1938) are interesting for a behind-the-scenes view of an 'insider' in British strategic and political affairs; while **The Diary of Edward Goschen 1900–14**, edited by C.H.D. Howard (1980) contains much useful material. There are some interesting essays on the role of governments in publishing documents related to war origins in Keith Wilson (ed.), *Forging the Collective Memory: Government and International Historians through Two World Wars* (Oxford, 1996).

There are numerous memoirs and autobiographies available – primarily from politicians and diplomats. These need to be approached with caution as, by their very nature, they tend to be self-serving in various ways – sometimes defending themselves from post-war charges for the failure of their policy or diplomacy, sometimes attacking their pre-war enemies. Nevertheless, such materials continue to provide interesting perspectives that might otherwise be neglected. For Germany, see Bernhard von Bülow, *Memoirs*, 4 vols (New York, 1930–32); the German ambassador to London, Prince Lichnowsky, *My Mission to London* (1918) and Alfred von Tirpitz, *My Memoirs*, 2 vols (1919). For France, we have the memoirs of two diplomats: Jules Cambon, *The Diplomat* (1931) and Maurice Paléologue, *An Ambassador's Memoirs*, 3 vols (1923–25). For Italy, we have the memoirs of the politician Giovanni Giolitti, *Memoirs of my Life* (1923).

Because of the interest in revolutionary Russia a surprising number of memoirs have appeared in English. Two especially helpful sources come from ministers of foreign affairs: Izvol'skii, *The Memoirs of Alexander Iswolki* (1920) and Serge Sazonov, *Fateful Years 1909–16* (1928). A number of diplomatic memoirs are available: D.I. Abrikossov, *Revelations of a Russian Diplomat: The Memoirs of Dmitrii I. Abrikossow* (Seattle, 1964); Nikolai Bazili, *Nicolas De Basily, Diplomat of Imperial Russia, 1903–1917: Memoirs* (Stanford, CA 1973); Andrei Kalmykov, *Memoirs of a Russian Diplomat; Outposts of the Empire, 1893–1917* (New Haven, CT, 1971); A.V. Nekliudov, *Diplomatic Reminiscences Before and During the World War, 1911–1917* (1920); A.A. Savinskii, *Recollections of a Russian Diplomat* (1927); and Evgenii Shelking, *Recollections of a Russian Diplomat; the Suicide of Monarchies* (New York, 1918). Useful political reminiscences may be found in: Sergei Witte, *The Memoirs of Count Witte* (1990); V.N. Kokovtsov, *Out of My Past; the Memoirs of Count Kokovtsov, Russian Minister of Finance, 1904–1914* (Stanford, CA, 1935); and P.N. Miliukov, *Political Memoirs, 1905–1917* (Ann Arbor, MI, 1967). A rare military memoir is Anton Denikin's *The Career of a Tsarist Officer: Memoirs, 1872–1916* (Minneapolis, MN, 1975), while an interesting 'bureaucratic' memoir is Aleksandr Mosolov's *At the Court of the Last Tsar; Being the Memoirs of A.A. Mossolov, Head of the Court Chancellery 1900–1916* (1935).

For Britain, the most useful sources are: the memoirs of Sir Edward Grey, *Twenty-five Years 1892–1916*, 2 vols (1925); R.B. Haldane, *Before the War* (1920); Charles Hardinge, *Old Diplomacy* (1947); Arthur Hardinge, *A Diplomatist in Europe* (1927); and the first volume of George Buchanan's *My Mission to Russia and Other Diplomatic Memories* (1923). Finally, an interesting journalistic perspective is provided by Valentine Chirol in *Fifty Years in a Changing World* (1927).

Historiography

Most of the early historical work on the war's origins were inspired by the war guilt controversy; notable among the revisionist accounts is Harry Elmer Barnes, *The Genesis of the World War: An Introduction to the Problem of War Guilt* (New York, 1927); this was replied to by Bernadotte Schmitt in *The Coming of the War, 1914*, 2 vols (New York, 1930) and Sidney B. Fay's *The Origins of the World War*, 2 vols (New York, 1928). Interesting articles on the war guilt controversy include Konrad H. Jarausch, 'World Power or Tragic Fate? The Kriegsschuldfrage as Historical Neurosis', *Central European History*, 5 (1972): 72–92; E.L. Evans and J.O. Baylen, 'History as Propaganda: The German Foreign Office and the "Enlightenment" of American Historians on the War Guilt Question', *Canadian Journal of History*, 10 (1975): 185–208; Selig Adler, 'The War-Guilt Question and American Disillusionment, 1918–1928', *Journal of Modern History*, 23 (1951): 1–28; and Holger Herwig, 'Clio Deceived: Patriotic Self-Censorship in Germany After the Great War', *International Security*, 12 (1987): 5–44. The book by Warren I. Cohen, *The American Revisionists: The Lessons of Intervention in World War I* (Chicago, IL, 1967) remains the standard work on American historiography. Brief excerpts from a variety of controversialists are given in Samuel R. Williamson Jr (ed.), *The Origins of a Tragedy: July 1914* (St Louis, MO, 1981).

No student of the subject should overlook several classic works: A.J.P. Taylor's *The Struggle for Mastery in Europe* (Oxford, 1954) – which was his masterpiece; the immensely detailed work by the Italian journalist Luigi Albertini, *The Origins of the War of 1914*, 3 vols (1952–7); and the two books by William L. Langer, *European Alliances and Alignments, 1871–1890* (2nd edn, New York, 1950) and *The Diplomacy of Imperialism, 1890–92* (2nd edn, New York, 1952). Other large-scale surveys and interpretations worth reading are: Laurence Lafore, *The Long Fuse* (1966) – who emphasises the role of Austria-Hungary and the problem of Balkan nationalism; L.C.F. Turner, who emphasises the role of the military and Russian ambitions in *Origins of the First World War* (1970) and James Joll's outstanding *The Origins of the First World War*, which, in essence, is a series of thoughtful and stimulating essays on each of the major 'interpretations' of war origins (1984).

The controversy that broke out after the publication of Fritz Fischer's *Germany's Aims in the First World War* (1967) has stimulated a considerable literature of its own – and also see Fischer's sequel, with a clearer exposition of the essential thesis, *War of Illusions: German Policies from 1911 to 1914* (New York, 1975). Valuable – and brief – introductions to the debate itself may be found in James Joll, 'The 1914 Debate Continues. Fritz Fischer and His Critics', *Past & Present*, 34 (1966): 100–13; and Fritz Stern, 'German Historians and the War: Fritz Fischer and His Critics', in Fritz Stern (ed.), *The Failure of Illiberalism: Essays on the Political Culture of Modern Germany* (New York, 1972): 77–118; and in Immanuel Geiss, 'The Outbreak of the First World War and German War Aims', *Journal of Contemporary History*, 1 (1966): 75–92. An overview of the debate from postwar revisionism onward is provided by John W. Langdon in *July 1914: The Long Debate, 1918–1990* (Oxford, 1991). Numerous additional essays may be found in the works edited by Hans W. Koch, *The Origins of the First World War: great power rivalry and war aims* (1972) and Gregor Schöllingen, *Escape into War? The Foreign Policy of Imperial Germany* (New York, 1990).

Another, more recent, debate was stimulated by the argument of Arno J. Mayer that the old socio-political élites of Europe resorted to war in order to forestall reform or revolution at home, which is briefly summarized in his 'Domestic origins of the First World War', in L. Krieger and F. Stern (eds), *The Responsibility of Power* (New York, 1967): 286–300; a larger exposition of this theme may be found in his *The Persistence of the Old Regime: Europe to the Great War* (New York, 1981). The responses to this argument include Donald Lammers, 'Arno Mayer and the British decision for war', *Journal of British Studies*, 12 (1973): 137–65; Wolfgang J. Mommsen, 'Domestic Factors in German Foreign Policy before 1914', *Central European History*, 6 (1973): 3–43; M.R. Gordon, 'Domestic conflict and the origins of the First World War: the British and the German cases', *Journal of Modern History*, 46 (1974): 191–226; David French, 'The Edwardian crisis and the origins of the First World War', *International History Review*, 4 (1982): 207–21; Standish Meacham, 'The sense of an impending clash: English working-class unrest before the First World War', *American Historical Review*, 77 (1972): 1343–64; and Niall Ferguson, 'Public Finance and National Security: The Domestic Origins of the First World War Revisited', *Past & Present*, 142 (1994): 141–68.

The great powers and the states system

Good overviews of the international history of the century preceding 1914 may be found in F.R. Bridge, and Roger Bullen, *The Great Powers and the European States System, 1815–1914* (1980), and in Norman Rich, *Great Power Diplomacy, 1814–1914* (New York, 1992). The survey by Joachim

Remak, *The Origins of World War I, 1870–1914* (New York, 1967) is still useful. Lectures on each of the great powers may be found in R. J. W. Evans and H. Pogge von Strandmann (eds), *The Coming of the First World War* (Oxford, 1988). A good survey of European affairs generally in the pre-war period is Oron J. Hale, *The Great Illusion, 1900–1914* (New York, 1971) while students who wish to grapple with economic developments should begin with Alan S. Milward and S.B. Saul, *The Development of the Economies of Continental Europe 1850–1914* (Cambridge, MA, 1977).

Germany

On Germany in general, see Gordon Craig, *Germany, 1866–1945* (Oxford, 1980); on foreign policy in particular, see Volker R. Berghahn, *Germany and the Approach of War in 1914* (1973) and/or Immanuel Geiss, *German Foreign Policy, 1871–1914* (1976); briefer introductions may be found in Holger H. Herwig, 'Industry, Empire and the First World War', in *Modern Germany Reconsidered*, Gordon Martel (ed.) (1991): 54–73; and/or David E. Kaiser, 'Germany and the Origins of the First World War', *Journal of Modern History*, **55** (1983): 442–74. On diplomats see Lamar Cecil, *The German Diplomatic Service 1871–1914* (Princeton, NJ, 1976). On nationalism see Geoff Eley **Reshaping the Right: Radical Nationalism and Political Change after Bismarck** (1980).

Biographical works on the most important personalities include Lothar Gall's **Bismarck: The White Revolutionary**, 2 vols (1986) and Otto Pflanze's **Bismarck and the Development of Germany**, 3 vols (Princeton, NJ, 1990), while a classic still worth reading is Joseph V. Fuller, **Bismarck's Diplomacy at its Zenith** (Cambridge, MA, 1922). On Kaiser Wilhelm II, there are an unusual number of very interesting works: John C.G. Röhl's, **Young Wilhelm** (Cambridge, 1998) is masterful and richly detailed, but ends with his accession in 1888; the second volume has been published in German and the translation should be available in 2003; Christopher Clark's **Kaiser Wilhelm II** (2000) covers his entire life, as does Lamar Cecil's **Wilhelm II**, 2 vols (1989 and 1996). There are two excellent studies of the Kaiser's inner circle: Isabel V. Hull, **The Entourage of Kaiser Wilhelm II 1888–1918** (Cambridge, 1982) and John Röhl, **The Kaiser and his Court: Wilhelm II and the Government of Germany** (Cambridge, 1994); see also the essays in Röhl and N. Sombart (eds), **Kaiser Wilhelm II: New Interpretations** (Cambridge, 1982) and Lamar Cecil, 'William II and his Russian "Colleagues"', in Carole Fink, Isabel Hull and MacGregor Knox (eds), **German Nationalism and European Response**, **1890–1945** (Norman, OK, 1985): 95–134. On Bethmann Hollweg, see K.H. Jarausch, **The Enigmatic Chancellor: Bethmann Hollweg and the Hubris of Imperial Germany** (New Haven, CT, 1973), but also the essay by Fritz Stern, 'Bethmann Hollweg and the war: the limits of responsibility', in Leonard

Krieger and Fritz Stern (eds), *The Responsibility of Power* (Garden City, NY, 1967): 252–85. On Bernhard von Bülow, see *The Chancellor as Courtier: Bernhard von Bülow and the Governance of Germany 1900–9* (Cambridge, 1990) and Terry Cole, 'Kaiser versus Chancellor: The Crisis of Billow's Chancellorship 1905–06', in Richard J. Evans (ed.), *Society and Politics in Wilhelmine Germany* (1978): 40–70. And finally, Wayne C. Thompson, *In the Eye of the Storm: Kurt Riezler and the Crises of Modern Germany* (Iowa City, IA, 1980).

The role of the army and navy in German politics may be followed in Ivo N. Lambi, *The Navy and German Power Politics, 1862–1914* (Boston, MA, 1984) and Martin Kitchen, *The German Officer Corps, 1890–1914* (Oxford, 1968). Some useful articles and essays are: Geoff Eley, 'Sammlungspolitik, social imperialism and the Navy Law of 1898', in Eley, *From Unification to Nazism* (1986): 110–53; Dennis Showalter, 'Army and Society in Imperial Germany: The Pains of Modernization', *Journal of Contemporary History*, 18 (1983): 583–618, and his 'Army, State and Society in Germany, 1871–1914: An Interpretation', in Jack R. Dukes and Joachim Remak (eds), *Another Germany: A Reconsideration of the Imperial Era* (Boulder, CO, 1988): 1–18; and Jonathan Steinberg, 'The Kaiser's navy and German society', *Past & Present*, 28 (1964): 102–10.

Austria-Hungary

On Austria-Hungary generally, see C.A. Macartney, *The Habsburg Empire, 1790–1918* (1968); John W. Mason, *The Dissolution of the Austro-Hungarian Empire, 1867–1918* (New York, 1985); the essays by Joachim Remak, 'The Healthy Invalid: How Doomed the Habsburg Monarchy?', *Journal of Modern History*, 41 (1969): 127–43; and the historiographical overview by Leslie C. Tihany, 'The Austro-Hungarian Compromise, 1867–1918: A Half Century of Diagnosis; Fifty Years of Post-Mortem', *Central European History*, 2 (1969): 114–38. On foreign policy in particular, see the survey by F.R. Bridge, *From Sadowa to Sarajevo: The Foreign Policy of Austria-Hungary, 1866–1914* (1972) which is still useful, but has been superseded by Samuel R. Williamson Jr, *Austria-Hungary and the Origins of the First World War* (1994). On the foreign office see István Diószegi, *Hungarians in the Ballhausplatz: Studies on the Austro-Hungarian Common Foreign Policy* (Budapest, 1983) and Helmut Rumpler, 'The Foreign Ministry of Austria and Austria-Hungary, 1848 to 1918', in Zara Steiner (ed.), *The Times' Survey of Foreign Ministries of the World* (1982): 49–58.

On politics and personalities see Gabor Vermes, *István Tisza: The Liberal Vision and Conservative Statecraft of a Magyar Nationalist* (New York, 1985); John W. Boyer, 'The End of the Old Regime: Visions of Political

Reform in late Imperial Austria', *Journal of Modern History*, 43 (1986): 159–93; Samuel R. Williamson Jr, 'Influence, power and the policy process: the case of Franz Ferdinand, 1906–1914', *Historical Journal, 17* (1974): 417–34; and Solomon Wank, 'The appointment of Count Berchtold as Austro-Hungarian Foreign Minister', *Journal of Central European Affairs*, 23 (1963–4): 143–51.

On the role of the military see Istvan Deak, *Beyond Nationalism: A Social and Political History of the Habsburg Officer Corps, 1848–1918* (New York, 1990); Gunther E. Rothenberg, *The Army of Francis Joseph* (West Lafayette, IN, 1976) and Norman Stone, 'Army and Society in the Habsburg monarchy, 1900–1914' *Past & Present*, 33 (1966): 95–111.

On the economy see David F. Good, *The Economic Rise of the Habsburg Empire 1750–1914* (Berkeley, CA, 1984). On Balkan policy see F.R. Bridge, 'Relations with Austria-Hungary and the Balkan states, 1906–1908', in F.H. Hinsley (ed.), *British Foreign Policy under Sir Edward Grey* (Cambridge, 1977): 165–77; and Solomon Wank, 'Aehrenthal and the Sanjak railway project: a reappraisal', *Slavonic and East European Review*, 42 (1964): 353–69.

On the issue of nationalities within the empire see Keith Hitchins, *The Nationality Problem in Austria-Hungary: The Reports of Alexander Vaida to Archduke Franz Ferdinand's Chancellery* (Leiden, 1974) and his article, 'The Nationality Problem in Hungary: István Tisza and the Rumanian National Party, 1906–1914', *Journal of Modern History*, 53 (1981): 619–51; F. Pölöskei, 'István Tisza's Policy toward the Romanian Nationalities on the Eve of World War I', *Acta Historica: Academiae Scientiarum* Hungaricae, 18 (1972): 267–91; and the two essays by Solomon Wank, 'Foreign Policy and the Nationality Problem in Austria-Hungary, 1867–1914', *Austrian History Yearbook*, 3 (1967): 37–56, and 'The Growth of Nationalism in the Habsburg Monarchy, 1848–1918', *East Central Europe/L'Europe du Centre-Est*, 10 parts 1–2 (1983): 165–79. See also Robert A. Kann, *The Multinational Empire: Nationalism and National Reform in the Habsburg Monarchy, 1848–1918*, 2 vols (New York, 1950); Charles Jelavich, *South Slav Nationalisms: Textbooks and Yugoslav Union Before 1914* (Columbus, OH, 1990) and 'The Croatian Problem in the Habsburg Empire in the Nineteenth Century' in *Austrian History Yearbook*, 3, pt. 2 (1967): 83–115; also in the same issue – Bogdan Krizman, 'The Croatians in the Habsburg Monarchy in the Nineteenth Century' (116–58) and Wayne Vucinich, 'The Serbs in Austria-Hungary' (3–47). Also see John Leslie, 'The Antecedents of Austria-Hungary's War Aims', *Wiener Beiträge zur Geschichte der Neuzeit*, 20 (1993): 307–94; and Nicholas Miller, 'Two Strategies in Serbian Politics in Croatia and Hungary Before the First World War' *Nationalities Papers*, 23 (1995): 327–51.

Italy

On Italy, the politics of united Italy may be studied in: R. Drake, *Byzantium for Rome: the politics of nostalgia in Umbertian Italy, 1878–1900* (Chapel Hill, NC, 1980); F.J. Coppa, *Planning, Protectionism and Politics in Liberal Italy: economics and politics in the Giolittian age* (Washington DC, 1971); A.W. Salamone, *Italy in the Giolittian Era: Italian democracy in the making, 1900–14* (Philadelphia, PA, 1960); and J.A. Thayer, *Italy and the Great War: politics and culture, 1870–1915* (Madison, WI, 1964).

The outstanding work on Italian foreign policy is to be found in two books by Richard J.B. Bosworth: the immensely detailed *Italy, the least of the Great Powers: Italian foreign policy before the First World War* (Cambridge, 1979) and the shorter survey, *Italy and the Approach of the First World War* (1983). For 1914–15 in particular, see W.A. Renzi, *In the Shadow of the Sword: Italy's Neutrality and Entrance into the Great War, 1914–15* (New York, 1987). See also R.A. Webster, *Industrial Imperialism in Italy, 1908–1915* (Berkeley, CA, 1975), and an older work that begins the story farther back is C.J. Lowe and F. Marzari, *Italian Foreign Policy, 1870–1940* (1975). Some articles worth reading are: C.G. Haines, 'Italian Irredentism during the Near Eastern Crisis 1875–78', *Journal of Modern History*, 9 (1937): 23–47; S. Jones, 'Antonio Salandra and the Politics of Italian Intervention in the First World War', *European History Quarterly*, 15 (1985): 157–74; A. Tamborra, 'The Rise of Italian industry and the Balkans (1900–1914)', *Journal of European Economic History*, 3 (1974): 87–120; W.A. Renzi, 'Italy's neutrality and entrance into the Great War: a re-examination', *American Historical Review*, 73 (1968): 1414–32; and R. Pryce, 'Italy and the outbreak of the First World War', *Cambridge Historical Journal*, 11 (1954): 219–27. Two good books on the role of the military are: John Gooch, *Army, State, and Society in Italy, 1870–1915* (New York, 1989) and J. Whittam, *The Politics of the Italian Army, 1861–1918* (1977).

Russia

On Russia, a good short survey of Russia generally is John F. Hutchinson, *Late Imperial Russia* (1999); more detailed is Hans Rogger, *Russia in the Age of Modernization and Revolution, 1881–1917* (1983). A broad survey of foreign policy may be found in Barbara Jelavich, *A Century of Russian Foreign Policy* (New York, 1964), but on the origins of the war in particular Dominic C.B. Lieven, *Russia and the Origins of the First World War* (1983) is excellent; and see Lieven as well on: *Nicholas II: Tsar of All the Russias* (1993) and *Russia's Rulers under the Old Régime* (New Haven, CT, 1989). Works on politics that are worth reading and bear upon Russia's role in war origins are: D.M. McDonald, *United Government and Foreign Policy in Russia 1900–1914* (Cambridge, MA, 1992); Peter Gatrell, *Government,* industry and rearmament in Russia, 1900–1914 (Cambridge, 1994); Geoffrey Hosking, *The Russian Constitutional Experiment: Government and Duma, 1907–1914* (Cambridge, 1973); Theodore Von Laue, *Sergei Witte and the Industrialization of Russia* (New York, 1974); E.C. Thaden, *Conservative nationalism in nineteenth-century Russia* (Seattle, WA, 1964) and the collection of essays edited by him, *Russification in the Baltic Provinces and Finland, 1855–1914* (Princeton, NJ, 1981); Louise McReynolds, *The News under Russia's Old Régime: The Development of a Mass-Circulation Press* (Princeton, NJ, 1991); Michael B. Petrovich, *The Emergence of Russian Panslavism, 1856–1870* (New York, 1958); and A. Walicki, *The Slavophile Controversy* (Oxford, 1975). W.C. Fuller Jr, *Civil-Military Conflict in Imperial Russia 1881–1914* (Cambridge, 1981) is good on the role of the military.

The revolution of 1905 was a vital turning-point in Russian politics and foreign policy. It can be studied in Abraham Ascher, *The Revolution of 1905*, 2 vols (Stanford, CA, 1988–92); Don C. Rawson, *Russian Rightists and the Revolution of 1905* (Cambridge, 1995); and Andrew M. Verner, *The Crisis of Russian Autocracy: Nicholas II and the 1905 Revolution* (Princeton, NJ, 1990).

The 'nationality' issue was an important one in Russia and is often overlooked by students of international history, except for the phenomenon of Panslavism. See Theodore R. Weeks, *Nation and State in Late Imperial Russia: Nationalism and Russification on the Western Frontier, 1863–1914* (DeKalb, IL, 1996); Robert E. Blobaum, *Rewolucja: Russian Poland, 1904–1907* (Ithaca, NY, 1995); Stephen Corrsin, *Warsaw before the First World War: Poles and Jews in the Third City of the Russian Empire, 1880–1914* (Boulder, CO, 1989); and William W. Hagen, *Germans, Poles and Jews: The Nationality Conflict in the Prussian East, 1771–1914* (Chicago, IL, 1980).

Articles and essays that bear particularly on foreign and military matters are: J. Bushnell, 'Peasants in Uniform: The Tsarist Army as a Peasant Society', *Journal of Social History*, 13 (1980): 565–76 and 'The Tsarist Officer Corps, 1881–1914: Customs, Duties, Inefficiency', *American Historical Review*, 86 (1981): 753–80; I.V. Bestuzhev, 'Russian foreign policy, February–June 1914', *Journal of Contemporary History*, 1 (1966): 93–112; John F. Hutchinson, 'The Octobrists and the future of Russia as a great power', *Slavonic and East European Review*, 50 (1972): 220–37; G.H. Bolsover, 'Izvol'sky and the Reform of the Russian Ministry of Foreign Affairs' *Slavonic and East European Review*, 63 (1985): 21–40; Dominic Lieven, 'Pro-Germans and Russian Foreign Policy 1890–1914', *International History Review*, 2 (1980): 34–54; D.R. Jones, 'Nicholas II and the Supreme Command: An Investigation of Motives', *Sbornik*, 11 (1985): 47–83; W.A. Renzi, 'Who

Composed "Sazonov's Thirteen Points"? A Re-Examination of Russia's War Aims of 1914', *American Historical Review*, 88 (1983): 347–57; two articles by E.C. Thaden in the *Journal of Central European Affairs*: 'Charykov and Russian foreign policy at Constantinople in 1911', 16 (1956–7): 25–44 and 'Montenegro: Russia's troublesome ally, 1910–1912', 18 (1958–9): 111–33; and E.R. Goldstein, 'Vickers Limited and the Tsarist Regime', *Slavonic and East European Review*, 58 (1980): 561–71.

France

On France generally, see R.D. Anderson, *France, 1870–1914, Politics and Society* (1977). Some interesting political aspects may be studied in: Allan Mitchell, *The German Influence in France after 1870: the formation of the French Republic* (Chapel Hill, NC, 1979); Eugen Weber, *The Nationalist revival in France, 1905–1914* (Berkeley, CA, 1959) and Gerd Krumeich, *Armaments and politics in France on the Eve of the First World War* (Leamington Spa, 1984). Two older articles on the role of politics still repay reading: John C. Cairns, 'Politics and Foreign Policy: The French Parliament, 1911–1914', *Canadian Historical Review*, 34 (1953): 245–76; and B.R. Leaman, 'The Influence of Domestic Policy on Foreign Affairs in France, 1898–1905', *Journal of Modern History*, 14 (1942): 449–79.

On foreign policy in particular, see J.F.V. Keiger, *France and the Origins of the First World War* (1983); Christopher M. Andrew, *Théophile Delcassé and the Making of the Entente Cordiale, 1898–1905* (1968); and Keith Eubank, *Paul Cambon, master diplomatist* (Norman, OK, 1960). The role of the bureaucracy is discussed in M.B. Hayne, *The French Foreign Office and the Origins of the First World War 1898–1914* (Oxford, 1993) – and more briefly in his 'The Quai d'Orsay and Influences on the Formulation of French Foreign Policy, 1898–1914', *French History*, 2 (1988): 427–52; D.R. Watson, 'The making of French foreign policy during the first Clemenceau ministry 1906–1909', *English Historical Review*, 86 (1971): 774–89; J.F.V. Keiger, 'Patriotism, politics and policy in the French foreign ministry, 1880–1914', in R. Tombs (ed.), *Nationhood and nationalism. From Boulangism to the Great War 1889–1918* (1991): 225–66; and 'Jules Cambon and Franco-German détente, 1907–14', *Historical Journal*, 26 (1983): 641–59. The role of the army is covered in Douglas Porch, *The March to the Marne: The French Army 1871–1914* (New York, 1981), and also see David B. Ralston, *The Army of the Republic. The Place of the Military in the Political Evolution of France, 1871–1914* (Cambridge, MA, 1967); and Allan Mitchell, *Victors and Vanquished: The German Influence on Army and Church in France after 1870* (Chapel Hill, NC, 1984).

Great Britain

On British foreign policy generally, see Kenneth Bourne, *The Foreign Policy of Victorian England 1830–1902* (Oxford, 1970) and Cedric J. Lowe, and Michael C. Dockrill (eds), *The Mirage of Power*, 3 vols (1972). The outstanding work on the subject of war origins remains Zara S. Steiner, *Britain and the Origins of the First World War* (1977), but see also the essays by Keith Wilson in *The Policy of the Entente: Essays on the Determinants of British Foreign Policy, 1904–14* (Cambridge, 1985) and the interpretation of John Charmley, *Splendid Isolation? Britain and the Balance of Power 1874–1914* (1999). The foreign policy of British foreign secretaries may be studied in: Cedric J. Lowe, *Salisbury and the Mediterranean, 1886–96* (1965); J. A. S. Grenville, *Lord Salisbury and Foreign Policy: the close of the nineteenth century* (1964); Rose L. Greaves, *Persia and the Defence of India 1884–92: A Study in the Foreign Policy of the Third Marquis of Salisbury* (1959); Gordon Martel, *Imperial Diplomacy: Rosebery and the Failure of Foreign Policy* (1986); and Keith Robbins, *Sir Edward Grey: A Biography of Lord Grey of Fallodon* (1971), as well as the essays in F.H. Hinsley (ed.), *British Foreign Policy under Sir Edward Grey* (Cambridge, 1977). An excellent monograph on the formation of the ententes is: George W. Monger, *The End of Isolation: British foreign policy, 1900–1907* (Edinburgh, 1963). Also useful are F.R. Bridge, *Great Britain and Austria-Hungary, 1906–14* (1972) and J. Heller, *British Policy Towards the Ottoman Empire, 1908–1914* (1983). On Lloyd George, see B.B. Gilbert, 'Pacifist to Interventionist: David Lloyd George in 1911 and 1914: Was Belgium an Issue?' *Historical Journal*, 28 (1985): 863–84.

The role of diplomats and bureaucrats is considered in Zara S. Steiner, *The Foreign Office and Foreign Policy, 1898–1914* (Cambridge, 1969) and in Ray A. Jones, *The British Diplomatic Service, 1815–1914* (Waterloo, Ontario 1983). On individual diplomats see Briton C. Busch, *Hardinge of Penshurst: a study in the old diplomacy* (Hamden, CT, 1980); Keith Hamilton, *Bertie of Thame: Edwardian Ambassador* (1990); D.H. Burton, *Cecil Spring Rice: A Diplomat's Life* (1990); and Sibyl Crowe and Edward Corp, *Our Ablest Public Servant: Sir Eyre Crowe 1864–1925* (Braunton, 1993). Shorter studies are: Zara S. Steiner, 'Grey, Hardinge and the Foreign Office, 1905–10', *Historical Journal*, 10 (1967): 415–39; R.A. Cosgrove, 'The Career of Sir Eyre Crowe: a reassessment', *Albion*, 4 (1972): 193–205; E.T. Corp, 'Sir Eyre Crowe and the Administration of the Foreign Office, 1906–1914', *Historical Journal*, 22 (1979): 443–54; and 'Sir William, Tyrrell: The *Eminence Grise* of the British Foreign Office, 1912–1915', *Historical Journal*, 25 (1982): 697–708; Keith Neilson, '"My Beloved Russians": Sir Arthur Nicolson and Russia, 1906–1916', *International History Review*, 9 (1987): 521–54; and Keith Wilson, 'The Question of Anti-Germanism at the British Foreign Office before the First World War', *Canadian Journal of History*, 18 (1983): 23–42.

The strategic dimension

There is a considerable literature on the role of strategy in the origins of the war. A good place to begin is with John H. Maurer, *The Outbreak of the First World War: Strategic Planning, Crisis Decision Making, and Deterrence Failure* (1995) and L.L. Farrar, *The Short-War Illusion* (Santa Barbara, CA, 1973). Two recent books that pay particular attention to the role of armaments in the making of policy are: David Stevenson, *Armaments and the Coming of War: Europe 1904–1914* (Oxford, 1996); and David G. Herrmann, *The Arming of Europe and the Making of the First World War* (Princeton, NJ, 1996). Books concentrating on naval affairs include: Paul Halpern, *The Mediterranean Naval Situation, 1908–14* (Cambridge, MA, 1971) which focuses on the significant changes in the balance and the strategies of France, Britain, Italy and Austria-Hungary; Jonathan Steinberg, *Yesterday's Deterrent: Tirpitz and the birth of the German battlefleet* (1965), which focuses on the politics and strategy in the origins of the 'risk' fleet; Holger Herwig, *'Luxury' Fleet: The Imperial German Navy 1888–1918* (1987), which takes a longer view; and Arthur J. Marder's classic *British Naval Policy, 1880–1905: the anatomy of British sea power* (1940). Jon Sumida examines the role of technology and finance: *In Defence of Naval Supremacy: Finance, Technology and British Naval Policy, 1899–1914* (1989). A useful historiographical essay is C.H. Fairbanks Jr, 'The Origins of the *Dreadnought* Revolution: A Historiographical Essay', *International History Review*, 13 (1991): 246–72.

Not surprisingly, much of the work on naval strategy focuses on the Anglo-German naval race. For German policy, see: P. Padfield, *The Great Naval Race: The Anglo-German Naval Rivalry, 1900–1914* (1974); Paul M. Kennedy, 'Tirpitz, England and the second Navy Law of 1900: a strategical critique', *Militärgeschichtliche Mitteilungen*, 2 (1970): 33–57 and his 'The development of German naval operations plans against England, 1896–1914', *English Historical Review*, 89 (1974): 48–76; Jonathan Steinberg, 'The Copenhagen complex', *Journal of Contemporary History*, 1 (1966): 23–46, and his 'The novella of 1908: necessities and choices in the Anglo-German naval arms race', *Transactions of the Royal Historical Society*, 5th ser., 21 (1971): 25–43. On the role of the navy in practice, see A.H. Ganz, 'The German navy in the Far East and Pacific: the seizure of Kiatschow and after', in J. Moses and P.M. Kennedy (eds), *Germany in the Pacific and Far East 1870–1914* (St Lucia, Queensland, 1977). For articles on British policy, see: D.C. Gordon, 'The Admiralty and Dominion Navies, 1902–1914', *Journal of Modern History*, 33 (1961): 407–22; Paul Haggie, 'The Royal Navy and war planning in the Fisher era', *Journal of Contemporary History*, 8 (1973): 113–32; and R.F. Mackay, 'The Admiralty, the German navy, and the redistribution of the British fleet, 1904–1905', *Mariner's Mirror*, 56 (1970): 341–6. On the 'race' itself, see Richard T.B. Langhorne, 'The Naval Question in Anglo-German Relations, 1912–1914', *Historical Journal*, 14 (1971): 359–70; and P. Hayes, 'Britain, Germany, and the Admiralty's Plans for Attacking German Territory, 1906–1915', in L. Freedman, P. Hayes and R. O'Neill (eds), *War, Strategy, and International Politics: Essays in Honour of Sir Michael Howard* (Oxford, 1992): 95–116.

Although most 'naval' literature concentrates on Britain and Germany, there is work on the other Great Powers: P. Gatrell, 'After Tsushima: Economic and Administrative Aspects of Russian Naval Rearmament, 1905–13', *Economic History Review*, 2nd ser., 43 (1990): 255–70; and Louis A. Gebhard Jr, 'Austria-Hungary's Dreadnought Squadron: The Naval Outlay of 1911', *Austrian History Yearbook*, 4–5 (1968–69): 245–58.

On military strategy the essays in Steven E. Miller (ed.), *Military Strategy and the Origins of the First World War* (Princeton, NJ, 1985) and Paul Kennedy (ed.), *The War Plans of the Great Powers 1880–1914* (1979) are a good place to begin. On German war planning and preparations, see Annika Mombauer, *Helmuth von Moltke and the Origins of the First World War* (Cambridge, 2001); Arden Bucholz, *Moltke, Schlieffen, and Prussian War Planning* (Oxford, 1991); Gerhard Ritter, *The Schlieffen Plan: Critique of a Myth* (Westport, CT, 1979); L.C.F. Turner, 'The significance of the Schlieffen plan', *Australian Journal of Politics and History*, 13 (1967): 47–66; Gunther Rothenberg, 'Moltke and Schlieffen', in Peter Paret (ed.), *Makers of Modern Strategy from Machiavelli to the Nuclear Age* (Princeton, NJ, 1986): 149–75; and Jack R. Dukes, 'Militarism and Arms Policy Revisited: The Origins of the German Army Law of 1913', in Jack R. Dukes and Joachim Remak (eds), *Another Germany: A Reconsideration of the Imperial Era* (Boulder, CO, 1988): 19–40. On British war planning, see John Gooch, *The Plans of War: the general staff and British military strategy, c.1900–16* (Oxford, 1974); David French, *British Economic and Strategic Planning, 1905–1915* (1982); J.P. Mackintosh, 'The Role of the Committee of Imperial Defence before 1914', *English Historical Review*, 77 (1962): 490–503; J. McDermott, 'The Revolution in British Military Thinking from the Boer War to the Moroccan Crisis', *Canadian Journal of History*, 21 (1986): 159–78; and Keith Nielson, 'Watching the "Steamroller": British Observers and the Russian Army before 1914', *Journal of Strategic Studies*, 8 (1985): 199–217. Anglo-French military affairs are covered in: J.W. Coogan and Peter F. Coogan, 'The British Cabinet and the Anglo-French

Staff Talks, 1905–1914: Who Knew What and When Did He Know It?',
Journal of British Studies, 24 (1985): 110–31; Keith M. Wilson, 'To the
Western Front: British war plans and the "military entente" with France
before the First World War', *British Journal of International Studies*, 3
(1977): 151–68; and J.D. Hargreaves, 'The Origins of the Anglo-French
military conversations in 1905', *History*, 36 (1951): 244–8.

There is a considerable literature on Franco-Russian military strategy and
planning. See Pertti Luntinen, *French Information on the Russian War
Plans, 1880–1914* (Helsinki, 1984); M. Perrins, 'Russian Military Policy in
the Far East and the 1905 Revolution in the Russian Army', *European
Studies Review*, 9 (1979): 331–50, and 'The Council for State Defence,
1905–1909: A Study in Russian Bureaucratic Politics', *Slavonic and East
European Review*, 58 (1980): 370–98; John C. Cairns, 'International politics
and the military mind: the case of the French Republic, 1911–14', *Journal
of Modern History*, 25 (1953): 273–85; Allan Mitchell, '"A Situation of
Inferiority": French Military Reorganization after the Defeat of 1870',
American Historical Review, 86 (1981): 49–62; and Roy A. Prete, 'French
Strategic Planning and the Deployment of the B.E.F. in France in 1914',
Canadian Journal of History, 24 (1989): 42–62, and 'The Preparation of the
French Army Prior to World War I: An Historiographical Reappraisal',
Canadian Journal of History, 26 (1991): 241–66.

Two noteworthy articles that should not be overlooked by any student of
strategic affairs are: Norman Stone, 'Moltke–Conrad: Relations between the
Austro-Hungarian and German general staffs, 1909–14', *Historical Journal*,
9 (1966): 201–28; and John C.G. Röhl, 'Admiral von Müller and the
Approach of War, 1911–1914', *Historical Journal*, 9 (1969): 651–73. The
role of intelligence is considered in several of the essays contained in Ernest
R. May (ed.), *Knowing One's Enemies: Intelligence Assessment Before
the Two World Wars* (Princeton, NJ, 1984). On British Intelligence in particular, see T.G. Fergusson, *British Military Intelligence, 1870–1914* (1984)
and on German see Ulrich von Trumpener, 'War Premeditated? German
Intelligence Operations in July 1914', *Central European History*, 9 (1976):
58–114.

The imperial factor

The literature on imperialism is vast, and imperialism as a cause of war is but
one theme in the genre. The works suggested here are those that pertain most
directly to the diplomatic/strategic dimension connected with war origins. A
good general introduction that considers to what extent economic motives
fuelled European expansion is David K. Fieldhouse, *Economics and Empire,
1830–1914* (1973), while Heinz Gollwitzer, *Europe in the Age of*

Imperialism 1880–1914 (1969) is a useful overview. A classic not to be overlooked is E.M. Winslow, *The Pattern of Imperialism: A Study in the Theories of Power* (New York, 1948). A useful summary of socialist interpretations of the phenomenon is A. Brewer, *Marxist Theories of Imperialism* (1980). On the radical-liberal interpretation see P.J. Cain, 'J.A. Hobson, Cobdenism and the Radical Theory of Economic Imperialism, 1898–1914', *Economic History Review*, 31 (1978): 565–84; Trevor Lloyd, 'Africa and Hobson's Imperialism', *Past & Present, 55* (1972): 130–53; and Eric Stokes, 'Late Nineteenth-Century Colonial Expansion and the Attack on the Theory of Economic Imperialism: A Case of Mistaken Identity?', *Historical Journal*, 2 (1969): 285–301. Interesting interpretive essays are: Ronald Robinson, 'Non-European Foundations of European Imperialism: Sketch for a Theory of Collaboration', in Roger Owen and Bob Sutcliffe (eds), *Studies in the Theory of Imperialism* (1972): 117–42; and Andrew Roberts, 'The Excentric Idea of Imperialism with or without Empire', in Wolfgang J. Mommsen and Jürgen Osterhammel (eds), *Imperialism and After* (1986): 267–89.

Imperial rivalries in central Asia are considered in David Gillard, *The Struggle for Asia 1828–1914: a study in British and Russian imperialism* (1977); F. Kazemzadeh, *Russia and Britain in Persia, 1864–1914* (New Haven, CT, 1968); and D. McLean, *Britain and Her Buffer State: The Collapse of the Persian Empire, 1890–1914* (1979). On Anglo-German rivalries in Africa see Matthew S. Seligmann, *Rivalry in Southern Africa, 1893–99: The Transformation of German Colonial Policy* (1998); D.M. Schreuder, *The Scramble for Southern Africa, 1877–1895* (Cambridge, 1980); P.H.S. Hatton, 'Harcourt and Solf: the search for an Anglo-German understanding through Africa 1912–14', *European Studies Review*, 1 (1971): 123–46; and R.T.B. Langhorne, 'Anglo-German Negotiations Concerning the Future of the Portuguese Colonies, 1911–14', *Historical Journal*, 16 (1973): 361–87. For the partition of Africa, useful introductory essays are: G.N. Sanderson, 'The European Partition of Africa: Origins and Dynamics', in Roland Oliver and G.N. Sanderson (eds), *Cambridge History of Africa*, vol. 6 (Cambridge, 1985): 96–158; John E. Flint, 'The Wider Background to Partition and Colonial Occupation', in Roland Oliver and Gervase Mathew (eds), *History of East Africa*, vol. 1 (1963): 352–90; and Juhani Koponen, 'The Partition of Africa: A Scramble for a Mirage?', *Nordic Journal of African Studies*, 2 (1993): 117–39; many of the essays in Prosser Gifford and W.R. Louis (eds), *Britain and Germany in Africa: Imperial Rivalry and Colonial Rule* (New Haven, CT, 1967) are outstanding. Also see W. Baumgart, *Imperialism: The Idea and Reality of British and French Colonial Expansion, 1880–1914* (Oxford, 1982).

Some unusual aspects of the imperial phenomenon are considered in: D.R. Headrick, *The Tools of Empire: Technology and European Imperialism in the Nineteenth Century* (Oxford, 1981); R.J. Hammond, *Portugal and Africa: A Study in Uneconomic Imperialism* (Stanford, CA, 1966); and Paul M. Kennedy, *The Samoan Tangle: A Study in Anglo-German-American Relations, 1878–1900* (New York, 1974). Two interesting articles are: Richard J.B. Bosworth, 'Great Britain and Italy's Acquisition of the Dodecanese, 1912–1915', *Historical Journal*, 13 (1970): 683–705; and F.R. Bridge, 'Tarde venientibus ossa: Austro-Hungarian colonial aspirations in Asia Minor, 1913–14', *Middle Eastern Studies*, 6 (1970): 319–30.

For Germany, see the detailed survey by Woodruff D. Smith, *The German Colonial Empire* (Chapel Hill, NC, 1978) and 'The Ideology of German Colonialism 1840–1906', *Journal of Modern History*, 46 (1974): 641–62; or the much briefer survey by W.O. Henderson, *The German Colonial Empire 1884–1919* (1993). Because Bismarck's decision to take territories in Africa seems, in retrospect, to have been a turning-point, this initiative has attracted considerable attention. See A.J.P. Taylor, *Bismarck's First Bid for Colonies* (1938); Hartmut Pogge von Strandmann, 'Domestic Origins of German Colonial Expansion under Bismarck', *Past & Present*, 42 (1969): 140–59; Klaus J. Bade, 'Imperial Germany and West Africa: Colonial Movement, Business Interests and Bismarck's "Colonial Policies"', in Stig Förster, Wolfgang J. Mommsen and Ronald Robinson (eds), *Bismarck, Europe and Africa* (Oxford, 1988): 121–47; H.P. Meritt, 'Bismarck and the German Interest in East Africa 1884–1885', *Historical Journal*, 21 (1978): 97–116; Hans-Ulrich Wehler, 'Bismarck's Imperialism 1862–1890', *Past & Present*, 48 (1970): 119–55; and Henry Ashby Turner Jr, 'Bismarck's Imperialist Venture: Anti-British in Origin?', in Prosser Gifford and W. Roger Louis (eds), *Britain and Germany in Africa* (1967): 47–82. Also see Roger Fletcher, *Revisionism and Empire. Socialist Imperialism in Germany 1897–1914* (1984); Holger Herwig, *Germany's Vision of Empire in Venezuela, 1871–1914* (Princeton, NJ, 1986); Richard A. Voeltz, *German Colonialism and the South West Africa Company, 1894–1914* (Athens, OH, 1988); Richard V. Pierard, 'A Case Study in German Economic Imperialism: The Colonial Economic Committee, 1896–1914', *Scandinavian Economic History Review*, 16 (1968): 155–66; Klaus Epstein, 'Erzberger and the German Colonial Scandals, 1905–1910', *English Historical Review*, 74 (1959): 637–63; and Helmuth Stoecker, 'The Expansionist Policy of Imperialist Germany in Africa South of the Sahara 1908–1918', in Walter Markov (ed.), *Afrika-Studien* (Leipzig, 1967): 129–41. The naval connection is discussed in A. Harding Ganz, 'Colonial Policy and the Imperial German Navy', *Militärgeschichtliche Mitteilungen*, 1 (1977): 35–52.

For France, see J.J. Cooke, *The New French Imperialism, 1880–1910: The Third Republic and Colonial Expansion* (Hamden, CT, 1973) and Henri Brunschwig, *French Colonialism, 1871–1914: myths and realities* (1966).

Articles by Christopher M. Andrew and A.S. Kanya-Forstner are essential reading: 'The French "Colonial Party": its composition, aims and influence, 1885–1914', *Historical Journal*, 14 (1971): 99–128; 'The *Groupe Colonial* in the French Chamber of Deputies, 1892–1932, *Historical Journal*, 17 (1974): 837–66; and two by Andrew alone – 'Gabriel Hanotaux, the Colonial Party and the Fashoda strategy', *Journal of Imperial and Commonwealth History*, 3 (1974): 55–104, and 'The French colonialist movement during the Third Republic: the unofficial mind of imperialism', *Transactions of the Royal Historical Society*, 5th ser., 26 (1976): 143–66; and also L. Abrams and D.J. Miller, 'Who were the French colonialists? A reassessment of the parti colonial, 1890–1914', *Historical Journal*, 19 (1976): 685–726. On resistance to French expansion, see Ross E. Dunn, *Resistance in the Desert: Moroccan Responses to French Imperialism, 1881–1912* (Madison, WI, 1977).

For Britain, see the influential study by Ronald Robinson and John Gallagher, *Africa and the Victorians: The Official Mind of Imperialism* (1961) and P.J. Cain and A.G. Hopkins, *British Imperialism: Innovation and Expansion, 1688–1914* (1993); Briton C. Busch, *Britain and the Persian Gulf, 1894–1914* (Berkeley, CA, 1967); G.N. Sanderson, *England, Europe and the Upper Nile* (Edinburgh, 1965); and A.N. Porter, *The Origins of the South African War: Joseph Chamberlain and the Diplomacy of Imperialism, 1895–99* (Manchester, 1980) explore areas of vital strategic significance. See also P.K. O'Brien, 'The Costs and Benefits of British Imperialism, 1846–1914', *Past & Present*, 120 (1988): 163–200; and W. Roger Louis, 'Sir Percy Anderson's Grand African Strategy, 1883–1896', *English Historical Review*, 81 (1966): 292–314.

For Russia, see D. Geyer, *Russian Imperialism: The Interaction of Domestic and Foreign Policy, 1860–1914* (Leamington Spa, 1987); B.H. Sumner, *Tsardom and Imperialism in the Far East and Middle East, 1880–1914* (New York, 1942); A. Malozemoff, *Russian Far Eastern Policy, 1881–1904: With Special Emphasis on the Causes of the Russo-Japanese War* (Berkeley, CA, 1958); G.A. Lensen, *The Russian Push Toward Japan: Russo-Japanese Relations, 1697–1875* (Princeton, NJ, 1959); R.A. Pierce, *Russia and Central Asia, 1867–1917* (Berkeley, CA, 1960); and S.G. Marks, *The Road to Power: The Trans-Siberian Railroad and the Colonization of Asian Russia, 1850–1917* (Ithaca, NY, 1991).

For Italy, see the monographs by W.C. Askew, *Europe and Italy's Acquisition of Libya, 1911–12* (Durham, NC, 1959); C.G. Segré, *Fourth Shore: the Italian colonization of Libya* (Chicago, IL, 1974); and R.L. Hess, *Italian Colonialism in Somalia* (Chicago, IL, 1966); and the articles by R.S. Cunsolo, 'Libya, Italian nationalism and the revolt against Giolitti', *Journal of Modern History*, 37 (1963): 186–207; and Richard Bosworth,

'The Albanian forests of Signor Giacomo Vismara: a case study of Italian economic imperialism during the Foreign Ministry of Antonino Di San Giuliano', *Historical Journal*, 18 (1975): 571–86.

The alliance system

The 'alliance system' as a cause of war has been a popular interpretation since the day it began. On the Anglo-German rivalry see Paul M. Kennedy, *The Rise of the Anglo-German Antagonism, 1860–1914* (1980); Pauline R. Anderson, *The Background of Anti-English Feeling in Germany, 1890–1902,* (New York, 1969); Ross J.S. Hoffman, *Great Britain and the German Trade Rivalry, 1875–1914* (New York, 1964); R.J. Crampton, *The Hollow Détente: Anglo-German Relations in the Balkans, 1911–14* (1980); S.L. Mayer, 'Anglo-German rivalry at the Algeçiras Conference', in P. Gifford and W.R. Louis (eds), *Britain and Germany in Africa* (New Haven, CT, 1967); and B.F. Oppel, 'The waning of a traditional alliance: Russia and Germany after the Portsmouth peace conference', *Central European History*, 5 (1972): 318–29. On the possibility of an Anglo-German alliance, see Paul M. Kennedy, 'German world policy and the alliance negotiations with England, 1897–1900', *Journal of Modern History*, 45 (1973): 605–25; Gordon Martel, 'The Limits of Commitment: Rosebery and the Definition of the Anglo-German Understanding', *Historical Journal*, 26 (1983): 387–404; and H.W. Koch, 'The Anglo-German alliance negotiations, missed opportunity or myth?', *History*, 54 (1969): 378–98.

On the Franco-Russian alliance and the ententes, see George Kennan, *The Fateful Alliance: France, Russia, and the Coming of the First World War* (New York, 1984); Samuel R. Williamson Jr, *The Politics of Grand Strategy: Britain and France prepare for war, 1904–14* (Cambridge, MA, 1969); John A. White, *Transition to Global Rivalry: Alliance Diplomacy and the Quadruple Entente, 1895–1907* (Cambridge, 1995); P.J.V. Rolo, *Entente Cordiale: the origins and negotiation of the Anglo-French agreements of 8 April 1904* (1969); R.P. Churchill, *The Anglo-Russian Convention of 1907* (Cedar Rapids, IO, 1939); Rose L. Greaves, 'Some Aspects of the Anglo-Russian convention and its working in Persia, 1907–14', *Bulletin of the School of Oriental and African Studies*, 31 (1968); B.J. Williams, 'The strategic background to the Anglo-Russian entente of August 1907', *Historical Journal*, 9 (1966): 360–73; and also his 'Great Britain and Russia, 1905 to the 1907 Convention', in F. Hinsley (ed.), *British Foreign Policy under Sir Edward Grey* (Cambridge, 1977): 133–47; D.W. Spring, 'Russia and the Franco-Russian Alliance, 1905–14: Dependence or Interdependence', *Slavonic and East European Review*, 66 (1988): 564–92; and his 'The

Trans-Persian Railway Project and Anglo-Russian Relations, 1909–14' in the same journal, 4 (1976): 60–82; Christopher Andrew, 'German world policy and the reshaping of the Dual Alliance', *Journal of Contemporary History*, 1 (1966): 137–52, and 'The Entente Cordiale from its origins to 1914', in Neville Waites (ed.), *Troubled Neighbours: Franco-British relations in the twentieth century* (1971): 11–39; D.N. Collins, 'The Franco-Russian Alliance and Russian Railways, 1891–1914', *Historical Journal*, 16 (1973): 777–88; and Keith A. Hamilton, 'Great Britain, France, and the Origins of the Mediterranean Agreements of 16 May 1907', in B.J.C. McKercher and D.J. Moss (eds), *Shadow and Substance in British Foreign Policy 1895–1939* (Edmonton, Alberta, 1984): 115–50.

On the Anglo-Japanese alliance, see Ian Nish, *The Anglo-Japanese Alliance: the diplomacy of two island empires, 1894–1907* (1977); Peter Lowe, *Great Britain and Japan, 1911–1915: A Study of British Far Eastern Policy* (New York, 1969); E.W. Edwards, 'The Japanese alliance and the Anglo-French Agreement of 1904', *History*, 42 (1957); R.J. Gowen, 'British Legerdemain at the 1911 Imperial Conference: The Dominions, Defense Planning, and the Renewal of the Anglo-Japanese Alliance', *Journal of Modern History*, 52 (1980): 385–413; Zara S. Steiner, 'Great Britain and the creation of the Anglo-Japanese alliance', *Journal of Modern History*, 31 (1959): 27–36; and Keith Wilson, 'The Anglo-Japanese Alliance of August 1905 and the Defending of India: A Case of the Worst Scenario', *Journal of Imperial and Commonwealth History*, 21 (1993): 334–56.

On the Triple Alliance, there is no good survey or synthesis in English, but see Oswald H. Wedel, *Austro-German Diplomatic Relations, 1908–1914* (Stanford, CA, 1932); and Ivan Scott, 'The Making of the Triple Alliance in 1882', *East European Quarterly*, 12 (1978): 399–423. On the Dual Alliance (Germany and Austria-Hungary) see R.A. Austensen, 'Austria and the "Struggle for Supremacy in Germany," 1848–1864', *Journal of Modern History*, 52 (1980): 195–225; and E.E. Kraehe, 'Austria and the Problem of Reform in the German Confederation, 1851–1863', *American Historical Review*, 56 (1951): 276–94; the strategic dimension is discussed in Graydon A. Tunstall Jr, *Planning for War against Russia and Serbia: Austro-Hungarian and German Military Strategies, 1871–1914* (New York, 1993). On Austro-Italian relations see Michael Palumbo, 'Italian-Austro-Hungarian Military Relations before World War I', in Samuel R. Williamson and Peter Pastor (eds), *Essays on World War I: Origins and Prisoners of War* (New York, 1983): 37–53; and W.C. Askew, 'The Austro-Italian antagonism, 1896–1914', in L.P. Wallace and W.C. Askew (eds), *Power, Public Opinion and Diplomacy* (Durham, NC, 1959): 172–221. See also Ulrich Trumpener, 'Liman von Sanders and the German Ottoman alliance', *Journal of Contemporary History*, 1 (1966): 179–92.

Crisis diplomacy

Generally, see Geoffrey Barraclough, *From Agadir to Armageddon: Anatomy of a Crisis* (New York, 1984); and D.E. Lee, *Europe's Crucial Years: The Diplomatic Background of World War I, 1902–1914* (Hanover, NH, 1974).

On the first Moroccan crisis see E.N. Anderson, *The First Moroccan Crisis, 1904–06* (Chicago, IL, 1930); and J. Kim Munholland, 'Rival Approaches to Morocco: Delcassé, Lyautey and the Algerian-Moroccan Border, 1903–1905', *French Historical Studies*, 5 (1968): 328–43. On the settlement of the crisis see E.W. Edwards, 'The Franco-German Agreement on Morocco', *English Historical Review*, 78 (1963): 483–513.

On the Russo-Japanese war see J.N. Westwood, *Russia Against Japan: A New Look at the Russo-Japanese War* (1986); J.A. White, *The Diplomacy of the Russo-Japanese War* (Princeton, NJ, 1965); R.A. Esthus, 'Nicholas II and the Russo-Japanese War', *Russian Review*, 40 (1981): 396–411; J. Long, 'Franco-Russian Relations during the Russo-Japanese war', *Slavonic and East European Review*, 52 (1974): 213–33; O.K. Fält, 'Collaboration Between Japanese Intelligence and the Finnish Underground during the Russo-Japanese War', *Asian Profile*, 4 (1976): 205–38; R.G. Griffith, 'Clandestine Japanese Activity in the Baltic During the Russo-Japanese War', *Journal of Baltic Studies*, 18 (1987): 71–8; Keith Nielson, '"A Dangerous Game of American Poker": Britain and the Russo-Japanese War', *Journal of Strategic Studies*, 12 (1989): 63–87; Jonathan Steinberg, 'Germany and the Russo-Japanese War', *American Historical Review*, 75 (1970): 1965–86; and B.J.C. McKercher, 'Diplomatic Equipoise: The Lansdowne Foreign Office, the Russo-Japanese War of 1904–5, and the Global Balance of Power', *Canadian Journal of History*, 24 (1989): 299–339.

On the Agadir crisis see Ima C. Barlow, *The Agadir Crisis* (Durham, NC, 1940); Keith M. Wilson, 'The Agadir crisis, the Mansion House speech and the double-edgedness of agreements', *Historical Journal*, 15 (1972): 513–32; J.S. Mortimer, 'Commercial interests and German diplomacy in the Agadir crisis', *Historical Journal*, 10 (1967): 440–56; and Michael L. Dockrill, 'British policy during the Agadir crisis of 1911', in F.H. Hinsley (ed.), *British Foreign Policy under Sir Edward Grey* (Cambridge, 1977): 271–87. On the radical view of the crisis see J. Jemnitz, *The Danger of War and the Second International* (1911) (Budapest, 1972).

On the Balkan crises generally, see A. Rossos, *Russia and the Balkans: Inter-Balkan Rivalries and Russian Foreign Policy, 1908–1914* (Toronto, 1981). On the Bosnian annexation crisis see Bernadotte Schmitt, *The Annexation of Bosnia* (Cambridge, 1937); F.R. Bridge, 'Izvolsky, Aehrenthal and the End of the Austro-Russian Entente, 1906–8', *Mitteilungen des österreichischen Staatsarchivs*, 29 (1976): 315–62; and D.W. Sweet, 'The

Bosnian crisis', in F.H. Hinsley (ed.), *British Foreign Policy under Sir Edward Grey* (Cambridge, 1977): 178–92. On the Balkan wars see E.C. Helmreich, *The Diplomacy of the Balkan Wars* (Cambridge, MA, 1938); E.C. Thaden, *Russia and the Balkan alliance of 1912* (Philadelphia, PA, 1965); Béla K. Király and Dimitrije Djordevic (eds), *East Central European Society and the Balkan Wars* (Boulder, CO, 1987); B. Raditsa, 'Venizelos and the struggle around the Balkan Pact', *Balkan Studies*, 6 (1965): 119–30; Richard J. Crampton, 'The Decline of the Concert of Europe in the Balkans, 1913–1914', *Slavonic and East European Review*, 52 (1974): 393–419, and his 'The Balkans as a factor in German foreign policy, 1911–1914', *Slavonic and East European Review*, 55 (1977): 370–89; E. Prevelakis, 'Eleutherios Venizelos and the Balkan Wars', *Balkan Studies*, 7 (1966): 363–78; Hans Heilbronner, 'The Merger Attempts of Serbia and Montenegro, 1913–1914', *Journal of Central European Affairs*, 18 (1958): 281–91; and József Galántai, 'Austria-Hungary and the War: The October 1913 Crisis – Prelude to July 1914', *Etudes Historiques Hongroises 1980* (Budapest, 1980): 63–89.

The mood of 1914: the crisis, culture and opinion

The July crisis is, of course, covered in much of the monographic literature referred to above. But there are numerous articles and essays that are well worth reading. Students may well begin with the classic Pierre Rénouvin, *The Immediate Origins of the War (28 June–4 August 1914)* (New Haven, CT, 1928), and then the debate between Joachim Remak, '1914 – the Third Balkan War: Origins Reconsidered', *Journal of Modern History*, 43 (1971): 259–78 and Paul W. Schroeder, 'World War I as "Galloping Gertie": a reply to Joachim Remak', *Journal of Modern History*, 44 (1972): 319–45. An interesting essay is James Joll, 'Politicians and the freedom to choose: the case of July 1914', in A. Ryan (ed.), *The Idea of Freedom, essays in honour of Isaiah Berlin* (Oxford, 1979): 99–114. The critical role of the military is discussed in Jack Snyder, *The Ideology of the Offensive: Military Decision Making and the Disasters of 1914* (Ithaca, NY, 1984); L.C.F. Turner, 'The role of the general staffs in July 1914', *Australian Journal of Politics and History*, 11 (1965): 305–23; and Stephen J. Cimbala, 'Steering Through Rapids: Russian Mobilization and World War I', *Journal of Slavic Military History*, 9 (1996): 376–98. On the assassination and its place in Serbian history, see Joachim Remak, *Sarajevo: The Story of a Political Murder* (New York, 1959) and the massively detailed *The Road to Sarajevo* by Vladimir Dedijer (1967).

The policy of Austria-Hungary during the July crisis is discussed in Samuel R. Williamson Jr, 'Vienna and July 1914: The Origins of the Great War Once

More' (9–36), and W. Jannen Jr, 'The Austro-Hungarian Decision for War in July 1914' (55–81), both in Williamson and Peter Pastor (eds), *Essays on World War I: Origins and Prisoners of War* (New York, 1983). See also Norman Stone, 'Hungary and the crisis of July 1914', *Journal of Contemporary History*, 1 (1966): 153–70. German policy is discussed in Konrad H. Jarausch, 'The illusion of limited war: Chancellor Bethmann Hollweg's calculated risk, July 1914', *Central European History*, 2 (1969): 48–76; and H.S.W. Corrigan, 'German-Turkish relations and the outbreak of war in 1914: a reassessment', *Past & Present*, 36 (1967): 144–52.

Various aspects of British policy are discussed in S.J. Valone, '"There Must Be Some Misunderstanding": Sir Edward Grey's Diplomacy of August 1, 1914', *Journal of British Studies*, 27 (1988): 405–24; Keith M. Wilson, 'The British cabinet's decision for war', *British Journal of International Studies*, 1 (1975): 148–59; Trevor Wilson, 'Britain's "Moral Commitment" to France in August 1914', *History*, 64 (1979): 380–90; Modris Ekstein, 'Sir Edward Grey and Imperial Germany in 1914', *Journal of Contemporary History*, 6 (1971): 121–31; P.H.S. Hatton, 'The First World War: Britain and Germany in 1914, the July crisis and war aims', *Past & Present*, 36 (1967): 138–43; Keith Wilson, 'Imperial Interests in the British Decision for War, 1914: The Defence of India in Central Asia', *Review of International Studies*, 10 (1984): 189–203; and Donald C. Watt, 'British press reactions to the assassination at Sarajevo', *European Studies Review*, 1 (1971): 233–47. On Russia see L.C.F. Turner, 'The Russian mobilization of 1914', *Journal of Contemporary History*, 3 (1968): 65–88.

'Public opinion' is discussed in two older works, which are still of value: O.J. Hale, *Publicity and Diplomacy: with special reference to England and Germany, 1890–1914* (New York, 1940); and E.M. Carroll, *French Public Opinion and Foreign Affairs, 1870–1914* (1931). Also see Wolfgang J. Mommsen, 'Domestic Factors in German Foreign Policy before 1914', *Central European History*, 6 (1973): 381–401; and Keith G. Robbins, 'Public Opinion, the Press and Pressure Groups', in F. Hinsley (ed.), *British Foreign Policy under Sir Edward Grey* (Cambridge, 1977): 70–88. Other works include: I.F. Clark, *Voices Prophesying War, 1863–1984* (1966); Roland Stromberg, *Redemption by War: The Intellectuals and 1914* (Kansas City, MO, 1982) and his 'The Intellectuals and the Coming of War in 1914', *Journal of European Studies*, 3 (1973): 109–22; and M.C.C. Adams, *The Great Adventure: Male Desire and the Coming of World War I* (Bloomington, IN, 1990).

There is a vast literature on 'nationalism' – both theoretical, dealing with the origins and contours of the concept, and practical, dealing with phenomena in particular historical settings (and many works devoted to nationalism are referred to in the 'Great Powers' section above). A recent influential study is Benedict Anderson, *Imagined Communities: Reflections on the Origin and Spread of Nationalism* (1983); a good, short and opinionated introduction to the subject is Elie Kedourie, *Nationalism* (3rd edn, 1966). See also Hugh Seton-Watson, *Nations and States: An Enquiry into the Origins of Nations and the Politics of Nationalism* (1977) and the essays in Paul Kennedy and Anthony Nicholls (eds), *Nationalist and Racialist Movements in Britain and Germany Before 1914* (1981).

There is much interesting work on the subject of militarism (and its relationship with patriotism). On Germany see Roger Chickering, *We Men Who Feel Most German: A Cultural Study of the Pan-German League 1886–1914* (1984) and 'Patriotic societies and German foreign policy, 1890–1914', *International History Review,* 1 (1979): 470–89; M.S. Coetzee, *The Army League: Popular Nationalism in Wilhelmine Germany* (Oxford, 1990); and W.H. Maehl, 'The Triumph of Nationalism in the German Socialist Party on the Eve of the First World War', *Journal of Modern History*, 24 (1952): 292–306. On Britain see Geoffrey F.A. Best, 'Militarism and the Victorian public schools', in B. Simon and I. Bradley (eds), *The Victorian Public School* (1975): 129–46; and R.J.Q. Adams, 'The National Service League and Mandatory Service in Edwardian Britain', *Armed Forces & Society*, 12 (1985): 53–74. See also Avner Offer, 'The Working Classes, British Naval Plans and the Coming of the Great War', *Past & Present*, 107 (1985): 204–26; Olive Anderson, 'The Growth of Christian Militarism in Mid-Victorian Britain', *English Historical Review*, 86 (1971): 46–72; and Anne Summers, 'Militarism in Britain before the Great War', *History Workshop*, 2 (1976): 104–23. Also see David MacKenzie, 'Serbian Nationalist and Military Organizations and the Piedmont Idea, 1844–1914', *East European Quarterly*, 16 (1982), 323–44; and J. Schwarzmantel, 'Nationalism and the French Working Class Movement, 1905–1914', in E. Cahm and V. Fisera (eds), *Socialism and Nationalism in Contemporary Europe (1848–1945)*, vol. 2 (Nottingham, 1979): 65–80.

On social Darwinism and the role of race see Robert C. Bannister, *Social Darwinism: Science and Myth in Anglo-American Social Thought* (rev. edn, Philadelphia, PA, 1988); David P. Crook, *Benjamin Kidd: Portrait of a Social Darwinist* (Cambridge, 1984); Alfred Kelly, *The Descent of Darwin: The Popularization of Darwinism in Germany, 1860–1914* (Chapel Hill, NC, 1981); Geoffrey G. Field, *Evangelist of Race: The Germanic Vision of Houston Stewart Chamberlain* (New York, 1981); Ted Benton, 'Social Darwinism and Socialist Darwinism in Germany: 1860 to 1900', *Rivista Di Filosofia*, 23 (1982): 79–121; Peter J. Bowler, 'Malthus, Darwin and the Concept of Struggle', *Journal of the History of Ideas*, 37 (1976): 631–50; David P. Crook, 'Darwin on War and Aggression', *Australian Journal of Politics and History*, 29 (1983): 344–53; Barry Gale, 'Darwin and the

Concept of a Struggle for Existence', *Isis*, 63 (1972): 321–44; John C. Greene, 'Darwin as a Social Evolutionist', *Journal of the History of Biology*, 10 (1977): 1–27; and J.A. Rogers, 'Darwinism and Social Darwinism', *Journal of the History of Ideas*, 33 (1972): 265–80.

On the subject of socialist internationalism see J. Braunthal, *History of the International, 1864–1914* (1966); G. Haupt, *Socialism and the Great War: The Collapse of the Second International* (Oxford, 1972); D.K. Buse, 'Ebert and the Coming of World War I: A Month from his Diary', *International Review of Social History*, 13 (1968): 430–48; Roger Fletcher, 'Revisionism and Militarism: War and Peace in the pre-1914 Thought of Eduard Bernstein', *Militärgeschichtliche Mitteilungen*, 31 (1982): 23–36; and B.D. Wolfe, 'French Socialism, German Theory and the Flaw in the Foundation of the Socialist Internationals', in J.S. Curtiss (ed.), *Essays in Russian and Soviet History* (Leiden, 1963): 177–97.

On the subjects of pacifism and internationalism see Roger Chickering, *Imperial Germany and a World without War: The Peace Movement and German Society, 1892–1914* (Princeton, NJ, 1975); A. Campanella, 'Garibaldi and the First Peace Congress in Geneva in 1867', *International Review of Social History*, 5 (1960): 456–86; J. Jemnitz, 'The First International and the War (1864–1866)', *Acta Historica*, 11 (1965): 57–93; A.J.A. Morris, *Radicalism Against War 1906–1914* (1972), and his 'The English Radicals' Campaign for Disarmament and the Hague Conference of 1907', *Journal of Modern History*, 43 (1971): 367–93; and Donald Newton, *British Labour and the Struggle for Peace, 1889–1914* (Oxford, 1985). On Norman Angell and 'economic' pacifism see J.B.D. Miller, *Norman Angell and the Futility of War: Peace and the Public Mind* (1986); A. Marrin, *Sir Norman Angell* (Boston, 1979); and Howard Weinroth, 'Norman Angell and *The Great Illusion*: An Episode in Pre-1914 Pacifism', *Historical Journal*, 17 (1974): 551–74. See also S.E. Cooper, 'Pacifism in France, 1889–1914: International Peace as a Human Right', *French Historical Studies*, 17 (1991): 359–86; D.L. Morrill, 'Nicholas II and the Call for the First Hague Conference', *Journal of Modern History*, 46 (1974): 296–313; Solomon Wank, 'The Austrian Peace Movement and the Habsburg Ruling Élite, 1906–1914', in Charles Chatfield and Peter van den Dungen (eds), *Peace Movements and Political Cultures* (Knoxville, TN, 1988): 40–64; and, in the same volume, Jost Dülffer, 'Citizens and Diplomats: The Debate on the First Hague Conference (1899) in Germany' (23–39) and Roger Chickering, 'War, Peace, and Social Mobilization in Imperial Germany: Patriotic Societies, the Peace Movement, and Socialist Labor' (3–22); A. Sidorowicz, 'The British Government, the Hague Peace Conference of 1907 and the Armaments Question', in B. McKercher (ed.), *Arms Limitation and Disarmament: Restraints on War, 1899–1939* (New York, 1992): 1–20;

C. Howard, 'MacDonald, Henderson, and the Outbreak of War, 1914', *Historical Journal*, 20 (1977): 871–918; H.S. Weinroth, 'British Radicals and the Balance of Power, 1902–1914', *Historical Journal*, 13 (1970): 653–82 and 'Left-Wing Opposition to Naval Armaments in Britain before 1914', *Journal of Contemporary History*, 6 (1971): 93–120; and R. Grant, 'The Society of Friends of Russian Freedom (1890–1917): A Case Study in Internationalism', *Journal of the Scottish Labour History Society*, 3 (1970): 3–24. On the origins of 'militarism' see Nicholas Stargardt, *The German Idea of Militarism: Radical and socialist critics, 1866–1914* (Cambridge, 1994); and J. Howorth, 'The Left in France and Germany, Internationalism and War: A Dialogue of the Deaf (1900–1914)', in E. Cahm and V. Fisera (eds), *Socialism and Nationalism in Contemporary Europe (1848–1945)*, vol. 2 (Nottingham, 1979): 81–100.

Miscellaneous

There are some interesting pieces of work that do not fit neatly into any of the above categories. Jonathan Helmreich considers Belgian policy in 'Belgian Concern over Neutrality and British Intentions, 1906–14', *Journal of Modern History*, 36 (1964): 416–27; while Barbara Jelavich considers Rumanian policy in 'Romania in the First World War: The Pre-War Crisis, 1912–1914', *International History Review*, 14 (1992): 441–51. Also see J.F.N. Bradley, 'Czech Pan-Slavism before the First World War', *Slavonic and East European Review*, 40 (1961–62): 184–205; L.B. Fritzinger, 'Friends in High Places: Valentine Chirol, *The Times*, and Anglo-German Relations, 1892–6', *Victorian Periodicals Review*, 21 (1988): 9–14; D.W. Sweet, 'The Baltic in British Diplomacy before the First World War', *Historical Journal*, 13 (1970): 454–74; Clive Trebilcock, 'British Armaments and European Industrialization, 1890–1914', *Economic History Review*, 2nd ser., 26 (1973): 254–72; John A. Moses, 'The "Ideas of 1914" in Germany and Australia: A Case of Conflicting Perceptions', *War and Society*, 9 (1991): 61–82; Ulrich Trumpener 'Turkey's entry into World War I: an assessment of responsibilities', *Journal of Modern History*, 34 (1962): 369–80; Keith Neilson, '"Greatly Exaggerated": The Myth of the Decline of Great Britain before 1914', *International History Review*, 13 (1991): 695–725; and in the same issue, Gordon Martel, 'The Meaning of Power: Rethinking the Decline and Fall of Great Britain' (662–94).

References

Albertini, Luigi, *The Origins of the War of 1914* (trans. and ed. by Isabella M. Massey), 3 vols (Oxford, 1952–7).

Andrew, C.M., *Théophile Delcassé and the Making of the Entente Cordiale, 1898–1905* (1968).

Berghahn, V.R., *Germany and the Approach of War in 1914* (1973).

Bosworth, R.J.B., *Italy, the least of the Great Powers: Italian foreign policy before the First World War* (1979).

Bosworth, R.J.B., *Italy and the Approach of the First World War* (1983).

Bury, J.P.T., *Gambetta's Final Years: 'The Era of Difficulties' 1877–1882* (1982).

Buthman, William C., *The Rise of Integral Nationalism in France* (New York, 1970).

Cecil, Lamar, *Wilhelm II*, 2 vols (Chapel Hill, NC, 1989, 1996).

Craig, Gordon, *Germany, 1866–1945* (Oxford, 1980).

Deak, I., *Beyond Nationalism: A Social and Political History of the Habsburg Officer Corps, 1848–1918* (New York, 1990).

Eley, Geoff, *Reshaping the Right: Radical Nationalism and Political Change after Bismarck* (1980).

Fay, Sidney B., *The Origins of the World War*, 2 vols (New York, 1966 [paperback reprint of the 1930 edn]).

Fieldhouse, D.K., *Economics and Empire, 1830–1914* (1973).

Fischer, Fritz, *War of Illusions: German Policies from 1911 to 1914* (New York, 1975).

Fuller, Joseph V., *Bismarck's Diplomacy at its Zenith* (Cambridge, MA, 1922).

Gall, Lothar, *Bismarck: The White Revolutionary*, 2 vols (trans. J.A. Underwood, 1986).

Geiss, Imanuel, 'The Outbreak of the First World War and German War Aims', *Journal of Contemporary History*, 1 (1966): 75–92.

Geiss, Immanuel, *German Foreign Policy, 1871–1914* (1976).

Gooch, John, *The Plans of War: the general staff and British military strategy, c.1900–16* (Oxford, 1974).

Gordon, M.R., 'Domestic conflict and the origins of the First World War: the British and the German cases', *Journal of Modern History*, 46 (1974): 191–226.

Hale, Oron J., *The Great Illusion, 1900–1914* (New York, 1971).

Herwig, Holger H., 'Industry, Empire and the First World War', in Gordon Martel (ed.), *Modern Germany Reconsidered* (1991): 54–73.

Howard, Christopher, *Splendid Isolation* (1967).

Howard, Michael, *The Continental Commitment* (1972).

Hull, Isabel V., *The Entourage of Kaiser Wilhelm II 1888–1918* (Cambridge, 1982).

Jane, Fred T., *The Imperial Russian Navy* (2nd edn, 1904).

Jarausch, K.H., *The Enigmatic Chancellor* (New Haven, CT, 1973).

Jelavich, Barbara, *A Century of Russian Foreign Policy* (New York, 1964).

Kehr, Eckhardt, *Battleship Building and Party Politics in Germany, 1894–1901* (Chicago, IL, 1975).

Keiger, John F.V., *France and the Origins of the First World War* (1983).

Kennedy, Paul (ed.), *The War Plans of the Great Powers, 1880–1914* (1979).

Kitchen, Martin, *The German Officer Corps, 1890–1914* (Oxford, 1968).

Lambi, Ivo N., *The Navy and German Power Politics, 1862–1914* (Boston, 1984).

Langer, William L., *European Alliances and Alignments, 1871–1890* (2nd edn, New York, 1950).

Lieven, D.C.B., *Russia and the Origins of the First World War* (1983).

Lowe, C.J. and Marzari, F., *Italian Foreign Policy, 1870–1940* (1975).

Mayer, Arno J., in L. Krieger and F. Stern (eds), *The Responsibility of Power* (New York, 1967): 286–300.

Mitchell, Allan, *The German Influence in France after 1870: the formation of the French Republic* (Chapel Hill, NC, 1979).

Offer, Avner, 'The Working Classes, British Naval Plans and the Coming of the Great War', *Past & Present*, 107 (1985): 204–26.

Pipes, Richard, *Struve: Liberal on the Right, 1905–1944* (Cambridge, MA, 1980).

Porch, Douglas, *The March to the Marne: The French Army 1871–1914* (New York, 1981).

Rich, Norman and M.H. Fisher (eds), *The Holstein Papers,* vol. 4 (Cambridge, 1963).
Rogger, Hans, *Russia in the Age of Modernisation and Revolution 1881–1917* (1983).
Röhl, John C.G., *1914: Delusion or Design?* (London, 1973).
Röhl, John C.G., *The Kaiser and his Court: Wilhelm II and the Government of Germany* (Cambridge, 1994).
Röhl, John C.G., *Young Wilhelm* (trans. Jeremy Gaines and Rebecca Wallach, Cambridge, 1998).
Rothenberg, Gunther E., *The Army of Francis Joseph* (West Lafayette, IN, 1976).

Schmitt, Bernadotte, in *The Coming of the War,* 1914, 2 vols, (New York, 1930).
Sondhaus, Lawrence, *Preparing for Weltpolitik: German Seapower before the Tirpitz Era* (Annapolis, MD, 1997).
Steinberg, Jonathan, *Yesterday's Deterrent: Tirpitz and the birth of the German battlefleet* (1965).
Stieve, Friedrich, *Isvolsky and the World War* (New York, 1926).

Taylor, A.J.P., *The Struggle for Mastery in Europe* (Oxford, 1954).
Taylor, A.J.P., *War by Timetable* (London, 1969).
Thaden, E.C., *Conservative nationalism in nineteenth-century Russia* (Seattle, WA, 1964).
Tint, Herbert, *The Decline of French Patriotism, 1870–1940* (1964).

Whittam, J., *The Politics of the Italian Army, 1861–1918* (1977).
Williams, Robert C., *Russia Imagined: Art, Culture and National Identity 1840–1995* (New York, 1997).

Index

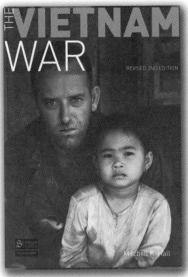

9781405874342

SEMINAR
STUDIES
IN HISTORY

9780582771895

9781405874366

9781405874359

9780582299085

9781405874311

9781405874304

9781405874328

9781405840583

9781405874335

9781405824699

9781405812535

Other books available in this series

Full Title	Author	ISBN
The First World War 2nd Edition	Stuart Robson	978-1-4058-2471-2
The Russian Revolution 2nd Edition	A. Wood	978-0-582-35559-0
Lenin's Revolution:Russia, 1917-1921	David Marples	978-0-582-31917-2
Fascism and the Right in Europe 1919-1945	Martin Blinkhorn	978-0-582-07021-9
Anti-Semitism before the Holocaust	Albert S. Lindemann	978-0-582-36964-1
The Holocaust: The Third Reich and the Jews	David Engel	978-0-582-32720-7
The Third Reich 3rd Edition	D.G. Williamson	978-0-582-36883-5
The Second World War in Europe	S. P. Mackenzie	978-1-4058-4699-8
Hitler and the Rise of the Nazi Party	Frank McDonough	978-1-582-50606-8
Japan in Transformation, 1952-2000	Jeffrey Kingston	978-0-582-41875-2
China since 1949	Linda Benson	978-0-582-35722-8
Eastern Europe 1945-1969: From Stalinism to Stagnation	Ben Fowkes	978-0-582-32693-4
The Khrushchev Era 1953-1964	Martin McCauley	978-0-582-27776-2
The Origins of the Vietnam War	Fredrik Logevall	978-0-582-31918-9
The Collapse of the Soviet Union, 1985-1991	David Marples	978-0-582-50599-1
The United Nations since 1945: Peacekeeping and the Cold War	Norrie MacQueen	978-0-582-35673-3
South Africa: The Rise and Fall of Apartheid	Nancy Clark and William H Worgew	978-0-582-41437-2
Race and Empire	Jane Samson	978-0-582-41837-0